DARKNESS
—IN—
PRIMETIME

ALSO BY MITCHELL HADLEY:

The Electronic Mirror: How Classic TV Helps Us Understand Who We Were and Who We Are

FICTION:
The Collaborator
The Car

DARKNESS IN PRIMETIME

How Classic-Era TV Foresaw
Modern Society's Descent into Hell

MITCHELL HADLEY

Foreword by
CHRISTIAN TOTO

THROCKMORTON PRESS
HUNTINGTON, INDIANA

© 2025 Mitchell D. Hadley
All rights reserved. No part of this publication may be reproduced, stored in a retrieval system, or transmitted in any form or by any means, electronic, mechanical, photocopying, recording, or otherwise, without the prior written permission of the publisher.

Throckmorton Pres
Huntington, Indiana 46750 USA

ISBN 978-1-7326207-4-2 (paperback)
ISBN 978-1-7326207-7-3 (e-book)
Library of Congress Control Number: 2025908684

First Edition, August 2025

Printed in the United States of America

Cover design by Hadco

For

Carol Ford

and

Jodie Peeler

Comrades-in-arms

and,

more important,

true friends

Contents

Notes on the Text iii
Foreword v
Acknowledgements xi
Introduction 1
ONE: EYES OF THE MACHINE 9
   1984 (*Studio One*, 1953) 11
   The General (*The Prisoner*, 1967) 27
   The Architects of Fear (*The Outer Limits*, 1963) 39
   O.B.I.T. (*The Outer Limits*, 1963) 51
TWO: MINDS IN CHAINS 65
   Number 12 Looks Just Like You (*The Twilight Zone*, 1964) 67
   The Children's Story (*Mobil Showcase*, 1982) 81
   A Sound of Different Drummers (*Playhouse 90*, 1957) 93
   One (*Kraft Television Theatre*, 1955) 109
THREE: SHADOWS OF DOUBT 125
   The Monsters Are Due on Maple Street (*The Twilight Zone*, 1960) 127
   The Brotherhood of the Bell (1970) 139
   They (*NET Playhouse*, 1970) 153
   The Invasion of Kevin Ireland (*The Bold Ones*, 1971) 167
FOUR: SCALES OF JUSTICE 181
   The Investigation (1967) 183
   Darkness at Noon (*Producers' Showcase*, 1955) 202
   A Taste of Armageddon (*Star Trek*, 1967) 215
   The Year of the Sex Olympics (*Theatre 625*, 1968) 229

FIVE: THE BLOOD OF THE MARTYRS 243
   The Obsolete Man (*The Twilight Zone*, 1961) 245
   Dialogues of the Carmelites (*NBC Opera Theatre*, 1957) 257
   Murder in the Cathedral (*Theatre Parade*, 1936) 271
   A Feasibility Study (*The Outer Limits*, 1964) 285
JOURNEY'S END 303
   The Horn Blows at Midnight (*Omnibus*, 1953) 305
Bibliography 317
Index 343

Notes on the Text

Several essays in this collection originally appeared, in substantially different form, on www.itsabouttv.com.

In this book, titles are formatted as follows:

- **Movie titles** are italicized (e.g., *The Brotherhood of the Bell*), even when broadcast on television.
- **Television series titles** are italicized (e.g., *Playhouse 90*).
- **Television episodes** and **broadcasts of plays or operas** appear in quotation marks (e.g., "Murder in the Cathedral," "Dialogues of the Carmelites").
- **Published versions of plays or scripts** are italicized (e.g., *The Investigation*), but the title of the play as broadcast is in quotation marks ("The Investigation").
- When a **book is adapted for television**, the book title is italicized (*The Children's Story*), while the title of the adaptation is in quotation marks ("The Children's Story").

These conventions help distinguish between original works and their televised adaptations.

Foreword
by Christian Toto
Founder of hollywoodintoto.com

Pop culture is as trivial as doom-scrolling on Instagram, or so we're told. In the past, we dismissed TV as the "Boob Tube," a distraction while we gulped down Hungry Man Dinners.

The advent of *My Mother The Car* didn't help that perception.

The big screen gets more respect, but not much in some circles. Hey, relax. It's just a movie. The "Fast & Furious" movies didn't help that perception, either.

Think again.

Consider Jennifer Aniston, or more specifically, her hairstylist during the 1990s. The "Rachel" 'do became a sensation after the actress made it fashionable on NBC's *Friends* sitcom.

Former President Joe Biden credited the rise of same-sex marriage laws to *Will & Grace* and *Modern Family*, sitcoms featuring flawed but lovable gay characters. We welcomed them into our homes each week. Their very presence changed enough hearts and/or minds.

There's a reason late-night comedians dedicate so many monologues to swaying political tastes. They think the right zinger could change the course of a news cycle, or even an election. Occasionally, they're right. Just ask Sarah "I can see Russia from my house" Palin, the former Alaskan governor disassembled by *Saturday Night Live*'s Tina Fey.

One skit did the trick.

No matter where you stand on Climate Change, Al Gore's 2006 documentary *An Inconvenient Truth* changed the conversation on the subject. The Daily Wire rocked the zeitgeist with both *What Is a Woman?* and *Am I Racist?* Those film's left-leaning targets took it on the chin, and cultural forces buckled under their weight.

The latter became the highest-grossing documentary in a decade. Months later, DEI-style programs began to crumble.

Pop culture matters more than we think. Stories can impact the culture or, in some cases, warn us about what might be lurking around the corner. And for every frothy sitcom or mind-numbing sequel, there are other stories that examine the past while considering what the future might look like. Even when writers don't realize it. Especially when that's the case.

The very best of the best understood western culture, the nature of humanity and an old saw from the great wordsmith Mark Twain: "History doesn't repeat itself, but it often rhymes."

That's never been more true than with *Darkness in Primetime*, a fascinating blast from the past which speaks volumes about the future. It's all about rhyming.

Mitchell Hadley exhumes forgotten TV classics, exploring what they said about the times in question. Their lessons aren't just valuable for today but darn near vital for tomorrow.

We've been warned. And warned. And darn it, we haven't listened.

Sure, we remember select *Twilight Zone* episodes, like a young William Shatner staring down a gremlin on an airplane's wing. George Orwell's *1984* feels like a transcript from Reuters of late, leaving even the most jaded consumer aware of its rumblings.

Orwell meant to do that, to warn us about what humanity's darkest impulses might evoke. He didn't pull any punches or hide his intentions.

Darkness in Primetime is different. It's the kind of pop culture deep dive that leaves the reader feeling both woozy and exhilarated. Wait. . . what did I miss? And how did they know so much about the 21st century without Doc Brown's time-traveling DeLorean?

His research reveals the recent TV Golden Age may have featured New Jersey mobsters and meth dealers, but classic TV scriptwriters had plenty on their minds, too. Yes, they worked with infinitely smaller budgets and FX teams that couldn't replicate a fraction of what today's wizards can achieve.

They also made do with "TV" level actors, unlike today, when Oscar-winners scramble to snag a streaming platform show at all costs.

What they created stands the test of time and mirrors our present day in ways that aren't just inconvenient. They're uncomfortable, unsettling and, sadly, far too predictable. Good luck finding many of these stories. They're not a click or two away on Tubi, but the exhaustive profiles here make them accessible.

We couldn't have foreseen the massive cultural overreach that a nasty flu would yield, but TV screenwriters saw that potential in all of us. Hadley's righteous fury against what he dubs "COVID Theater" is palpable and refreshing.

If only modern storytellers shared this righteous fury. Maybe the young minds forever impacted by school closures will tell those tales someday soon. They might appear on our smartphones or devices we can't even imagine yet.

They will leave a mark all the same.

TV screenwriters of yore worked from instinct and life experience, bypassing tribal thinking and cultural biases. That's increasingly rare in the 21st century, another reason they had an advantage over their modern-day successors.

Our current fight for privacy, a war we're losing byte by byte in the digital age, is neither new nor unexplored. We've been waging those battles for decades, just not with smart phones pinging in our pockets. You don't need technology to lose your soul.

The tales here prove it.

Darkness walks us through these incendiary stories, offering the kind of thoughtful, nuanced observations that make them pop. Political. Social. Economic. Cultural. Hadley covers all sides, transporting us back to the thinking within each era and why the stories merit inclusion now.

There are no accidents, apparently.

The stories themselves do plenty of heavy lifting. Heck, if any studio executives are reading this book they may glean a dozen or so stories they could reboot with little need for updates. The source material isn't as well-known as, say, a shape-shifting car or star-spangled Avenger, but these yarns never go out of style. That's depressing, given the tenor of the tales.

One lost TV production of "The Investigation" is suddenly too topical for some. The fact that it's been memory-holed adds another maddening layer. The more we try to forget a narrative, the more obvious it becomes we need to relive it.

It's impossible to read *Darkness in Primetime* without having a profound respect for the writer class. They not only entertain us but force us to consider larger questions, the kind that leave us vulnerable, even scared. It's a vital process to step out of our lives and consider those of others.

And, more importantly, how the two overlap.

The great *Seinfeld* sitcom removed potentially dated references in its storylines. Co-creator Jerry Seinfeld wanted the show to have legs, to be interpreted as funny first and foremost but not become an artifact, like a *Brady Bunch* episode with dated fashions and lingo.

Technological advances make that impossible. If George Costanza picks up a landline we're already transported to the analog age. Still, Seinfeld's approach has kept the 1990's show surprisingly fresh.

The same is true of the stories showcased here. Their creators understood the ravages of time and how humanity's foibles mean their imagination won't grow stale. Perhaps that explains their ability to dissect the present and predict the future.

This "Descent into Hell" isn't a political screed, but, understandably, the fear of Big Government isn't just justified. It's prescient.

Reading *Darkness in Primetime* may make you recoil at the notion of another vapid reality show or film reboot. It'll also make you lean into today's elite storytellers and what they might have to share about the future.

Maybe this time we'll listen.

Acknowledgements

An author doesn't get to give people a piece of his mind without a lot of help from others, and I'm deeply grateful to the friends, researchers, television historians, and assorted partners in crime—some of whom may not even realize the trouble they've caused—who made this book possible.

First and foremost, my thanks go to my wife, Judie, my finest editor and most trusted reader. By patiently enduring my endless talk about television, she has become a reluctant historian herself. Her insight and patience have been invaluable.

I am deeply grateful to Christian Toto for his graciousness in agreeing to write the Foreword, and for the insight and generosity of his words. His thoughtful perspective not only honors this project, but makes me want to read the book myself.

Jodie Peeler and Maureen Carney generously scoured newspaper archives for articles, reviews, and contemporary accounts that brought these often-obscure programs to life. Without their efforts, many shows—some barely mentioned online—would have remained unknown to me.

David Hofstede offered vital encouragement and suggested expanding this project beyond its origins as essays for It's About TV. Paul Mavis and Bob Sassone provided thoughtful advice on introducing the book to new readers. Carol Ford, as always, gave unwavering support, advice, and friendship. Herbie J Pilato, one of the best and most elegant writers about television, was generous with his time and gracious in his support. Rodney Marshall, a fine writer on classic television in his own right, believed I had another TV book in me. Marc Ryan always provided a positive word in general.

Special thanks to Jane Parr, Archivist for Acquisitions at the Howard Gotlieb Archival Research Center at Boston University Libraries, for her extraordinary work scanning and sending hundreds of pages from the David Karp collection. Her efforts with Karp's *Kraft Television Theatre* teleplay "One," adapted from his novel, were crucial in understanding the key differences—especially the ending—between the teleplay and the novel.

My opinions, as you'll see, are strong, and those who helped me most may not always agree with them. Yet their generosity, friendship, and shared passion for television history made this book possible. Any errors that remain are mine alone.

Finally, I am grateful to the readers of It's About TV! for their support over the past fourteen years. Most essays in this book began as shorter pieces on the blog, and your encouragement inspired me to develop them into a full-length work.

AMDG
June, 2025

*Necessity is the plea for every infringement of human freedom.
It is the argument of tyrants; it is the creed of slaves.*

—William Pitt the Younger (November 18, 1783)

Introduction

This instrument can teach, it can illuminate; yes, and it can even inspire. But it can do so only to the extent that humans are determined to use it to those ends.

—Edward R. Murrow [1]

The future!
How often we looked forward to it with anticipation and excitement, confident that advancements in science, technology, and education would continue to make things better. There were no challenges we couldn't overcome, no obstacles we couldn't master.

Just look at the slogans from the World's Fairs of the 20th Century: *A Century of Progress; Dawn of a New Day; Century 21 Calling; Man and His World*; and the most famous of all, *The World of Tomorrow*. Even in the face of economic calamities and despite wars that came and went, there was always a sense—sometimes no more than a *hope*—that tomorrow was on the way, that *next year* would be the year that brought peace and prosperity.

It was at the 1939 World's Fair that we discovered the greatest of modern marvels, television. It had been on the way for a decade, and now, thanks to RCA, it had landed in America; in opening the fair, Franklin D. Roosevelt became the first president to appear on TV. No longer would we have to go to the theater to see our favorite stars in action—now, they would come to us, in the comfort of our own living rooms. Movies, sports, dramas, comedies, musicals, variety shows—they'd all be there for us to see at the flip of a switch.

As we watched, we were treated to symbols of the future, the limitless potential promised by America's postwar prosperity: the latest new cars, traveling down modern highways linking cities throughout the country; electric appliances, such as washers and dryers, refrigerators and stoves, providing comfort and convenience for the American homemaker; travel to the moon and the stars beyond, and more. Providing a better future for our children was no longer just a hope—it was now more like a *certainty*.

There was, however, another vision that appeared on television: that of a darker future, imagined by those who recalled the lessons of history and understood how easily men could turn a future full of hope into one of violence, oppression, totalitarianism, and death.

Darkness in Primetime is a collection of essays reflecting my perspective on how these programs predicted today's surveillance and tyranny. As a conservative, I see these threats often stemming from progressive social engineering—language manipulation, censorship, and the erosion of individual freedoms under the guise of safety or equity. I recognize, however, that authoritarianism can manifest across the political spectrum, from conservative-led surveillance policies to liberal overreach, and I aim to explore these dynamics through the lens of television's prophetic narratives. These essays are not objective histories but subjective reflections, meant to provoke thought and draw parallels between past fictions and present realities.

I

The art of storytelling has played a crucial role in human culture since antiquity. The earliest records of sacred dramas date back as far as 2,000 years before Christ, and long before the written word, oral communication served as a way of preserving those things that a people valued: their history, their forms of entertainment, their traditions, their sacred beliefs. Stories were told through drawings, by song and dance, on stage, and in manuscripts. The advent of television presented yet another way of telling a story, one that allowed the storyteller to reach millions of people all at once, in the most intimate setting possible: not a theater, not a public square, but a person's home.

It is the job of the storyteller to engage the audience in such a way that they are entertained, illuminated, or educated. It doesn't have to be all three, of course; only a sadist would be "entertained" by the massacre of nuns or the extermination of Jews, to cite just two of the stories presented in this book. But the storyteller understands the necessity to grab the audience and not let them go, commanding their attention through the sheer drama of the telling; only then will there be a chance for the storyteller's message to be transmitted.

The storytellers responsible for the scripts that were turned into these television dramas were moved by events past and present, and by their insights into human nature. They sought to communicate their observations, hopes, and fears, to viewers, either by adapting stories written by others, or by creating original works: stories that used historical allegories, science fiction parables, and contemporary warnings of how even those who fought against evil could succumb to using that very evil in support of what they thought was good. The results were occasionally inspiring, often frightening, and without exception, disturbing. And the irony of it all is that these broadcasts, which in so many ways have turned out to be prophetic, came to us through the same technology that the brighter future promised.

A dry recitation of the facts, however accurate or well-intended it may be, doesn't always accomplish that objective. George Orwell wrote his memoir *Homage to Catalonia* (1938) in an attempt to convey his growing disillusionment with totalitarianism and communism. After reading Arthur Koestler's *Darkness at Noon*, he realized he could communicate that story much more effectively through fiction, and the result was *1984*. David Karp was influenced by both *1984* and *Darkness at Noon*, and added his own perspectives in writing *One*. Peter Weiss realized that nothing could compare to the story of Auschwitz as told by the survivors themselves, and relied on trial transcripts in writing "The Investigation." And so on.

Most of the stories in this book are fictional, although many of them—particularly the Cold War stories—have their basis in fact. But even when the story being told is one based on a specific historical event—the extermination camps of the Holocaust, the assassination of Archbishop Thomas Becket, or the French Martyrs of Compiègne—the television adaptations of those stories had, as an underlying component, a way of dealing with contemporary events through the backdrop of historical drama. T.S. Eliot had one eye on the past, the assassination of Becket in 1170; but the other eye was set squarely on the future—the rise of Hitler's Germany.

The results—programs that aired during some of the most tumultuous times in modern history—were meant to function on multiple levels. They had to succeed, of necessity, as entertainment programs suitable for broadcast on network television. It is clear, though, that their authors intended them also to be taken as cautionary tales—no, I think it needs to be stronger than that. They were warnings, modern-day morality plays pitting good versus evil in such a way that the opposing sides were on display for all to see.

II

The COVID crisis—what I call "COVID Theater"—brought home the fragility of freedom and liberty, not only in supposedly democratic countries such as the United States, but around the world. It was also a dramatic demonstration of how relevant these totalitarian dystopias had become. Events that had, in their time, been considered fantasy and science fiction were now very real, and very threatening. When neighbors began reporting each other for mask violations and outdoor gatherings—echoing the paranoid citizens of "The Monsters Are Due on Maple Street"—or when governments tracked citizens' movements through smartphone data—bringing to life the surveillance state of "1984"—it causes one to view episodes from familiar programs such as *The Twilight Zone* and *The Outer Limits* in a different—and more disturbing—light.

The growth of the surveillance state, and with it the diminishment of personal privacy, is evident in "1984" and "The Invasion of Kevin Ireland," while "One" illustrates the horror of thought crimes and the lengths to which the State goes to eliminate them. "The Children's Story" and "The General" demonstrate how easily the education system can be used for indoctrination purposes, and "A Taste of Armageddon" shows the folly of leaders who will do anything to keep wars going. The cult of celebrity obsession and the unreality of reality television are prophesied in "The Year of the Sex Olympics," the desire for immortality and cosmetic perfection is portrayed in "Number 12 Looks Just Like You," and the suspicion and paranoia of COVID Theater can be neatly summed up in "The Monsters Are Due on Maple Street." Themes ranging from religious intolerance to cancel culture appear as undercurrents throughout the stories.

These programs come from a variety of genres: made-for-television movies; episodes from weekly series; comedies and dramas that appeared on anthology programs; and an opera. They come from the United States and Great Britain; the earliest was originally broadcast in 1936, while the most recent dates to 1982; and they are set in the past, the present, and the future. Some of them are quite well-known, but many have lapsed into a kind of limbo, unseen since their original telecasts.

That so many of them remain unknown to most people, even those who consider themselves classic television aficionados, is partly the fault of the television industry itself, an industry that failed to realize the historical significance of what it was programming.

The television industry's neglect of its heritage is striking given its moral potential. John Gardner wrote: "Television—or any other more or less artistic medium—is good (as opposed to pernicious or vacuous) only when it has a clear positive moral effect, presenting valid models for imitation, eternal verities worth keeping in mind, and a benevolent vision of the possible which can inspire and incite human beings toward virtue, toward life affirmation as opposed to destruction or indifference"[2]

If television can, therefore, be considered an art form, then what the industry has done with its heritage is no less egregious than if painters were to throw out their canvases following an exhibition, or playwrights burned their manuscripts after a performance. It's understandable that no filmed record exists of television's first dramatic production, 1936's "Murder in the Cathedral," but even after kinescopes and video recording became available, the industry took little care to preserve or promote its output beyond a few scattered examples.

Even the internet, which has done much to make obscure video available (and to catalog information about programs that no longer exist) has at times fallen short. As I point out, the 1967 broadcast of "The Investigation," heralded as one of the most important programs ever shown on television, isn't even mentioned in the IMDb (or anywhere else online, for that matter). There's precious little information to be found about "One," either—not even a cast list. Information on these programs had to come through the kind of research that is personally satisfying, but often frustrating in its incompleteness.

It has to be said, though, that if more of the people who had seen these programs took their messages seriously, rather than dismissing them as "far-fetched" and "improbable," we might not find ourselves in this mess in the first place. Is that an exaggeration, a case of wishful thinking? Perhaps, but history is strewn with examples of those who ignored the messages from the prophets to their eternal regret.

III

You might wonder, apart from burnishing the historical record, why anyone would be interested in these programs other than the historian dedicated to the documentation of obscure television programs from 40, 50, even 60 years ago. Even if they did prophesy the future, even if their warnings were eerily prescient, isn't this a little like closing the barn door after the horses have already escaped?

I suppose there's some truth in that. But history serves many purposes, and one of them is to show us that history is never static; it never stays in one place for long. We no longer seem to view the future with unbridled optimism, and most of us doubt that our children will grow up in a better world than we did. We spend our lives just trying to hang on, waiting for the next shoe to drop, and fearing that the shoes belong to a centipede.

We indeed live in what Aldous Huxley called a Brave New World, and it does indeed take bravery to live in it, let alone try to change it. But for all the alienation and despair present in the worlds presented to us in these programs, there can also be found an undercurrent of hope. Not the same hope that made the future look so positive back in The World of Tomorrow, perhaps, but hope nonetheless. Hope that one man alone can throw a monkey wrench into the machinery and stop the inevitable. Hope that a group of people acting together can change things, even though no one will ever recognize their sacrifice. Hope that by remaining true to your values, you can make a difference, even if you aren't alive to see it.

If things are to turn around, if the world is to change for the better, then it is important to learn from history. The stories told in these programs are part of that history.

---

1. Murrow, "RTNDA Speech," 364–71.
2. Gardner, *On Moral Fiction*, 15.

ONE
EYES OF THE MACHINE

1984

Written by William P. Templeton
Based on the novel by George Orwell
Produced by Felix Jackson
Directed by Paul Nickell
First broadcast on *Westinghouse Studio One*, September 21, 1953

I hardly know an intellectual man, even, who is so broad and truly liberal that you can think aloud in his society.

—Henry David Thoreau[1]

Just as the Rose Bowl is considered the Granddaddy of all college football games, George Orwell's *1984* presentation of everything encapsulated by that description. That doesn't mean it was the first—Aldous Huxley's *Brave New World* precedes it by more than a decade, and several of the programs reviewed in this book are adapted from stories that came out prior to Orwell's classic work—nor does it necessarily suggest that it is the best, the most thrilling, or the most compelling; such judgments are often in the eyes of the consumer.

There is no doubt, though, that *1984* is the most iconic, its most famous elements now comfortably entrenched in our lexicon. The title no longer describes just a year; it has become a synonym for an entire way of thinking, shorthand for a world in which everything has become a contradiction—concepts such as Big Brother, the Thought Police, and thoughtcrime; banal (but telling) sayings such as War is Peace, Freedom is Slavery, Ignorance is Strength, and 2+2 = 5; and even the use of the author's name—Orwellian—as shorthand for the nightmarish, and the oppressive, that which cannot be believed until one finds himself in the middle of it.

Therefore, it seems only logical to begin here, in Oceania, the place from which all other nightmares emerge. The themes that are present throughout the programs in this book—fear, alienation and loneliness, naivete, the loss of privacy, and perhaps above all the search for truth—can all be seen here.

It also seems appropriate to look to the first-ever television adaptation of Orwell's story, which appeared on the CBS television network in 1953, only four years after the book's publication. It may not be the best adaptation of 1984; in fact, almost certainly it is neither the best nor the most comprehensive, given the limitations imposed by the one-hour timeslot and the mores of the era. But it is the first, and as such, that ought to count for something.

I

The world in the year 1984 is an ugly place. The three great superstates—Oceania, Eurasia, and East Asia—have been in a permanent state of war for the last 25 years. The State rules by brute force; books have long since been outlawed, personal freedom is a thing of the past, telescreens in every room monitor all that is said and done, and the Thought Police are constantly on the alert for the merest suggestion of independent thought, expression of emotion, or expression of beauty.

Winston Smith (Eddie Albert), a faceless bureaucrat in the Ministry of Truth, spends his day revising history—erasing "unpersons," tweaking "misprints"—to align with Big Brother's latest narrative, ensuring the past conforms to the State's current dictates.

In his dim flat, Winston huddles in a telescreen's blind spot, a corner of shadow where he dares to defy. In his forbidden diary, he scrawls repeatedly: "Down with Big Brother." A knock at the door startles him—he hides the diary, heart pounding—but it's only Parsons, his neighbor, with his daughter Selina, a zealous Youth Spy. "She's turned in thoughtcriminals," Parsons boasts, proud of her vigilance. They walk to the Chestnut Tree Café, ordering "Victory Gin," the Party's favored drink. Julia (Norma Crane), a striking Anti-Love League member, passes by, her dark hair catching Winston's eye. Parsons warns him not to look at her with such open desire, as expression like that can get you in trouble.

Seeking solace, Winston visits Charrington's antique shop, a dusty haven run by an old widower who recalls pre-Revolution days. A glass orb with Indian Ocean coral, useless yet luminous, captivates Winston; he buys it, drawn to its defiance of utility. Charrington shows him an upstairs room, once his home with his late wife, now empty—no telescreen. "My world," Charrington murmurs, gesturing to shelves of delicate relics. Winston, leaving, spots Julia again, captivated by her beauty.

At work, Winston's supervisor, O'Brien (Lorne Greene), praises his erasure of traitors' photos, calling him "valuable." O'Brien's cryptic aside—"I'd like to talk sometime"—hints at subversion, intriguing Winston. The daily Two Minutes Hate interrupts, a ritual frenzy where workers denounce Cassandra, a Trotsky-like archenemy, and kneel to Big Brother's image, chanting his name. Julia, nearby, slips Winston a note: a declaration of love, forbidden and electric. They meet in the countryside, beyond the gaze of telescreens. She sensed that he didn't belong, that he wasn't one of them. "They can't own love." Their affair blooms—stolen moments, always alert for the sound of footsteps, posing as strangers at work.

Darkness in Primetime

Winston suggests Charrington's room as a meeting place. There, Julia unveils smuggled Inner Party luxuries—real sugar, white bread, jam, coffee, and milk—and dons a dress. For the moment, it feels as if they've escaped. The mood is broken when a rat skitters across the room, causing Winston to react in terror, but Julia eases his mind: "We all have something we fear more than anything else."

Despite their growing love—or perhaps because of it—Winston's desire for resistance continues to grow. He confronts O'Brien, declaring that he and Julia want to join the underground. O'Brien probes their commitment—Winston replies that they will do anything, except lose each other. O'Brien promises to get Winston a copy of Cassandra's book, a key to the Party's origins. Winston shares this with Julia, but she balks: she cares not for revolution, but only the happiness of the present.

In Charrington's room, their haven shatters. A telescreen, hidden behind a mirror, blares: "Treason!" Charrington, a Thought Police agent, betrays them. Arrested, Winston lands in a cell with Parsons, nabbed for muttering "Down with Big Brother" in his sleep. His daughter had turned him in, he says, oddly proud. "It shows that I brought her up in the right way."

And then O'Brien enters—not a prisoner, but an official with the Thought Police. He has had Winston under observation for seven years, and Winston now realizes that O'Brien's earlier hints of rebellion were a calculated trap to ensnare dissenters.

The interrogation begins: Julia, O'Brien reveals, betrayed Winston instantly. Holding up four fingers, O'Brien asks, "How many fingers am I holding up, Winston?" he asks. "Four," Winston answers. O'Brien replies, "And if Big Brother were to say, not four but five, then how many?" Winston receives a charge from the machine, and as he cries out, he changes his answer to five. "You are lying," O'Brien says. "You still *think* you see four. Two and two do not always make four, Winston. Sometimes they make five."

Room 101 is next. What lies behind the door, O'Brien says, is "the worst thing in the world" for each individual. Recalling the incident in Charrington's room, O'Brien says he knows what Winston's fear will be, and we hear the squealing of rats. growing louder and louder. Terrified, Winston screams, "Take Julia, not me. Not me." O'Brien nods malevolently; he knows that the brainwashing is complete, that Winston now belongs to them.

Released, Winston sits at the Chestnut Tree, scrawling "2+2=5" on paper, Big Brother's lie has now become his truth. Julia passes; they speak as strangers. Each admits betraying the other in the terror of Room 101. "I couldn't stand up to the threats," she says. "*Do it to someone else.* Do it to anyone. Do it to so-and-so, and afterwards you might pretend that it's a trick, but when it happens, you do mean it," she says. "And after that, you don't feel the same toward that person any more." Winston hollowly repeats the phrase: "*You don't feel the same.*" As she leaves, a song lingers in the background:

> *Under the spreading chestnut tree,*
> *I sold you and you sold me,*
> *There lie they, and here lie we*
> *Under the spreading chestnut tree.*

II

"Nineteen Eighty-Four" opened the sixth season of CBS's dramatic anthology series *Studio One* on September 21, 1953, at the height of the McCarthy era. Felix Jackson, the show's producer, told the press that he "had been hoping to get the Orwell book on the TV screen ever since it was published several years ago," but had never found the "proper program" until now. One of Jackson's priorities was to emphasize that 1984 was a story of ideas and not to overwhelm it with futuristic elements:

> [T]he thing above all that we had to avoid was anything fantastic—in the science fiction manner—in the way of costumes, sets, and action. Orwell's description of things in his imaginary country was pretty thorough, and we have done our best to stick to it.[2]

The depiction of the telescreen was a subject of great curiosity prior to the broadcast and proved to be a technical challenge. After various experiments, Jackson explained, "our technicians came up with an apparatus that almost gives the impression of being a living thing as it dominates the lives of the characters. Even when there is no image on the screen, you are conscious of the power it holds over the people."*

In the world of live television, the selection of a director is always critical, and for "1984," Jackson bypassed Franklin J. Schaffner, an experienced hand when it came to current affairs stories, in favor of Paul Nickell, who was nearly overwhelmed by the assignment but came through brilliantly; he would later say that "1984" was the most important show he'd ever directed.[3] The cast included Eddie Albert, unfortunately miscast (in this writer's opinion) as the protagonist, Winston Smith; Norma Crane as Julia, his colleague and forbidden lover; and Lorne Greene as O'Brien, the underground member who turns out to be an agent of the Thought Police (you'll never watch

---

* Incidentally, the male telescreen voice belongs to a very young Robert Culp (later to portray Kelly Robinson in *I Spy*), in only his second television credit—a rare instance of an actor appearing in "1984" before becoming famous for a role involving espionage.

Bonanza in quite the same way again). Altogether, Jackson assembled roughly 50 actors and a crew of 100, the largest company ever seen on American television.[4]

Music for the play was composed and conducted by Alfredo Antonini, musical director for CBS and conductor of the CBS Orchestra, and a past contributor to *Studio One*. Antonini's effort produced an extremely effective soundtrack, combining a melancholy string motif that captured the story's tension between longing and despair, with Russian-flavored martial music that left no doubt as to the source of that despair.

Unsurprisingly, the script, written by British playwright William Templeton, required several compromises to bring Orwell's vision to 1950s television. The production dramatically condensed the story to about 50 minutes, and saw many of its more graphic elements either toned down (as in the case of Room 101) or, as with Orwell's frequent philosophical digressions, removed completely. (In the case of the latter, it appears more likely that the running time, rather than any political considerations, resulted in the cuts.) As for Cassandra, the traitor now leading the resistance, his name was changed from Emmanuel Goldstein in the book, possibly due to concerns that the name sounded too Jewish. (Remember, Julius and Ethel Rosenberg had been executed as Soviet spies earlier in 1953.)

The sexual content of the novel required discretion as well. Not only was the Junior Anti-Sex League (the group to which Julia belongs) renamed the Anti-Love League—a touch of Orwellian irony—the costuming presented Jackson with a challenge: "Orwell had his men and women in similar attire, a sort of overall garment," he explained.

> We decided we certainly couldn't have a man and woman in a romantic clinch while both were wearing pants... So

we compromised a little by dressing the woman in a mannish-type blouse, but we put a skirt of sorts on her.[5]

On the other hand, some of the accommodations proved to be quite effective, in particular the conceptualization of the infamous Room 101, the room in which a prisoner is confronted by his worst fear. Though some critics wanted a more graphic Room 101, its unseen horror—marked by squeals and Winston's screams—served to intensify the Party's psychological terror, forcing viewers to imagine the depths of totalitarian control.

Also effective was the claustrophobic, expressionist set, designed by Kim Swados and Henry May and dominated by two elements: pairs of eyes, appearing randomly on the backdrop, seemingly peering out from the darkness; and an abstract rendition of Big Brother that, according to Jackson, was meant to avoid identification with any specific dictator. "As a matter of fact, Orwell wasn't writing about Russia at all," Jackson pointed out. "We wound up with a poster that shows a face only from eyebrows to lower lip. Without forehead and chin, it doesn't look like anyone."[6]

The broadcast was a resounding commercial success, garnering a 53 percent share of the market (8.7 million homes),[7] which would stand as the highest-rated *Studio One* presentation of the season. Numerous viewers reported being unable to sleep following the broadcast, so disturbed were they by what they'd seen. Reviews heaped praise on the production. *The New York Times* television critic Jack Gould called it "a masterly adaptation that depicted with power, poignancy, and terrifying beauty the end result of thought control—the disintegration of the human mind and soul."[8] Walter Winchell said it "deftly dramatized the stark terror" of the novel, adding, "You've met nicer folks in your nightmares."[9] Philip Hamburger, writing in *The New Yorker*, called it "stunning," praising Templeton's script for reflecting "the chill terror" of the novel and singling out Crane's performance, one that "made me, for one, believe that she was literally fighting for the very right to think and breathe and remain human."[10]

From his perch at the *Herald Tribune*, John Crosby opined that Albert was perhaps a little too timorous as Smith, and that Crane might turn into a very good actress, but "isn't yet." Still, he wrote that while "1984" "could hardly have equaled the book, . . . it was a pretty thought-provoking experience, all around."

Crosby also noted something both ironic and disturbing, the mention of which could not help but tweak executives at CBS:

> It was very nice of CBS to put on this protest against the totalitarian future but a good many of the practices which are decried in this drama are practiced at CBS right now.
>
> "Here's to the time when thought is free," says Eddie Albert in a toast at one point in the play. It's a great toast—until you stop to think that thought is not at all free at CBS.
>
> Every single actor on that show had to be cleared by the upper floors to be sure they had never had a politically incorrect thought. If they'd ever had one, they'd never have been on that show. As I said, I'm glad CBS is publicly opposed to Thought Police, as in this show.[11]

III

George Orwell's world is one that has become familiar in both literary and political history, a world built on censorship, government surveillance, mutual suspicion, and the suppression of all forms of dissent, populated by agencies with names like the Ministry of Truth, which controls the distribution of information and makes appropriate "adjustments" to the historical record to conform to the latest pronouncements of the government; and the Ministry of Love, home of the infamous Thought Police, charged with the arrest and "rehabilitation" of those who practice dissent against the government. Orwell's concepts entered the lexicon almost from the very beginning, perhaps none more iconic than "Big Brother" himself, which has become synonymous with malevolent omniscience, oppressive totalitarianism, and (most terrifying of all) reality television.

As we look back from the perspective of seven decades, it's easy to see how much of Orwell's vision has come true: the concept of thoughtcrime, the mindless (and dangerous) babble of Newspeak, the promulgation of fake news through constant historical revision, and—particularly—the creation and use of technology as a weapon. Bob Francis, reviewing "1984" in *The Billboard*, complained that the script was "cluttered with fantastic, pseudo-scientific devices" that made it "more ridiculous than moving."[12] And yet, as we will see repeatedly throughout these stories, nightmarish visions that were written off as absurd or even impossible have not only come to pass, but they have also been accepted as normal (or at least here to stay) by vast portions of society.

Although there have been relatively few video adaptations of the novel—the 1953 *Studio One* broadcast was followed by BBC productions in 1954 and 1965, big-screen adaptations in 1956 and 1984, and a memorable Apple Macintosh TV commercial in 1984—the book itself has never gone out of print, nor has it ever really gone out of style. Undoubtedly, one of the reasons for the book's timelessness is that both the left and the right can point to its contents as representing an existential threat to freedom and liberty. In a letter from Orwell to Sidney

Sheldon,* who had purchased the stage rights to *1984* soon after its publication in 1949, he wrote that the book "was based chiefly on communism, because that is the dominant form of totalitarianism, but I was trying chiefly to imagine what communism would be like if it were firmly rooted in the English-speaking countries, and was no longer a mere extension of the Russian Foreign Office."[13]

But while many, quite reasonably, assumed the villains of the piece were communists, and Big Brother modeled on Stalin (in fact, the 1956 movie was secretly funded by the CIA, with a $100,000 subsidy from the United States Information Agency),[14] † the convergence of the *Studio One* broadcast with the era of the McCarthy hearings meant the plot could be interpreted in multiple ways. Both producer Felix Jackson and director Paul Nickell suggested McCarthyism as at least a subtext of the production; when asked years later if he had intended to draw a parallel between the story and McCarthyism, Nickell said that although it was not done overtly, "That's what I wanted to come out subconsciously."[15] And after all, the word socialism is missing from "1984" altogether.

But how does Orwell's message translate to today's ideological divide? Unfortunately, due to the running time, the *Studio One* "1984" ignores the manipulation of language inherent in Newspeak. However, in the novel, the character Syme explains the potency of such manipulation:

> By 2050, earlier, probably—all real knowledge of Oldspeak will have disappeared. The whole literature of the past will

---

* Yes, the same Sidney Sheldon who wrote *The Other Side of Midnight*, created *I Dream of Jeannie*, and won an Oscar, a Tony, and an Emmy for his various writing projects.
† The CIA also contributed to the funding of an earlier movie based on Orwell's *Animal Farm*. At least it wasn't USAID.

have been destroyed. Chaucer, Shakespeare, Milton, Byron—they'll exist only in Newspeak versions, not merely changed into something different, but actually changed into something contradictory of what they used to be.[16]

And indeed, it's hard not to see Newspeak at work in the efforts by the left to advance social engineering and indoctrination, efforts that would be ripe for satire, were satire itself not considered a form of subversive thoughtcrime. One might question an ideology that defines abortion as a "reproductive right," sex-change operations as "gender-affirming care," and mothers as "inseminated persons."[17] These are just a few of the ways in which this indoctrination proceeds, and simultaneously compels its adherents to tie themselves in such knots that they struggle to define what a woman is, and fear offending fragile ego structures to such a degree that they substitute the term "unalive" for suicide,[18] and refuse to print the nicknames of professional sports teams if those nicknames refer to Native American terminology. In their world, words have the power to hurt, to offend, and to do everything, in fact, except tell the truth. Control language, as someone once said, and you control the masses.

There's more; take the media's groupthink, where outlets parrot identical phrases like the Ministry of Truth's lies, or the Memory Hole, swallowing inconvenient facts unless social media preserves them. The Two Minutes Hate lives in the frenzy of Trump Derangement Syndrome, whipped up by media, political operatives, and influencers to drown out dissent.

And then there's one of the most insidious, intrusive elements in Orwell's world, the telescreen. Orwell must have been familiar with the technology behind television, given that the

BBC began regular television service in 1936.* It would have been no great stretch to imagine that while you were watching your television, it was watching you back (in fact, there were many anecdotes of people back in the day who thought the new device was doing just that), and listening to what you had to say as well. Which, of course, our phones do constantly; I'm not sure how Orwell would feel about a portable telescreen that people not only didn't try to avoid, but willingly—obsessively—carried around with them.

Of course, the right has its own history of surveillance and control: post-9/11 policies like the Patriot Act expanded government overreach, and recent 2025 proposals for nationwide facial recognition under a conservative administration continue this trend.[19]

The intrusiveness of technology has, I think, a more corrosive effect even than the loss of privacy. In "1984," Winston yearns for a time "when men are different from one another and don't live alone." Is there anything that has contributed more to that feeling of isolation and alienation than technology? We text instead of talk; look at our screens instead of at each other; watch television shows on demand and movies at home, rather than as shared or group experiences. It is one of the most insidious ways in which a regime demoralizes and controls the population, separating people from each other communally and spiritually. It keeps them from organizing. From plotting.

IV

In the end, much is left unsaid and unknown about the world in "1984." Is Cassandra a real person, for instance, and

---

* More on this later!

does he speak the truth? Or is he a creation of Big Brother, a straw man performing a *Wag the Dog*-like scenario that distracts the people of Oceania from their own miseries? What about Cassandra's book, which supposedly explains how the State works, and which O'Brien uses to tempt Winston: did he write it, as Big Brother says, or was it actually written by the Party, as O'Brien alleges? Is there an actual Resistance, or is it a fiction of the Thought Police, meant to keep people stirred up and to lure dissidents into a trap that will lead to their reeducation?

What about the never-ending wars? Are they real, or is the truth as Cassandra says,

> The primary aim of modern warfare is to use up the products of the machine without raising the general standard of living, for if leisure and security are enjoyed by all alike, great masses of human beings who are normally stupefied by poverty will become literate and learn to think for themselves. And once they have done this, they would sooner or later realize that the privileged minority has no function and they would sweep it away.

For that matter, does *Big Brother* even exist, or is he simply a symbol: a face on a poster, a puppetmaster's front, a propaganda tool used by the Party to focus fear and loyalty? "You'll never know," O'Brien tells Winston. The true power might lie with unseen elites, like the Party's faceless rulers, orchestrating control through wealth and influence, a military-industrial complex thriving on endless conflict like Oceania's wars, or a former leader pulling strings from the shadows, unseen yet ever-present.

We'll never know. Or will we?

In "1984," O'Brien says that power is not a means, but an end in and of itself. "One does not establish a dictatorship in order to safeguard a revolution; one makes the revolution in order to establish the dictatorship. The object of persecution is persecution. The object of torture is torture."

Essayist and critic Scott Bradfield wrote that, "For Orwell, the horror of totalitarianism was not that someone would impose it on you, but rather that you might be all-too-prepared to submit."[20] Or, as Benjamin Franklin put it, "Those who would give up essential Liberty, to purchase a little temporary Safety, deserve neither Liberty nor Safety."[21]

That, my friends, is what we face today. It takes no great stretch to make the connections between Orwell's creation and our world today; if you glance at the headlines on any day of the week—"Communist crackdown in China is 'Beyond George Orwell's Imaginings'"[22]—the parallels become clearer. And if you think that it can't happen here, in the land of the free and the home of the brave, you haven't been paying attention.

So the next time someone—perhaps in the government or the media—tells you that Freedom is Slavery and Ignorance is Strength, remember the words of the prophet: "Woe unto them that call evil good, and good evil; that put darkness for light, and light for darkness; that put bitter for sweet, and sweet for bitter!"[23] And then ask yourself: when someone asks what two plus two equals, what will *you* answer?

All dialogue quoted is from "1984" (*Studio One*).
1. Thoreau, *Life Without Principle*, 488.
2. United Press, "Tough Problems," 2.
3. Ryan, *Orwell on Screen*, 15-16.
4. Ibid., 15.
5. United Press, "Tough Problems," 2.
6. Ibid.

7. Ryan, 19.
8. Gould, "Television in Review," 44.
9. Winchell, "Actress Working," 4.
10. Hamburger, quoted in Ryan, *Orwell on Screen*, 20.
11. Crosby, "Radio and Television," 24.
12. Francis, quoted in Ryan, 20.
13. *New American*, "60th Anniversary," para. 6.
14. Morris, "All in the Family," para. 31.
15. Nickell, quoted in Ryan, *Orwell on Screen*, 21.
16. Orwell, *1984*, 77.
17. Marshall, "Creeping Totalitarianism," para. 3.
18. Ibid.
19. Birnbaum, "Facial Recognition," para. 5.
20. Bradfield, "'1984' Still Relevant," para. 5
21. Franklin, "Reply to the Governor," 19.
22. Pentin, "Communist Crackdown," para. 4.
23. Isaiah 5:20 (*KJV*).

The General

Written by Lewis Greifer (as Joshua Adam)
Produced by Patrick McGoohan (Executive Producer)
and David Tomblin (Producer)
Directed by Peter Graham Scott
First broadcast as the sixth episode of *The Prisoner*, November 3, 1967

indoctrinate *(in·doc·tri·nate) verb. 1: to teach or inculcate a doctrine, principle, or ideology, especially one with a partisan or sectarian opinion or specific point of view.*[1]

—*Merriam-Webster's Collegiate Dictionary*

In man's eternal quest for knowledge, it sounds like a panacea, manna from heaven: an online learning program that allows a student to take a three-year college-level course in history in just three minutes. It's the most egalitarian of educational opportunities: no tuition, no classrooms, just knowledge beamed straight into your living room via your television screen. And if you think you're the kind of person who can't learn like that, just ask The Professor: "It can be done," he says. "Trust me."

What could *possibly* go wrong?

I

The Village, a pastel prison of surreal calm, hums with its latest gift to residents: "Speed Learn," a three-part history course beamed through its sole TV channel. Promising mastery of "Europe Since Napoleon" in a 15-second burst, it's the brainchild of the Professor, whose posters beam assurance: "It can be done. Trust me." A cryptic "General" guarantees "100% entry, 100% pass." Number 6 (Patrick McGoohan), ever wary of the Village's benevolence, strolls its cobblestone paths when Number 12 (John Castle), a self-described "cog in the machine," nudges him to enroll. "The Professor's interesting," he says, eyes glinting with unspoken intent. Number 6's instincts flare—nothing here is as it seems.

En route to his cottage, a commotion erupts. Villagers chase a fleeing figure, security pouncing like hounds. To Number 6's shock, it's the Professor himself, wild-eyed, dragged away. In the aftermath, Number 6 discovers a tape recorder hidden in the sand. Listening to the recording, he hears the Professor's voice: "I have an urgent message for you . . ." Number 6 quickly shuts off the machine and reburies it.

Curious about what he has seen and heard, Number 6 decides to investigate further, starting by tuning into Speed Learn. The Professor's face fills the screen, hypnotic music swelling as the camera zooms into his left eye. Fifteen seconds later, the broadcast ends. Number 2 (Colin Gordon), the Village's overseer, barges into Number 6's cottage, quizzing him. To his own surprise, Number 6 recites flawlessly—the Treaty of Adrianople (1829), Greek independence (1830), Bismarck's ally in the Second Schleswig War (Austria). Every villager he meets parrots the same, their minds eerily synchronized.

Afterward, Number 6 returns to the beach to retrieve the recorder, but finds Number 12 there ahead of him. The two men agree to work together to get to the bottom of whatever is going on.

At a "voluntary" art class, the Professor's wife oversees residents sculpting oddities. A man tears book pages, and Number 6, puzzled, asks why. "He's creating a fresh concept," she replies. "Construction from destruction's ashes." She adds, voice strained, that her husband suffered a breakdown from lecture stress, now under a doctor's care—likely Village coercion to keep him compliant.

Number 6's suspicion deepens. Along with Number 12, he replays the tape. The Professor's voice resumes: "You are being tricked. Speed Learn is an abomination. It is slavery. If you wish to be free, there is only one way: destroy The General. Learn this and learn it well: the General must be destroyed!" Number 12 proposes swapping the next lecture with the warning. Handing Number 6 a security pass disc, he instructs him to infiltrate the Administration's projection room at dawn.

The plan unravels, as Village schemes often do. Number 6, recognized, is hauled to a boardroom where Number 2 and Number 12—maintaining his cover—grill him. This time, the question shifts from "Why did you resign?" to "Who leads your conspiracy?" Number 2 ridicules Number 6 over his insignificant attempt. "This reactionary drivel that you were on the point of sending out to our conscientious students: 'the freedom to learn,' 'the liberty to make mistakes,' old-fashioned slogans. You are an odd fellow, Number 6, full of surprises." He explains why the conspiracy must be crushed: "I'm sure that a man of your caliber will appreciate that rebels... must be kept under the closest possible surveillance with a view to their extinction if the rebellion is absolute."

Escorting Number 6 to a vast chamber, Number 2 reveals the Professor, hunched over a typewriter, scripting lectures. "Allow me to introduce—The General," he says, parting curtains to unveil a hulking supercomputer, lights pulsing like a heartbeat. "The Professor's creation," Number 2 boasts. "No more rote learning, no wasted schools—a course subliminally absorbed, verified by infallible authority." "A row of cabbages,"

Number 6 observes sardonically. Number 2 corrects him: "*Knowledgeable* cabbages."

The Professor, pale and tethered to his machine, barely glances up, his passion for The General now a chain. Number 2, frustrated by Number 6's silence, plans to feed data into The General to unmask conspirators: Number 6's security pass, issued only through Number 12's department. But Number 6 seizes the moment, daring Number 2 to ask The General a question it can't answer. Unwilling to back down in the face of Number 6's dare, Number 2 allows him to ask the question.. Number 6 approaches the terminal, his fingers deliberate — four keys: W, H, Y, question mark. He feeds the tape into The General. Dials spin, lights flare. Smoke curls as the machine groans, circuits frying. The Professor lunges to save it, Number 12 at his side. An explosion rocks the room, flames claiming both men. The General lies in ruins, its "infallible" mind shattered.

Number 2, ashen, stammers, "What was the question?" Number 6 replies coldly, "It's insoluble, for man or machine." Pressed again, he answers, "W. H. Y. Question mark." Number 2 echoes, "*Why?*"

Number 2 is left mumbling, " . . . Why?" as Number 6 leaves the room.

II

Airing on November 3, 1967, in the UK and July 13, 1968, in the US as a CBS summer replacement for *The Jackie Gleason Show*, 'The General' showcases the Village's latest control mechanism: Speed Learn, a program that imprints historical facts instantly, raising Number 6's suspicions of a deeper agenda.

The General

The premise of *The Prisoner* is key to understanding the series, though it often plays a minor role in individual episodes. The show emerged as a quasi-spin-off of the 1960s British espionage series *Danger Man* (known as Secret Agent in the U.S.), starring Patrick McGoohan as John Drake, an agent battling England's enemies and occasionally his own superiors. Unlike James Bond, Drake, at McGoohan's insistence, used violence only as a last resort and avoided romantic entanglements. Despite—or perhaps because of—this approach, *Danger Man* ran for three seasons, with the first featuring 30-minute episodes, and had begun a fourth in color when McGoohan left to create *The Prisoner*.

The Prisoner seemingly continues from *Danger Man*. Its opening credits depict an unnamed secret agent who resigns, only to be kidnapped while planning a vacation and taken to a mysterious place called the Village. There, everyone is assigned a number instead of a name, with some as prisoners and others as agents of the Village, leaving their true allegiances unclear.

The Village is run by—well, that's just one of the mysteries. It could be an Eastern bloc country—the Soviet Union, East Germany, Red China—or a Western agency like the CIA, suspicious of defectors, or even a modern elite like Klaus Schwab or George Soros, wielding unseen influence.

In this world, nothing and no one is above suspicion. We know only that the supreme leader of the chimera-like city-state, the Big Brother of the Village, is the unseen, unheard, Number 1.

Number 1's majordomo is aptly called Number 2, and, as an individual, is completely disposable: we see a different actor in the role virtually every week. While Number 2's responsibilities encompass the whole of the Village, he appears to have one overriding obsession: the new prisoner, who has been dubbed Number 6. Specifically, he demands to know why Number 6 resigned; it is a question that Number 6 stubbornly refuses to answer: "My reasons," he says, "are my own."

Subsequent episodes feature the struggle of the Village's overlords, under the direction of Number 2, to obtain the answer to their question "by hook or by crook," while Number 6 fights his twin battles: to escape from the Village and to resist their questioning. All the while, one overriding question hangs over the series: Who's in charge here? Who is Number 1?

As for the Village itself—well, that's perhaps the most perplexing of all. Unlike the other interrogation centers we've seen, the Village is not a grim underbelly, a vista dominated by Brutalist architecture swathed in uniform grayness. It is, in fact, beautiful: the small flats in which Number 6 and his fellow inmates reside are neat and tidy—all the comforts of home, really. The architecture of the civic and social buildings is playful and imaginative, the grounds manicured and colorful. It's almost too pleasant—comfortable enough that you might never want to leave. But that's precisely the trap: What if the perfect village hides the perfect prison?

III

Isn't Speed Learn an interesting concept? "A three-year course indelibly impressed upon the mind in three minutes." Imprinted—downloaded, if you will—right onto your brain while you're hypnotized by what's on the screen; I wonder if that's what the Chinese used in *The Manchurian Candidate*. And the machine that facilitates it is called the Sublimator—a nice touch. You remember how subliminal images of food and drink used to be inserted into movies to make people in the theater hungry and get them to buy popcorn and soda, all without them being aware? We didn't like it then, so why should we tolerate it anywhere else? Even the word *Sublimator* has a sinister connotation, as if you're trying to get away with something you shouldn't be doing. It's a very effective tool for indoctrination.

Indoctrination, of course, isn't limited to education (or filmmakers); in fact, many educators would denounce it. But there's more than one way to "educate" people. Take, for instance, the media. It doesn't matter what kind of media we're talking about; it all has to do with presenting the news in such a way as to mold your reaction to it, to ensure that your opinion conforms. They control access to the facts they choose to present, the video they choose to show, the people who face their cameras and write on their pages; you could say that they control access to the access.

You notice how, after taking the course, everyone answers the questions by rote, right down to the use of the same words? Their answers don't vary, even by a comma. Haven't you ever gotten curious when newscasters do the same thing: report a story using virtually the same words, the same phrases, on every national network, every local station, in every part of the country? Almost as if they're all working from the same script, isn't it?[2]

IV

Interestingly, Thesaurus.com presents both *instruction* and *training* as synonyms for indoctrination, as if it could somehow infuse the word with a kind of value-free meaning.[3] Indoctrination deservedly carries with it a negative connotation, because it's not education so much as it is re-education, a way of presenting information to ensure conformity—or Groupthink—as a natural way of thinking. Groupthink encourages infantilism: it teaches people not to think, but to defer—to trust the experts, the authorities, the system, lest they *hurt* themselves trying.

Rote learning has an important role to play in education; imagine multiplication tables, forms of grammar, or remembering world capitals otherwise. At the same time, and especially when it comes to understanding and analyzing the meaning behind ideas and concepts, one also has to have the ability to comprehend, to put things in context, and thereby draw conclusions from them. For example, Corporate America loves to preach the gospel of embracing change as if it's some divine mandate, but without teaching folks how to determine whether the change is actually *necessary*, it's little more than empty calories, education-style. Alas, the art of critical thinking is too often left on the cutting-room floor.

This is nowhere more apparent than in the discovery of the secret behind the General. Even in 1967, the idea of a computer pulling all the strings was becoming something of a cliché, used in science fiction for decades. However, even though the visual concept of a giant supercomputer dates the series, the logic behind it remains sound. And what does it mean that these electronic brains, seen by the writers as threats to our freedom, have evolved into items of convenience for modern living? One would have to be a fool to deny how easy we've made it for machines to do our thinking for us—outsourcing judgment to apps, bots, and algorithms. And the more we rely on them, the less we seem to rely on ourselves.

The Prisoner is a series composed of questions, challenging not only the viewers but the characters themselves, and "The General" is no exception: "Who is Number 1?" "Why did you resign?" "Who is the General?" "Who is the head of the conspiracy?" It comes as no surprise, therefore, that the most devastating moment of the episode is also sparked by a question: "Why?"

When Number 6 challenges the computer, he does so not as *Star Trek*'s Captain Kirk might, by using its own logic against it, but by posing the most natural of questions: *Why?* And consider: it is a natural question, one of the first that we learn as infants; we ask our parents "why" this and "why" that, and the answer we get is always the same: *Because*. There's no need to go any further in justifying the answer, because they're the adults and we're not; they know more than we do. They provide us with what they think we ought to know.

So the instinct to ask questions comes to us early on. As we grow older, we discover that asking questions leads to knowledge. After all, how many times have we been told that "there are no stupid questions"? According to Plato, Socrates believed that "the disciplined practice of thoughtful questioning enables the scholar/student to examine ideas and be able to determine the validity of those ideas."[4]

In *The Prisoner*, the knowledge came from the General. Today, the State props up experts as all-knowing parents, infantilizing the population to justify its control. These authorities, cloaked in credentials, demand conformity, warning of calamities to suppress dissent, substituting paranoia for caution and censorship for discussion, leaving no room for individual judgment.

And the body politic, fearful of being left out, ostracized, or accused of not getting it, nods their heads and goes along, and heaven help those who dare to stand out. It is impossible to free a man who has come to love his jailer.

As Number 2 says of the Professor, "People love him, they'll take anything from him. It's the image, you see, that's important: the kindly image."

One of the biggest lies in history: I'm from the government and I'm here to help.

Let me repeat: *Groupthink encourages infantilism.* It makes us five years old again.

V

In a series set in a prison—an unconventional one, to be sure, but a prison nonetheless—where every individual finds himself trapped in a cell, "The General" is an episode that is particularly clear on this point, that we are all our own jailers, imprisoned in the cells we create for ourselves.

There are many kinds of prisons, however; fear, as we've seen in these programs, is one of them.

In his 1933 inaugural address, Franklin Roosevelt famously told us that the only thing to fear was fear itself.[5] Fear has the ability to hold us in its grip, like a vise. And when fear is wielded by the powerful over the powerless, it becomes one of the most potent weapons in the arsenal, with an ability not only to imprison but to crush totally.

Fear is a fickle mistress, though, and her sword cuts both ways. The Professor is as much of a prisoner as everyone else in the Village. His greatest creation, The General, is also his warder; Number 2 shows a great deal of perception in identifying the computer as both the Professor's greatest love and his greatest hate. As has been the case in so many "mad scientist" stories, he has come to fear his own creation.

And what about Number 2? His role as an architect of fear serves only to underline his own insecurity, his tenuous hold on power. Our knowledge that Number 2 is an interchangeable figurehead, destined to be replaced next week by yet another, shows that he, too, is ultimately a prisoner, subject to the whims of Number 1.

The powerful thrive on fear, which is why it must be resisted; otherwise, we wind up imprisoning ourselves. After all, it's hardly a coincidence that the one phrase appearing in the Bible more often than any other is "fear not"[6]. Likewise, the prophet Isaiah promises that the Lord's anointed one will "proclaim liberty to the captives, and the opening of the prison to them that are bound."[7]

That's a promise no tyrant, no algorithm, and no Village can ever silence.

All dialogue quoted is from "The General" (*The Prisoner*).
1. *Merriam-Webster's Collegiate Dictionary,* s.v. "indoctrinate."
2. Shapiro, *Ben Shapiro Show,* para. 2.
3. Thesaurus.com, s.v. "indoctrination," para. 1.
4. Plato, *Theaetetus,* 155d.
5. Roosevelt, "First Inaugural," *Public Papers,* 2:11.
6. Goodrick and Kohlenberger III, *NIV,* s.v. "afraid" and "fear.".
7. Isaiah 61:1 (*KJV*).

The Architects of Fear

Written by Meyer Dolinsky
Produced by Joseph Stefano
Directed by Byron Haskin
First broadcast on *The Outer Limits*, September 30, 1963

The scientists of today think deeply instead of clearly. One must be sane to think clearly, but one can think deeply and be quite insane.

—Nikola Tesla[1]

"Follow the science" has become quite the mantra in certain quarters these days, repeated with an almost religious fervor, like a Catholic praying the Hail Mary, a Jew reciting the Shema, a Hindu chanting the Gayatri Mantra, or a Muslim praying the Salah.

As such, those who follow the science, like any devout religious believer, have their holy men, the scientists, whom they follow with fanatical devotion. And they accept their prophecies with a belief that borders on superstition. For these scientists are nothing less than gods, the science they preach illuminating the day.

And then, in the lateness of the hour, comes the setting of the sun, and the twilight of the gods.

I

In the shadow of a nuclear clock ticking toward midnight, a cadre of scientists and doctors at United Laboratories grapples with mankind's brinkmanship. Plagued with wars and rumors of war, and with tensions running high in every corner of the world, the apocalypse seems ever more inevitable. Their solution is radical: only a common enemy can avert a nuclear holocaust. Blurring the line between science and madness, they create a living hoax: an alien invader from the distant planet Theta. Their plan is audacious: land a Thetan spaceship on the UN terrace, incite global panic, and watch nations unite against the threat, ushering in an era of cooperation. The catch? A member of this group must agree to become the Thetan, allow himself to be transformed beyond humanity.

Dr. Allen Leighton (Robert Culp), a quiet, intense young scientist, draws the short straw. He accepts the irreversible cost: injections and surgeries will remake every organ, rendering him alien, unfit for Earth's air or life. Dr. Gainer (Leonard Stone), overseeing the process, is blunt: they'll change "every organ in your body"—lungs, kidneys, blood—to match an alien world. The physical toll will be immense, the emotional strain worse. Allen, deeply in love with his wife, Yvette (Geraldine Brooks), carries a heavier burden. They've just learned she's pregnant—a miracle they feared impossible—yet he must abandon her and their unborn child; due to the need for secrecy, he won't even be allowed to tell her goodbye. Yvette will hear he died in a plane crash en route to a Peruvian conference, never knowing his pain, his fear, or his choice. Allen's resolve hardens: despite the personal toll, he remains grimly committed to the cause of world peace.

Preparations hum with precision. The spaceship, a sleek marvel, balances alien oddity with aerodynamic grace. It can float, ensuring survival if Allen misses the UN and hits the East River. His transformation is grueling. Cells shift to thrive on nitrogen, not oxygen; his digestive tract, kidneys, and blood chemistry morph under relentless surgeries. Pain fractures his mind—a schizophrenic episode leaves him raving, strapped down, sedated. Doctors talk of risks, but Allen, lucid again, presses on, haunted by Yvette's absence. Meanwhile, Yvette, shattered by the crash report, visits United Labs to collect his belongings. Grief sharpens her intuition—she confronts Gainer, voice trembling: "I feel him here, somehow." Gainer, stone-faced, deflects, but Allen, listening from a sterile chamber, writhes in agony.

The launch nears. Disguised as a weather satellite, Allen's ship will trace a reentry path mimicking an interstellar voyage, bolstered by a staged alert of an approaching alien craft. Gainer briefs him: Land at the UN, face the General Assembly, and declare yourself the vanguard of an invasion. The goal: fear of the common threat will lead to global unity and world peace. When he asks if it really *will* work, Gainer gives it a 70 to 80 percent chance of success, adding, "Millions of soldiers have gone into battle in wars of hate with less odds and with less cause." Allen, now barely human, his skin taut and eyes unearthly, nods.

However, it turns out those scientists weren't so smart after all. A navigational glitch caused by misaligned coordinates sends the ship off course, and instead of landing in front of the UN, it crashes in dense woods near the lab. Allen, battered but alive, emerges from his damaged craft, where he's set upon and shot by a group of frightened hunters.

In the meantime, Yvette, drawn by an unshakable hunch, arrives at the lab. Her suspicions, sparked by Gainer's evasiveness during her earlier visit, drive her to return, searching for answers.

Mortally wounded, Allen staggers back to the lab, where he sees Yvette. Their eyes meet, his still holding a spark of the man he once was, and he traces a gesture, a private sign from their shared nights that only she will recognize. Yvette gasps, recognition flooding her. "Allen," she whispers, reaching, but his strength fades. Yvette kneels beside him, sobbing, as he dies, a martyr to the cause of science.

II

"The Architects of Fear" remains one of the most memorable episodes of *The Outer Limits*, and, in the opinion of many critics, one of the very best. (It was, incredibly, only the third episode of the series.)[2]

Meyer Dolinsky's script never allows the heavy moral and ethical questions inherent in its premise to overwhelm the human scale of its tragedy, brought to life with tenderness and believability by Robert Culp and Geraldine Brooks. Neither of them attempts to milk the pathos of the situation; they simply trust the script to do the heavy lifting. Culp brilliantly conveys the sense of loss hanging over Allen, all while he's pretending to Yvette that everything is normal—he won't even be able to tell her goodbye. The torment he experiences is almost palpable.

For her part, the sudden revelation of Allen's death, as she's preparing for the birth of her child, is devastating to Yvette, and to us; Brooks achingly conveys the marital love that causes her to feel her husband's pain on the operating table, the kind of love that continues even after death. It is, in a sense, the antithesis of the love experienced by Rick and Ilsa in *Casablanca*: in "The Architects of Fear," Allen and Yvette's love *does* amount to more than a hill of beans, because, in the end, it proves that love is the only truly redemptive force. After all, what does it profit the world to gain peace and lose love?

Byron Haskin, who had previously directed the 1953 big-screen version of *The War of the Worlds*, as well as several film noir thrillers, would direct six episodes of *The Outer Limits* in all;

we'll see his name again later. Three-time Oscar winner Conrad Hall is masterful with his black-and-white cinematography that is equal parts noir and classic science fiction, its heavy shadows and sharp delineations producing a stylish yet foreboding atmosphere seldom seen on television. And Dominic Frontiere's affecting original score, beautiful even as it breaks one's heart, is so good that it shows up as music cues in future *Outer Limits* episodes, as well as other Frontiere-scored programs such as *Stoney Burke*.[3]

Let's talk for a minute about the alien, the so-called Thetan, created, as were all monsters on *The Outer Limits*, by Project Unlimited, Inc. Our first look at the Thetan is chilling; the scientists at United Labs have been conducting experiments on an animal, presumably some kind of primate, and at the meeting where they discuss their plan, they unveil their creation. We don't see it directly, only in grotesque shadow; we do, however, hear its unearthly squeals and screeches. The subtlety of that initial experience is extremely effective, in the great tradition of horror movies in which the monster is only intimated. Regardless of how it looks, it couldn't possibly be as horrifying as the image conjured up in our mind's eye.

Later, when Allen's transformation is complete, we see the Thetan full-on. And it remains grotesque, although we can tell that there is a human inside the costume. (One can only imagine the kind of non-human creature that today's special effects could have conjured up.) While less subtle than its initial shadowy glimpse, the Thetan's grotesque reveal underscores the scientists' hubris, transforming a human into a monstrous parody to serve their scheme. This stark visibility drives home the human cost of their arrogance, making Allen's transformation viscerally real. And that human dimension is, of course, the point of everything.

However, let's not underestimate the effect the Thetan had on viewers in 1963; some of ABC's affiliates judged its appearance to be so monstrous as to cause them to black out the screen when it appeared (which basically meant the entire final act), while other stations tape-delayed the footage containing the Thetan until after the late local news. There were even a few affiliates that didn't air the episode at all.* So it was still nasty enough to make one wonder how scientists could ever do that to someone.[4]

III

So what, exactly, are the bioethics involved in converting a human being into an alien life form? It's a death sentence for Allen, no matter how you look at it. In all likelihood, he'll be killed, perhaps even in front of the United Nations building; any sci-fi fan can tell you that this is how Earthlings deal with alien visitors, especially if they come bearing hostile intentions. Killed, and then dissected for examination, which is why it was so important to the scientists to create a convincing, non-human alien in the first place.

A non-human. But, you see, there's the rub. Because Allen is a human being, and always will be, created with a soul and everything that makes us human. No amount of conversion can alter that fact. And if Allen does somehow manage to survive, either through escape or by being held as a prisoner subject to the protection of the Geneva Convention and so forth, what kind of life does he have to look forward to? Alone, in what is now, to his transformed biology, an alien atmosphere, never

---

* The Thetan was portrayed by Hungarian stuntman and acrobat Janos Prohaska, who would go on to play the Horta in *Star Trek* and the Cookie Bear on *The Andy Williams Show*, among many credits.

again to know the companionship of one of his own. The scientists, presuming to remake Allen's God-given nature, strip away his humanity as if they could override the soul's sacred design.

And what about the Nazi doctors in World War II, Mengele and the others, conducting experiments in the concentration camps? There were others, in other countries, experimenting on humans without their consent. Those doctors all used the excuse that the work they were doing was important, perhaps even critical to the continuation of human life. Maybe they even believed it themselves. They didn't have that right, any more than the scientists at United Labs did. That no one was forced, that they all had an equal chance of being the one chosen—that doesn't make what they did somehow less evil. And Allen, too, bears some culpability; he consented not just to his own fate, but would have accepted another's had the draw gone differently.[5]

Not only was Allen Leighton given a death sentence, he was surgically and psychologically stripped of his humanity, except for one thing. Even the doctors weren't able to remove the human capacity to love.

IV

There are other moral and ethical considerations at work here as well, relating to the manipulation of others' lives, the desire to assume the God mantle. It's tough when you assume that mantle of being smarter, better, and worthy of making decisions in the name of "world peace."

Allen's sacrifice is intended to be noble and selfless. That's how the scientists at United Labs see it, anyway, but we can see immediately that this is absurd on the very face of it, that there is something tremendously immoral—wicked—about what they're up to. Fully in thrall to the "ends justify the means" school, they scheme—for that is what it is, with all its negative connotations—to employ a massive deception on Earth's population. And even if this harebrained scheme were to work, what kind of megalomania would these scientists have to possess to take upon themselves the authority to engage in an act with such global consequences? Who made them God? They were neither elected nor appointed; they simply take it upon themselves to manipulate the lives of others. It is, without doubt, a characteristic of all totalitarian societies. And where does it end? Having achieved world peace, do they now undertake a similar deception to end other ills? Mandatory sterilization to stop overpopulation? Deindustrialization to end air pollution? Rationing of food to cure obesity?

I know—how about something like locking down the entire world over a supposedly deadly pandemic? We isolated those who were most vulnerable, the sick and the elderly and the shut-ins, even though we understood that the deprivation of love, of human contact, would demoralize those who hadn't already lost hope, and would make them feel like outcasts. Then we impressed upon the public an untested, unproven "vaccine," making its use all but mandatory, and we threatened those who didn't follow the rules with a different kind of isolation—ostracism, quarantine, even the possibility of internment—for "the good of society." We knew just how potent that deprivation could be. Consider global lockdowns, where unelected officials isolated the vulnerable and mandated untested vaccines, claiming it was for society's good, much like the scientists' presumptuous scheme.

The thing about playing God is that once you go down that road, it becomes pretty hard to pull over to the side.

V

I don't know if C.S. Lewis coined the term "scientism"—I think he did, but in any event, he certainly provided the modern understanding of the concept, and why it was something to be feared. Lewis defined scientism as "science characterized by principles and practices tending toward controlling rather than investigating nature," resulting in what he termed a "moral devolution of science."[6]

In his book *The Abolition of Man*, Lewis predicted that if "scientific planning [was] cut free from traditional values" it would eventually become "joined to modern ideologies," the result of which would be a not-so-distant future in which the values and morals of the majority are controlled by a small group who rule by a thorough understanding of psychology, and who, in turn, being able to see through any system of morality that might induce them to act in a certain way, are ruled only by their own unreflected whims. In surrendering rational reflection on their own motivations, the controllers will no longer be recognizably human, the controlled will be robot-like, and the Abolition of Man will have been completed.[7]

In "The Architects of Fear," the scientists embody this scientism, their plan to deceive mankind illustrating Lewis's warning of science untethered from moral restraint. To our eyes, there is something tremendously immoral—something *evil*, if we're being accurate—about this plan. Undoubtedly, the scientists have assured themselves that their motives are benign, even noble. And fully in thrall to the "ends justify the means" school, they feel that, as men of science, they're not only equipped, not only justified, but entitled, to make this monumental decision—to employ a massive deception on Earth's population. It's the Achilles heel of scientists.

However—and this is important to consider—being critical of scientism is not the same as being anti-science. As James A. Herrick says of Lewis in *The Magician's Twin: C.S. Lewis on Science, Scientism, and Society*,

> Lewis respected scientific work that pursued knowledge of the natural world. Science, for Lewis, was a means of seeing and thus of appreciating nature, and the inviolability of nature was the principal value guiding its investigations. By contrast, the new science, or scientism, developed out of an impulse to see through nature by deconstructing its processes until everything in it—including the human being—was explained as a matter of mere physical causality. Scientism's ultimate goal is placing all of nature under human control.[8]

VI

The human tragedy of "The Architects of Fear" is heartbreaking. Forget whether or not what the scientific cabal is up to passes moral scrutiny; what happens to Allen and Yvette is simply painful to watch. It's a human dimension that science fiction doesn't often explore, so focused is it on science. It's the human dimension that the scientific cabal so totally overlooks; they're so intent on saving all of humanity, they forget the wonder of the individuals that make up the leviathan. In a sense, they can't see the trees for the forest.

The stories emanating from *The Outer Limits* were often skeptical of science, especially when it was placed in the hands of powerful men answerable to no one. "The Architects of Fear" is no exception, for these powerful men, these scientists who thought they could bring the peoples of the world together,

The Architects of Fear

were not only trying to create fear; they were acting out of fear themselves. The episode's closing narration:

> Scarecrows and magic and other fatal fears do not bring people closer together. There is no magic substitute for soft caring and hard work, for self-respect and mutual love. If we can learn this from the mistake these frightened men made, then their mistake will not have been merely grotesque. It will have been at least a lesson—a lesson at last to be learned.

What these men didn't realize, what those who use fear—or fall victim to it—don't realize, is that fear is not the most powerful emotion. Love is. And in the end, fear is no match for it.

We have, in our lifetimes, seen the triumph of scientism, not just in the way we live our lives, but in the terms by which the battle is defined: the words that can be used, the concepts that can be discussed, the opinions that can be held in public. And, as is always the case, to be on the other side is to be not just different but wrong. As Christopher O. Blum writes in the article "C.S. Lewis and the Religion of Science," "It is alarming to learn how the rise and growth of a scientific culture has been linked with the most blatant subjectivism."[9] Now, of course, everything is subjective, thanks to scientism.

And if that subjectivism continues, where does it end? We've seen vaccine mandates and social credit systems emerge, echoing the episode's warning of fear-driven control that dehumanizes individuals. And if it doesn't stop, what comes next? Life and death itself, perhaps—decided not by God, but by algorithms, experts, and unelected panels. And by then, will any of us be recognizably human?[10]

There is, of course, one more lesson to take from all this, one that we would all do well to remember: "except the LORD keep the city, the watchman waketh but in vain."[11]

And the Architects of Fear will continue to live in the night, and thrive.

All dialogue quoted is from "The Architects of Fear" (*The Outer Limits*).
1. Tesla, "Radio Power Will Revolutionize."
2. Schow, *Outer Limits Companion*, "Architects."
3. Ibid.
4. Ibid.
5. Lifton, *Nazi Doctors*, 180–92.
6. Herrick, "Lewis, Science, and Science Fiction."
7. Herrick, "Abolition of Man."
8. Herrick, "Lewis, Science, and Science Fiction."
9. Blum, "Lewis and Science," para. 6
10. Ibid.
11. Psalm 127:1 (*KJV*).

O.B.I.T.

Written by Meyer Dolinsky
Produced by Joseph Stefano
Directed by Gerd Oswald
First broadcast on *The Outer Limits*, November 4, 1963

Experience should teach us to be most on our guard to protect liberty when the Government's purposes are beneficent. Men born to freedom are naturally alert to repel invasion of their liberty by evil-minded rulers. The greatest dangers to liberty lurk in the insidious encroachment by men of zeal, well meaning but without understanding.

—Louis D. Brandeis[1]

You might remember that slasher movie from about 30 years ago called *I Know What You Did Last Summer*. It was based on a novel and spawned a couple of sequels and even a TV series. Pretty successful, in other words, and based on the primal desire for privacy, the fear that one's deepest secrets might be made public.

Now imagine that a machine exists that enables you to know what *everybody* does, not only last summer, but last week, last night, two hours ago, even what they're doing right now. How would you feel about that—would you make use of it, just one time? More than once? All the time?

And since we're kicking the idea around, how would you feel if you found that others could use that same machine to spy on *you*?

This is the world according to O.B.I.T.

I

At the Cypress Hills Research Center, a top-secret U.S. government facility, Captain James Harrison dies under mysterious circumstances. His erratic behavior and apparent mental deterioration prompt concerns beyond just his death—morale at the center is reported to be in steep decline, with strange, widespread psychological effects on the staff.

In response, a Senate investigative committee is convened. The episode opens with Senator Jeremiah Orville (Peter Breck) arriving at the center to conduct a series of tense hearings into both the death and the facility's increasingly hostile and dysfunctional atmosphere. From the beginning, it is clear that the staff are deeply uneasy. The senator's presence is met with reluctance and fear. Everyone seems on edge, as if being watched—or hiding something.

Orville questions a number of personnel, including technicians and military officers. Their testimonies reveal a pervasive climate of distrust and tension. One witness bluntly says that everyone suspects everyone else, and that people have stopped talking to one another. Another describes the center as a "slaughterhouse of the human spirit."

As Orville digs deeper, references to a mysterious device called O.B.I.T. begin to surface more frequently, though staff remain tight-lipped and visibly frightened. What troubles the Senator even more than the device's existence is the ambiguity surrounding its origin. No one—not even high-ranking officials—seems to know who invented the machine, where it came from, or how it was installed in the tightly secured facility. Its presence is treated like a fact of life, unquestioned yet omnipresent. The secrecy surrounding it, combined with the fear it inspires, suggests a conspiracy operating well above the command structure. It becomes clear that O.B.I.T. is not merely a controversial surveillance tool, but something more insidious—something whose very existence has undermined the institution's foundations without anyone fully understanding how or when it took root.

Eventually, Orville is taken to see the machine itself. O.B.I.T.—the Outer Band Individuated Teletracer—is kept in a darkened, sealed room, monitored by a technician. Through its screen, Orville observes a man being watched in another part of the facility, completely unaware. The machine allows for total, covert surveillance of any individual within range. No walls or barriers can shield one from its gaze.

Colonel Grover (Alan Baxter), a high-ranking officer involved with the machine's deployment, testifies before the committee and provides one of the most damning insights into O.B.I.T.'s impact. He says while the device was originally introduced under the guise of safeguarding national security, the military's rapid adoption of it twisted its purpose—turning it into a kind of institutional "Peeping Tom" and an addictive trap. He reveals that 18 O.B.I.T. machines are currently operating at military installations across the country and that their influence has spread well beyond defense: "industry, education, communication networks—all over the country."

As his composure falters, Groves admits the psychological toll; "It's like a debilitating disease," he says, echoing Senator Orville's own later phrasing. At first, Groves had supported O.B.I.T., believing in its utility, but he now sees the horror it breeds. "It's the most hideous creation ever conceived," he cries. "No one can laugh or joke. It watches. It saps the very spirit." His voice trembling, he admits the device's deepest cruelty: "And the worst thing of all is... I watch it. I can't not look. It's like a drug, a horrible drug. You can't resist it. It's an addiction." The implication is devastating: even those who recognize the evil cannot break free from its grip.

While Orville is horrified by what he learns, he senses there's more to the story. He arranges to meet Dr. Clifford Scott (Harry Townes), a former scientist at the center who has since been institutionalized. Scott is withdrawn but lucid. He reveals that he once operated the O.B.I.T. machine and became obsessed with using it. Prompted by Lomax, Scott began spying on his wife, consumed by jealousy. "I literally drove her away from me," he confesses. He watched her constantly, suspecting infidelity, until she eventually did fall into another man's arms. Yet no matter how much he scrutinized her with the machine, he could never identify her lover—until he realized the truth: Lomax had ensured that his own wavelength was undetectable by the device. Scott then reveals that Harrison, too, had seen the same monstrous image on the O.B.I.T. screen, which led to his murder. Harrison's death was a direct consequence of his exposure to the same horrifying sight that shattered Scott's mind.

Dr. Scott desperately wants to believe he imagined all of it, that he is simply ill, delusional. But he cannot deny what he saw, and what he now understands. He admits that staying in the institution is a form of self-preservation; it's the only place he feels safe from those behind O.B.I.T. He knows that what he witnessed—the extent of its power, the manipulation he endured—is real. Orville, now fully convinced of the machine's danger and the insidious motives surrounding it, believes him.

The final hearing is convened. Dr. Byron Lomax (Jeff Corey), the acting director of the facility, is called to testify. Throughout the episode, Lomax has been calm, calculating, and eerily composed. But under questioning, he drops his disguise and reveals his true identity: an alien agent from a race that has seeded the O.B.I.T. machines across Earth.

Their goal, he explains, is not immediate conquest by force, but social disintegration. Through endless surveillance and the destruction of trust, the world will become too paranoid, fragmented, and spiritually weakened to resist when the final invasion begins. "You'll learn to live with it," he says. "You'll have to."

Lomax then disappears without interference. The final shot returns to the O.B.I.T. machine, now glowing alone in a dark room. The control voice informs us that while the Justice Department is rounding up the machines, the threat posed by them remains; "In the last analysis, dear friends, whether O.B.I.T. lives up to its name or not will depend on you."

II

Airing just three weeks before John F. Kennedy's assassination, "O.B.I.T." paints a darkly sinister picture of a deep state functioning outside the U.S. government's official channels, steered by a foreign power—a *really* foreign one, this being sci-fi and all. Don't let the extraterrestrial angle fool you, though; the idea presented by the titular machine is coldly realistic, one that would work even without the show's famous Bear making a final-act appearance.

With its themes of surveillance, vanishing privacy, paranoia, distrust, and authoritarian control, "O.B.I.T." was an obvious choice for this book—so obvious, in fact, it was almost overlooked. It made it into the lineup at the eleventh hour, and a good thing it did, fot it's another case of today's world channeling 1960s art, and for viewers, its message probably hits harder now than it did back then.

Many critics today rank "O.B.I.T." among *The Outer Limits'* best. The website *Films from Beyond*, looking back nearly 60 years later, called it a spooky preview of our smartphone and social media age, dubbing "O.B.I.T." an "unholy union of an

NSA supercomputer and the ever-present, all-seeing, all-knowing Facebook app."[2] Even critics who aren't totally sold agree on the episode's eerie foretelling of the electronic future; Critic Billie Doux put it bluntly: "I kept flashing to Big Brother and 1984. If this is what dooms humanity, folks, we're already there."[3]

The story comes from Meyer Dolinsky, who you'll recall explored similar scientific hubris in "The Architects of Fear" in the last chapter; he doubles down on those same uneasy themes here. Behind the camera is Gerd Oswald, in the first of his 14 episodes as an *Outer Limits* director, far more than anyone else. The episode includes some nice visual touches that accentuate Dolinsky's sardonic commentary on things; O.B.I.T.'s viewscreen, for example, looks very much like a 1960s-era television set, and I'd have to think that's not a coincidence.

The cast is led by Peter Breck as Senator Jeremiah Orville—I'll bet that name looks good on a campaign poster—who starts out as your typical ambitious politician but ends up dead-set on uncovering the truth. The excellent Harry Townes gives a moving performance as Dr. Scott, a man who's had the life drained out of him, forced to flee to a mental institution for safety, his vision so terrifying that he *hopes* he is proven insane. Alan Baxter is effective as Colonel Grover, a typical military martinet who breaks down when admitting O.B.I.T.'s addictive grip on him. Jeff Corey proves a worthy adversary as Lomax, the sinister (yet, apparently, seductive) alien who spills his planet's plot against Earth with an enigmatic mix of pride and justification, pointing the finger directly at us.

III

Oh, these meddling scientists! Airing not long after "The Architects of Fear," Dolinsky doubles down with his cynical view that these men just can't seem to resist developing technology that they naively believe will improve "human understanding," all the while apparently remaining oblivious to the potential the technology has to destroy humanity itself, if not human life.

It's as if the thought of some sinister organization exploiting such technology for its own nefarious purpose has never occurred to them. (Scientists really *do* live sheltered lives, don't they?) The loss of privacy is not something to be taken lightly, even when it appears to be done for the right reason; as Justice Brandeis says in the opening epigraph to this chapter, "The greatest dangers to liberty lurk in the insidious encroachment by men of zeal, well meaning but without understanding."[4] Such zeal paves the way for authoritarian tools like O.B.I.T., as Lomax's claim reveals. And, at least until they experience the corrosive effects of O.B.I.T., most of the scientists, unlike Dr. Scott, seem clueless about O.B.I.T.'s potential misuse. (Apparently, they have no time for watching shows like *The Outer Limits*, which warn of these threats constantly.)

But then, as if we're supposed to derive comfort from it, there's always Lomax's reassuring statement that "People with nothing to hide have nothing to fear from O.B.I.T."—the authoritarian mantra that's every bit as instinctive to tyrants as "I was just following orders" is to the guilty. I mean, if it's only used against wrongdoers, and it's done in a good cause, it can't possibly be that bad, can it?

This justification for surveillance has its modern parallels, such as those Craig Beam notes in his excellent blog *My Life in the Glow of The Outer Limits*. Beam makes an interesting comparison to Christopher Nolan's 2008 Batman movie, *The Dark Knight*, in which "Batman hacks into all the cell phones in Gotham to create a highly-detailed echolocation network, an O.B.I.T.-like approach that's likely possible in the real world (and might already be happening)."⁵ It's all very much a part of that "ends-justify-the-means" mantra, and while it's very cool to see in a movie, it's a hell of a lot more disturbing when you think about the possibilities in real life, especially if it's happening with your iPhone.

Lomax's bland assertion is answered by Senator Orville's dry retort, "I'd hate to have that thing trained on me when I was cussing out fellow Senators or the president of the United States or my former law partner, to say nothing of my wife." No one, Orville implies, can possibly be "that perfect" to withstand such scrutiny. That, I think, is what we should be most worried about, for when we're that willing to blithely debase the basic dignity of the human individual, where does it end?

IV

You might have detected, in the "security" use of O.B.I.T., an echo of the McCarthy-era Blacklist of the 1950s, and you wouldn't be wrong. Dolinsky had a keen interest in what governments were capable of doing when driven by fear. "[I'm] also concerned that we do have restraints against extreme totalitarianism," he told author David J. Schow.

> The political focus of 'O.B.I.T.' is all mine; it's a reverse on the H.U.A.C. [House Un-American Activities Committee] thing. These people, far from helping a free society, are really its worst enemy, in the sense they breed so much hostility and fear that they curiously accomplish the very thing they are trying to prevent. Witch-hunting is the wrong way to go about it.⁶

Indeed, the actions taken by both O.B.I.T. and HUAC were driven, at least in part, by a paranoid zeal to root out perceived threats at the cost of liberty. Both systems justified their excesses as national security imperatives, yet the result, often as not, was fear, conformity, and ruined lives. The lesson should be obvious, but bears repeating nonetheless: when the state wields unchecked power to "protect," it often tramples on the very principles it claims to defend.

Jeff Corey, who played the sinister Lomax, knew this cost firsthand, having been blacklisted for refusing to name names before HUAC in 1951. Corey, who never joined the Communist Party despite attending some meetings, ridiculed the committee's tactics, a defiance that cost him his acting career for over a decade. As we'll see in later chapters, Corey was not the only actor featured in this book to endure the Blacklist's wrath; others, too, faced similar economic and social exile for their beliefs or associations. The Blacklist, like O.B.I.T., thrived on this kind of atmosphere—eventually, over 300 Hollywood professionals, from actors to writers, were denied work, their careers affected, sometimes beyond repair, often by suspicion alone.

The irony certainly wasn't lost on Corey. In a 1989 interview with Kathryn M. Drennan, he said that while he wasn't sure if he'd been deliberately cast in the role as a political statement, "I had a lot of fun doing that." Of the Blacklist, he said, "I just couldn't be an informer. I know I've got guts, and I know I care so much for my country. I demonstrated it."[7]

V

There's another aspect to this story that, I think, bears some thought. Orville's evolution during the episode from ambitious politician to determined truth-seeker illuminates the government's conflicted role in safeguarding or subverting personal freedom. O.B.I.T. embodies the shadow of the Deep State, operating beyond accountability, its origins obscured as Grover admits that nobody knows who authorized its purchase. This opacity epitomizes the Deep State's unaccountable power. Yet Orville, a government figure himself, emerges as a defender of liberty, his determination undeterred in the face of continued stonewalling.

We can't really be surprised at this duality, nor can we be surprised that it becomes most apparent only in retrospect. One of the high points of "O.B.I.T.," most critics agree, is how it has actually become *more*, not less, relevant over the years. At the time the episode was aired, the assassinations of the Kennedys and Martin Luther King, the Vietnam War, Watergate, and a host of other events had yet to occur, and the overarching cynicism with which we view the government today had yet to be the cultural norm; the Pew Research Center notes that in a 1964 poll conducted by the American National Election Study, 77 percent of those responding said "they could trust the federal government to do the right thing nearly always or most of the time."[8]* Today, it's far more likely that the government itself would be shown as instigating the development of O.B.I.T. (no need for aliens at all), and that the senator would probably be involved in a cover-up of the whole thing—or, alternatively, that if he insisted on persisting in his investigation, he'd wind up, as Lomax suggests, going down to electoral defeat.

Or worse—because you can't ignore the retroactive irony of the episode's timing. When viewers originally saw it, on November 4, 1963, they had no clue as to the events less than three weeks in the future, and the theories that would soon erupt.

---

* By contrast, when asked the same question in May 2024, only 22 percent answered in the affirmative—up from *16 percent* in 2023. (Pew Research Center, June 2024.)

JFK's death (combined with the murder of Lee Harvey Oswald three days later), followed by the assassination of Robert F. Kennedy in 1968, fueled theories of Deep State involvement, a notion that seems all-too reasonable considering O.B.I.T.'s untraceable origins. And so one must wonder: could Orville meet the same fate as JFK and RFK, given the threats Lomax hints at for those who probe too deeply? Regardless of how you feel about conspiracy theories, the fact that such a scenario can even be considered underscores the shift from 1963's optimism to today's distrust, where the government's role as guarantor of individual freedom is met with derision.

All this is probably less an indication of the government's unchecked power (although it is), and more a sign of how naïve we were, how we should have been asking more questions. Still, even if it's true that the "good old days" weren't really all that good, they did provide us with something of a breather. For cynicism, even when it's justified, is a corrosive force, a postmodern form of self-hatred. It is so very, very tiring.

VI

When Dr. Scott testifies to his opposition to O.B.I.T., he mentions how his protests to the Department of Defense went unheeded. "I got the view," he tells Orville, "that they thought that the machine was highly successful in eliminating undesirable elements."

I suppose we should be grateful that O.B.I.T. didn't exist during the years of the Bush Administration.* The Patriot Act—billed in the post-9/11 panic as a necessary protection against

---

* Although you can bet that Dick Cheney would have been on the phone to the studio in a New York minute, asking if they could share the technology behind it.

terrorism—opened the gates to mass surveillance, leaving every citizen's liberty dangling like a piñata for bureaucratic whacking.[9] The Biden administration, not to be outdone, stretched this intrusion into schools, banks, churches, and social media, where "misinformation" witch hunts justify rifling through private lives.

Both Bush's bureaucratic spies and Biden's tech commissars, in their words and deeds, betray the soul of liberty. They deny the truth that individual freedom, not state omniscience, fortifies the republic; O.B.I.T., both the episode and the machine, shows how easy it is for such surveillance to ensnare governments and souls in a moral abyss.

Added to that is today's digital serfdom—doom-scrolling, chasing "likes"—what Grover called a "debilitating disease." The personal wreckage of O.B.I.T.'s temptation leaves its victims as exposed as Adam and Eve after the fall, demoralized and disillusioned under a totalitarian shadow: Grover, crumbling on the stand, admits his early zeal for the machine, only to sob, "It's the most hideous creation ever conceived. No one can laugh or joke. It watches. It saps the very spirit. And the worst thing of all is. . . I watch it. I can't not look. It's like a drug, a horrible drug. You can't resist it. It's an addiction."

Dr. Scott, who'd suspected it from the start, paid a steeper price: O.B.I.T. shattered his marriage, and his jealousy—stoked by Lomax—pushed him to spy until, as he admits, "I literally drove her away from me" into another's arms. Discovering Lomax shielded himself from the machine's gaze, Scott fled to a mental institution, his only protection against those hunting him for his defiance. Like our first parents in the Garden of Eden, they were lured by the serpent's promise of godlike knowledge—the forbidden fruit of O.B.I.T.'s omniscience. And yet, where Christ spurned the devil's desert temptations, Scott and Grover faltered, their spirits broken by their own devices.

I wonder—how many of us feel the same way today, yet remain paralyzed by fear or dependency on that which we so willingly embrace?

VII

Well, this is the part where now I'm supposed to point out how the threat from O.B.I.T. was vanquished, and everyone lived happily ever after. I'm not sure I can do that, though.

The closing narration, while assuring us that "Agents of the justice department are rounding up the machines now," reminds us that "these machines, these inventions of another planet have been cunningly conceived to play on our most mortal weakness."

Defiantly, Lomax reveals the plans of his home planet to conquer Earth through the use of the machines, which, he says, are everywhere. "Oh, you'll find them all," he says. "You're a zealous people! And you'll make a great show of smashing a few of them, but for every one you destroy, hundreds of others will be built. And they'll demoralize you, break your spirits, create such rips and tensions in your society that no one will be able to repair them!" The downfall and subjugation of Earth will occur, he says, "without even a single shot being fired."

He makes it clear, however, that this is not a problem that they *created*, merely a condition they are *exploiting*. "You're all the same. Dark, persuasive. You demand, insist on knowing every private thought and hunger of everyone. Your family's, your neighbor's, everyone, but yourselves."

Isn't that always the way? The only window we choose not to look out is the one that is a mirror to our own lives, our own souls. Lomax's vision of societal collapse finds its echo in our surrender to technology. As noted earlier, the Patriot Act's legacy persists, now joined by Silicon Valley overlords capturing our every click, like, and late-night pizza order. As the Founding Fathers spin in their graves, most of us shrug, too busy scrolling to notice our digital chains tightening.

Beyond social media, countless individuals live publicly, their lives an open feed, yet an inner voice whispers that this is *unnatural*, a violation of the soul's need for privacy and freedom. Just as Adam and Eve hid their shame, they bury this truth, too afraid to break free, too scared to confess the addiction that defines their existence.

If our future hinges on breaking free from our addiction to electronic devices, the prognosis for our society is grim. Our obsession with smartphones, social media, and endless streaming has eroded personal responsibility and self-reliance, chaining us to Big Tech's whims while numbing our capacity for critical thought. With government surveillance and corporate data grabs thriving on our dependency, the path to reclaiming liberty demands a cultural reckoning. Yet we seem unwilling—or unable—to break its grip.

And in that, we will be writing our own O.B.I.T.

All dialogue quoted is from "O.B.I.T." (*The Outer Limits*).
1. *Olmstead v. U. S.*, 277 U.S. 438, 479 (1928) (Brandeis, J., dissenting).
2. Scoleri, "Outer Limits of Spying," para. 3.
3. Doux, "O.B.I.T.," para. 2.
4. *Olmstead v. U. S.*, 277 U.S. 438, 479 (1928) (Brandeis, J., dissenting)..
5. Beam, "O.B.I.T.," para. 4.
6. Schow, *Outer Limits Companion*.
7. Drennan, "Test of Character," 52, 70.
8. Pew Research Center, "Public Trust."
9. Greenwald, "Patriot Act Legacy," para. 5.

TWO
MINDS IN CHAINS

Number 12 Looks Just Like You

Written by John Tomerlin (credited to Charles Beaumont)
Based on the short story "The Beautiful People" by Charles Beaumont
Produced by William Froug
Directed by Abner Biberman
First broadcast on *The Twilight Zone*, January 24, 1964

Whoso would be a man must be a nonconformist

—Ralph Waldo Emerson[1]

A red rose is not selfish because it wants to be a red rose. It would be horribly selfish if it wanted all the other flowers in the garden to be both red and roses.

—Oscar Wilde[2]

A *person*, according to the *Catholic Encyclopedia*, is defined as "an individual substance of a rational nature. It implies independence or existence in itself." It goes on to state that, "The strongest proof of the reality of human beings in the world around us rests therefore on the evidence for human personality, and for each of us ultimately on the proof of our own personality."[3] It is what makes us different from animals; only persons exist as rational beings (though some, through their actions, certainly seem bent on disproving that fact); and therefore only persons can be said to be self-conscious, aware of such things as reason, ethics, and truth.

That self-consciousness, combined with one's collective memories, limitations, and free will, is what guarantees our continued existence as an individual human being, as "a free, self-conscious, separate personality, possessed of a genuine individual existence"[4] that belongs to no one else. As John Stuart Mill would write, individuality is essential to the development and refinement of the self; it becomes a moral necessity for the individual to have freedom to make choices based on his or her own experiences and beliefs, else they have no more character "than a steam engine has a character."[5]

And so the individual human being, with all those characteristics and traits, with free will and consciousness and the knowledge of right and wrong, could therefore be said to be the majesty of God's very creation, the shining jewel in the crown.

I

In a future world, those reaching the age of 19 undergo a "Transformation," swapping their natural body for a designer model chosen from a catalog. The options guarantee stunning beauty—astoundingly beautiful women or extraordinarily handsome men. The process eliminates most illnesses, extends lifespans two to three times, and is hailed as "the most marvelous thing that could happen to a person."

Marilyn (Collin Wilcox), a plain 19-year-old, should be thrilled, but she's not. She tells her gorgeous mother (real-life supermodel Suzy Parker), "I want to stay ugly." Alarmed, her mother takes her to Dr. Rex (Richard Long), who insists the Transformation is a normal rite of passage, signaling maturity and aiding "psychological adjustment." Marilyn resists, haunted by her late father, a nonconformist who called the process a "tragedy" that erased individuality before taking his own life post-Transformation. His words echo in her mind: "There's got to be more to life," she insists. "Being like everybody. . . isn't that the same as being nobody?"

Dr. Rex confines Marilyn to the hospital, claiming, "I am afraid that for now, you must let *us* decide what's best for *you*." Her best friend Val (Pam Austin) urges her to comply, saying, "It isn't as if it hurts or anything." When Marilyn vows, "I won't let them change me," Val responds with an inane ditty, "Life is pretty, life is fun, I am all and all is one."

Though the Transformation isn't legally mandatory, Marilyn sees through the pretense—it's inescapable. Realizing the hospital is, in reality, a prison, she flees through the hospital's empty corridors, dodging nurses and recoiling at the sight of a transformed body on a gurney, before darting through a doorway that locks behind her. Two nurses await, saying, "Come in, my dear, we've been expecting you. Sooner or later, everyone wants to be beautiful."

The Transformation proceeds; afterward, Marilyn emerges identical to Val, beaming as she admires her reflection. "The nicest part," she tells Val, "is I look *just like you*." The process has reshaped her body and mind, erasing her resistance.

Rod Serling's closing narration presents the dismal truth: "Portrait of a young lady in love. With herself."

II

One of the most disturbing episodes of *The Twilight Zone*'s much-maligned fifth and final season is "Number 12 Looks Just Like You," written by John Tomerlin, based on Charles Beaumont's short story "The Beautiful People."* As Marc Scott Zicree

---

* The episode's credits list Beaumont as the author, but Tomerlin wrote the script in its entirety as a favor to Beaumont, who was unable to

points out in *The Twilight Zone Companion*, Tomerlin's adaptation is an improvement on the original in that Beaumont's story had Marilyn standing trial and being forced to submit. Tomerlin's change makes things more subtle, more seductive, more insidious.[6]

The key element in "Number 12"—the only science fiction element in the story; everything else is psychological—is a process known as the "Transformation." Professor Sig explains the origins of Transformation:

> Many years ago, wiser men than I decided to try and eliminate the reasons for inequality and injustice in this world of ours. They saw in physical unattractiveness one of the factors which made men hate. So, they charged the finest scientific minds with the task of eliminating ugliness in mankind."

But that's not all:

> As we learned to reshape the features, remold the body, we also learned to eliminate most of the causes of illness and thus to prolong life. Before the Transformation, you could have expected to live 70, 80, perhaps 90 years. But now you can live twice that long. Perhaps three times. This is a good thing, is it not?"

If the Transformation erases physical ugliness, why not reprogram minds to purge 'racist' or 'bigoted' thoughts through reeducation or cancellation? What about the "criminal gene," the genetic anomaly that some scientists believe to be responsible for the most violent behavior in certain individuals?

---

write any longer due to the Pick's Disease that would claim his life in 1967. Beaumont's name was used to sell the episode to the program.

Wouldn't that perfect society, just as Marilyn's world demands uniformity?

In the meantime, people like that have to be kept from attaining positions of influence in business or government. The education of their children has to be turned over to a more responsible authority, one not tainted by such dangerous ideas. Think of what a wonderful world it would be if we all saw things the same way.

III

There are two great reveals in "Number 12," or perhaps we should say one reveal and one discovery that shouldn't come as a surprise to anyone who knows how these things work. The reveal comes in Marilyn's hospital room, where she is "resting." Marilyn's mother and her friend Valerie continue to press her on why she's so unhappy. After all, her mother says, "all they want to do is make you pretty." That's not true, Marilyn replies, recalling what her father had once told her: "When everyone is beautiful, no one will be, because without ugliness there can be no beauty."

As Marilyn becomes more agitated, the doctor suggests they leave her alone, but Valerie asks to stay behind for a moment. She truly cannot understand why Marilyn feels the way she does; furthermore, why does she care so much about what her father said? He's dead, and she's had plenty of fathers since then. "I cared about him," Marilyn says. "He was good and he was kind and he cared about me. Not what I wore, not the way I looked, but what I thought, what I felt. He cared about himself and his dignity as a human being."

And then she tells Valerie what really happened: her father didn't die in an accident; he committed suicide following his own Transformation. "Because when they took away his identity he had no reason to go on living."* Her defiance suggests a deeper motive: by resisting the Transformation, she seeks to give her father's suicide meaning, proving he died defending the individuality that defined his humanity.

As for the discovery, it is the revelation that the Transformation process is mandatory, despite the assurances that everyone makes—"No one has ever been forced to take Transformation if he didn't want it," Dr. Rex had told Marilyn, but that was a lie, and any of you out there could have told her that she was in deep trouble, that if she actually believed she had a choice in the matter, she had another think coming. No government, no regime, is ever going to pass up an opportunity to make something mandatory if it helps them stay in power. In her desperate dash through those bleak, antiseptic corridors of the "hospital," Marilyn finds herself in a rat's maze with no way out; no matter which way she goes, she's always going to end up running through that doorway into the waiting arms of the nurses who, of course, only want to "help" her.

Elk verzet volledig zinloos, as the Nazis put it in their declaration of war against the Netherlands: Resistance is useless.[7]

IV

There is a subtext to "Number 12 Looks Just Like You," one that is impossible to ignore: a commentary on the obsession with youth, particularly among women. Today, we're obsessed not only with looking young, but also with *acting* young. As we

---

* It's quite possible Dr. Rex is making an oblique reference to this when, speaking of the transformation process, he mentions how "we've improved methods since the old days and now it always turns out well."

will see in the chapter on "They," there's a specific tyranny connected with such thought that is particularly insidious.

It encourages us to value things superficially, to equate perception with reality, to judge a book by its cover. And just as beauty is more than skin deep, the poison from such thought goes much deeper than the surface.

This ideology—and it is an ideology—rejects history and tradition, the lessons passed down from generation to generation, that which unites families and communities and nations in a common heritage. It rejects the old in favor of the new, and the hereafter in favor of the here and now. And in doing so, it also rejects the idea of permanency in favor of a dictatorship of relativism, of constant reinterpretation, a floating definition of truth that eventually forgoes truth altogether. That which is wrong today? Just wait a while, and it will be right tomorrow.

As for the consequences, the desire we all have—whether we admit it or not—to make things good before we die? Well, what if that isn't a concern? In a recent article, Venezuelan futurist Jose Luis Cordeiro says, "the evidence suggests death and aging really aren't the inevitable facts of life most people imagine.

> "If we make it to 2030, we will basically live long enough to live forever because we will gain one year per year we survive and more and more," he says. He believes that by 2045, we will start to be able to reverse aging use rejuvenation therapies on cells and organs, making us as "young" as we choose to be.[8]

The claim is bold, almost utopian (as well as being disturbingly similar to the claim of "Number 12"'s Professor Sig). But if Marilyn's world shows us anything, it's that the promise of eternal youth may come at a steep price—not just biological, but existential. What becomes of purpose, of individuality, when aging—and by extension, the arc of a human life—is erased?

Consider, as well, the parallels to what we delicately dub "gender-affirming surgeries"—Orwell would've had a field day with that euphemistic gem—where we mutilate the human body to match someone's latest identity whim. From a moral perspective, rooted in the sanctity of the created order, such procedures echo the Transformation's seductive promise: to remake oneself into something "better," free from the supposed flaws of birth. But what is lost in this?

Marilyn's world strips away individuality for uniformity; might these surgeries, often urged by cultural currents or medical mandates, risk erasing the unique, God-given essence of a person for a fleeting ideal? The pressure to conform—to adopt a new gender as the only path to happiness—how different is that from the nurses' insistence that Marilyn must become Number 12? And once the scalpel falls, there's no going back. Is this freedom, or a deeper captivity to a society that demands we all look—and think—the same?

The mind recoils at this slippery slope, not out of malice, but from a conviction that truth is not so malleable. If gender, like beauty, becomes a construct to be reshaped at will, what, then, anchors us? The Transformation offered Marilyn a longer life, but at the cost of her soul; what price do we pay when we trade the permanence of our created selves for a transient affirmation? These operations, cloaked in compassion, may lead not to liberation but to a labyrinth of regret, where, like Marilyn, we find no exit from the maze of our own making.

V

One of the main benefits of Transformation is that it eliminates illness, lengthens lifespans, makes us happy. And whenever the inhabitants of Marilyn's world get stressed or upset, they just have a glass of Instant Smile. It's like those little pills, Mother's Little Helpers, isn't it? So enticing. If Instant Smile wipes away suffering, isn't that what Marilyn's world sells—a life free of pain but empty of self? Tempting, sure, but who'd trade their soul for that?

Nietzsche didn't agree. He saw suffering as "a necessary, indispensable part of a full life." A life free of suffering was, for him, "absurd and worthless," just like the "desire to get rid of bad weather." [9] This theme echoes in unlikely places, such as in *Star Trek V*, when Captain Kirk, given the chance to erase his bad memories, insists: "I need my pain." [10] In both cases, the message is clear: remove hardship, and you risk hollowing out the very soul of a person.

There is beauty and majesty at the heart of every person, a uniqueness woven into creation itself: no two snowflakes ever alike, fingerprints distinct to each soul. The power of one person to shape the world—magnificent yet daunting in its scope—runs as a constant thread throughout this book, binding the examples we've explored and those yet to come.

Although the theme of "Number 12 Looks Just Like You" seems obvious, and its message a sobering one, not everyone feels the same way. In an in-depth look at the episode at the blog "Shadow & Substance," one commentator wasn't sure that this "utopia" was such a bad thing:

> Come on, she was quite happy afterward. I suppose other races had their own change machines. They're just making everybody perfect. Sounds good to me. . . . after the

Transformation is there no more racism, murder, poverty,...etc.? If so, having to live a sanitized existence is a small price to pay.[11]

For some people, free will isn't that big a deal. Maybe some of you feel the same way.

VI

Would we be willing to give up everything that makes us who we are, in return for such a life? What would a life like that mean?

In "A Man for All Seasons," Robert Bolt's play about the martyrdom of St. Thomas More, the future saint is confronted at his trial by the betrayal of his former friend Richard Rich, who, as part of the deal for providing damaging evidence against More, has been made Attorney-General for Wales. With his characteristic humor, More looks at the chain of office that Rich wears, and wryly comments on the sellout, "For Wales? Why Richard, it profit a man nothing to give his soul for the whole world. . . but for Wales?"[12]

But then, when all is said and done, it is as Cromwell had predicted to Rich when they made the deal to betray Thomas. "That wasn't too painful, was it?" Cromwell asks. "No," Rich concedes. "No," Cromwell agrees. "And you'll find it easier next time."[13]

It's always easier *next time*, isn't it?

When they ask you to sacrifice for a few weeks—wear the mask, close the stores and offices, shut down the churches—that's a small price to pay for the common good, isn't it? And when they ask you to keep at it, when a few weeks stretch into months and then a year—well, if you've gone this far, it's simpler to carry on, isn't it?

And to live twice as long, or three times as long, as you used to? What would it be worth to you?

Would you accept an unproven vaccine, urged as a civic duty, just as Marilyn faced pressure to conform for society's 'good'? And if you have to get another shot, or a different one for the next virus that comes up—well, it didn't sting much last time, so it's fine to do it again, isn't it? Would you trade your freedom, your very uniqueness, for a shot at immortality? Would you surrender *your* soul for Wales?

VII

"The combination of all these causes forms so great a mass of influences hostile to Individuality, that it is not easy to see how it can stand its ground," John Stuart Mill wrote in his treatise *On Liberty*:

> The demand that all other people shall resemble ourselves, grows by what it feeds on. It will do so with increasing difficulty, unless the intelligent part of the public can be made to feel its value—to see that it is good there should be differences, even though not for the better, even though, as it may appear to them, some should be for the worse.[14]

We are, I think, entitled to wonder why "Number 12 Looks Just Like You" ends as it does, with no miracle, no last-gasp reprieve. Like 'Number 12,' the iconic Twilight Zone episode 'Eye of the Beholder'—familiar to fans of the series—exposes the tyranny of conformity, where beauty becomes a uniform mask. Yet, unlike Marilyn's total surrender, it offers a faint hope of community for the 'ugly,' highlighting 'Number 12' 's bleaker warning of a soul crushed by sameness.

Here, there is no such hope, no prospect for escape: just soul-crushing conformity. Even worse, our heroine seems to have succumbed wholeheartedly; she goes through the Transformation and comes out on the other side as "one of them." No regrets, no prospect of martyrdom, not even the sidelong glance that suggests the Transformation was not, after all, quite complete. There is no Pyrrhic victory, but one that can leave the viewer feeling especially discouraged.

So, you might ask, *what, then, is the point?*

The point, I think, is that this is meant to serve as a warning, a reminder that not all stories end with the characters living happily ever after. It's a warning of how easy it is to lose your individuality, your soul. And for what? For a lifetime expanded far beyond what we know today, a life filled with pleasure, happiness, free from want, free from fear. How enticing such an offer can be.

There's got to be more to life.

John Stuart Mill concludes: "If resistance waits till life is reduced nearly to one uniform type, all deviations from that type will come to be considered impious, immoral, even monstrous and contrary to nature. Mankind speedily become unable to conceive diversity, when they have been for some time unaccustomed to see it."[15]

And then? *Elk verzet volledig zinloos.*

All dialogue quoted is from "Number 12 Looks Just Like You" (*The Twilight Zone*).
1. Emerson, "Self-Reliance," 29.
2. Wilde, *Soul of Man*, 88.
3. *New Advent*, "Individualism," para. 2.

4. *Catholic Answers*, "Individual," para. 1.
5. Mill, *On Liberty*, 265.
6. Zicree, *Twilight Zone Companion*, 400–402.
7. de Jong, *Koninkrijk der Nederlanden*.
8. Fenton, "Biologically Immortal Organisms," para. 5.
9. "Suffering is Necessary," *Philosophy Break*.
10. Loughery, quoted in *Star Trek V: The Final Frontier*.
11. Steve Wynn, quoted in Gallagher, "Lure of Forced Utopia," para. 3.
12. Bolt, *Man for All Seasons*, 95.
13. Ibid., 45.
14. Mill, *On Liberty*, 280.
15. Ibid.

The Children's Story . . . but not just for children

Written and Directed by James Clavell
Based on his short story of the same name
Produced by James Clavell and John R. Sloan
First broadcast on *Mobil Showcase*, February 18, 1982

All it takes is one generation to brainwash a population and convince them that reality doesn't exist.

—Marie Lu[1]

"The teacher was afraid," the story begins. "And the children were afraid. All except Johnny. He watched the classroom door with hate. He felt the hatred deep within his stomach. It gave him strength.

"It was two minutes to nine."

This, in its entirety, is the first page of James Clavell's "The Children's Story," first published in *Ladies' Home Journal* in October 1963.[2]

The story was made into a half-hour drama, written and directed by Clavell himself, and telecast in most markets on February 18, 1982, on the syndicated *Mobil Showcase*. Unfolding in real time, it remains, to this day, one of the most subversive television shows ever aired, a deceptively simple story that tackles indoctrination, brainwashing, and a unique form of child abuse.

I

The story opens in a classroom set in the near future, shortly after "THEY have just conquered us." Miss Warden (Mildred Natwick), an elderly teacher, nervously fidgets at her desk, facing her young students. She reads an official document aloud: "All current teachers will turn over their classes to new teachers." Fear grips the room, except for Johnny, who boldly echoes his father's words: "We're scared too much. We're dead even though we're alive. We not to ever be afraid."

At 9:00, the New Teacher (Michaela Ross), young and dressed in olive green, enters with a warm smile. She gently directs Miss Warden to the principal's office, prompting tears from some children. Surprisingly, the New Teacher greets each student by name, explaining she memorized their seating chart over three days. It's lazy for a teacher to forget who's here, she says, instantly winning their admiration.

Their education begins subtly. When asked how school starts, a student mentions the Pledge of Allegiance. The New Teacher questions its meaning, noting none of them understand it—a failure of their parents and teachers. Allegiance means loyalty to "a king or president or leader or to your government." But you can't pledge allegiance to a flag—"that's like saying the flag is more important than a person." She admires the flag's beauty, suggesting they each take a piece. Finding scissors, she lets Leslie, the birthday girl, cut first. Excitedly, the children divide the flag.* When a student jokingly proposes tossing the bare flagpole out the window, she encourages them to do it, steering their loyalty to her cause as they comply.

---

* Clavell made the point in interviews that an actual flag was not used in the filming of this scene.

By 9:12, the New Teacher fields questions. Why was Miss Warden crying? She was probably tired and needed a rest, the Teacher replies. "She's going to have a long rest. We think the teachers should be young. I'm 23." Is the war over? Yes, she replies: "Now all of your daddies will be home soon." When she's asked if "we" won or lost, she replies, "We—that's you and I and all of us—we won. We're all one world now."

Johnny, silent until now, demands, "What have you done to my dad?" Sitting beside him, she explains that his father needed reeducation for "wrong thoughts" that misled others. "It's not right for others to believe wrong thoughts. Is it?" she asks. She adds that parents neglecting their children's questions is also a wrong thought. "Perhaps my mom should go back to school," one student says. "There's a good boy," the New Teacher replies.

Next, she announces they'll stay overnight at school and can stay up until 8:30—an exciting adventure. A girl mentions prayers, so the New Teacher suggests praying for candy. When no candy appears, she questions if they're using the wrong name. "Let's pray to Our Leader instead," she proposes. As they kneel, eyes closed, she slips Hershey's Kisses from her satchel. The children are thrilled, believing their prayer worked. Johnny, however, accuses her of placing the candy. To their surprise, she admits it, telling them that it doesn't matter who you pray to—"Even Our Leader. No one will ever give you anything. Only another human being. But if you work hard, *I* will." The children are excited. "Only I or someone like me can give you things."

For his perceptiveness, she names Johnny monitor for the week, and he beams as classmates applaud. "Teacher's right," he tells a friend, who vows to avoid wrong thoughts. "Me too," Johnny adds. "Not like dad."

The New Teacher gazes out the window, arms around her students. "It's a fine, fine land. A land to breathe in," she muses. "And you know, all over our new world, everyone's being taught, just like I'm teaching you. Each according to his age group, each according to his need."

The time is 9:23.

II

By the time "The Children's Story" was adapted for television, James Clavell was a household name. He'd authored four best-selling novels (*King Rat*, *Tai-Pan*, *Shōgun*, and *Noble House*), written screenplays for several movies (including *The Great Escape* and *The Fly*), and directed several others (including the Sidney Poitier smash *To Sir, With Love*, which he also wrote). The 1980 television miniseries of *Shōgun*, running for 12 hours over five nights, was the biggest hit in NBC's history, and one of the biggest ever seen on television.[3] With those credentials, anything by Clavell was sure to attract attention.

Compared to the books that made him famous, "The Children's Story" represents something of a change of pace. As opposed to epic sagas set in faraway exotic locales, this story is brief (only about 4,300 words), takes place in an intimate, almost claustrophobic setting, and deals overtly with contemporary politics.

The story's genesis came from a conversation Clavell had with his six-year-old daughter, Michaela, who'd proudly told him that she had learned the Pledge of Allegiance in school. What most struck him was that, while she'd memorized it completely, she had "no idea what many of the words meant." Clavell went on to ask "people of every age" about the Pledge, and discovered that "in every case . . . not one teacher, ever —

or anyone—had ever explained the words to any one of them. Everyone just had to learn it to say it." It was then, he wrote, that "I realized how completely vulnerable my child's mind was—any mind for that matter—under controlled circumstances."[4]

The subtitle of "The Children's Story," both in print and on television: "*But not just for children.*"

Oh, and that young actress playing the New Teacher? Her professional name was Michaela Ross; her real name was Michaela Clavell. The same Michaela who started the whole thing in the first place.[5]

If "The Children's Story" was a departure from Clavell's typical fare, its broadcast on *Mobil Showcase* marked a similar shift from that series' previous offerings. *Showcase* was a kind of commercial television companion to PBS's *Masterpiece Theatre* (also sponsored by Mobil). Its first presentation, in 1975, was a sensation: the 12-part British miniseries "Edward the King," hosted by journalist Robert MacNeil, which ran on Wednesday nights via an ad-hoc lineup of nearly 50 stations around the country, including 27 network affiliates. It was a huge success, not only for the stations airing it but for Mobil, which had the opportunity to air its commercials during the program instead of being limited to brief mentions at the beginning and end of *Masterpiece Theatre.*

Showcase followed the success of "Edward the King" with a series of distinguished programs from British television, including the ten-part BBC documentary series "Ten Who Dared"; Charles Dickens' sprawling "The Life and Adventures of Nicholas Nickleby," a triumphant nine-hour saga broadcast over four consecutive nights; "Edward & Mrs. Simpson," the seven-hour story of the ill-fated romance between Edward VIII and American divorcée Wallis Simpson (which won the Emmy for Best Limited Series); and an acclaimed production of "King

Lear," featuring Laurence Olivier in the title role. (Olivier would win a Best Actor Emmy for this, his last Shakespearean performance.)[6]

By contrast, "The Children's Story" was neither a period piece nor a multi-part miniseries. It was, instead, a piece of speculative fiction, a stand-alone, single-night production dealing with a controversial topic, with a running time of only 30 minutes; an announcer's voice stated at the beginnt that "because of the unusual nature and importance of the program," it was being presented without commercial interruption. An appropriate and effective choice, given that the story unfolds in real time.

Reaction to "The Children's Story" was predictable. Janet Maslin, writing in the liberal *New York Times*, described it as "a half-hour alarmist fable that has a numbingly obviousness, and plenty of other objectionable aspects," and compared it to "the cold-war hysteria of Rod Serling's *The Twilight Zone* without any of the ingenuity."[7] Gene Triplett, writing for *The Oklahoman*, saw it differently, calling it "a riveting and thought-provoking half-hour of television viewing," and praised Ross's "effective portrayal of the soothing, manipulative instructor [through which] we are given a disturbing demonstration in how charm and fallacious logic can seduce and subvert young minds."[8] *The Christian Science Monitor*'s Arthur Unger described it as a "unique horror show," and "an unnerving lesson in the danger of the hidden message." He added, "This slight but important half-hour in class is a shocking lesson about the sometimes forgotten power over our children which we delegate to our schools."[9]

In a way, though, perhaps Janet Maslin was right. The one thing you can depend on when it comes to evil is that it does exactly what it tells you it's going to do. If that makes it "numbingly obvious," so be it.

III

When *Showcase* host Peter Ustinov appeared on camera to introduce the program, which he hoped viewers would find "as chilling and as thought-provoking as we do," he did so not from an elaborate set or a comfortable chair, as Alistair Cooke might have, but from a library, surrounded by some of the most dangerous elements known to mankind: books. His singularly disturbing introduction, running barely a minute, concludes with a question as prescient today as it was 40 years ago.

We take so much for granted in this wonderful world of ours. Free speech, freedom to question, to choose what we read, where our children go to school, where we live, what we say, what we think. All our glorious inalienable rights. So solid, so permanent. But are they?

It's quite true; we do take these things for granted, and when anyone calls their continued existence into question, we want to believe that, in Sinclair Lewis's words, "*It Can't Happen Here.*"[10]

IV

In this discussion, you can't really separate education from truth. Plato believed that they were one and the same: "The true lover of learning then must from his earliest youth, as far as in him lies, desire all truth."[11] But, in the words of Pilate's eternal question, "What is truth?"[12]

I'm reminded of what Katherine Mayer, CEO of National Public Radio in the United States (and former CEO of Wikipedia) said in a 2024 speech: "Our reverence for the truth might be a distraction that is getting in the way of finding common ground and getting things done," she said. "That is not to say that the truth doesn't exist or to say that the truth isn't important. Clearly the search for the truth has led us to do great things. . . [but] one reason we have such glorious chronicles to the human experience and all forms of culture is because we acknowledge there are many different truths." She concluded, "I'm certain that the truth exists for you. And probably for the person sitting next to you. But this may not be the same truth."[13]

Well, not to put too fine a point on it, but this really is *1984* territory, isn't it? You know, 2+2 = 5 and all that? And we all know how that turned out. (Apropos of nothing, I wonder what Katherine Mayer would see in Room 101?)

The early Christians believed that to mislead people about the spiritual truth was, in a sense, a form of brainwashing, an indoctrination into falsehoods that threatened not the physical lives of those individuals, but their spiritual lives as well. Should one die while under the control of such false beliefs, their soul could very well end up in Hell, a fate far more disastrous than anything that could happen to them through torture or killing.

As such, to manipulate the young, while in their most vulnerable intellectual stage of life, came in for particularly severe judgment. I referred to this earlier as a form of child abuse; Christ Himself warned of the consequences: "But whoso shall offend one of these little ones which believe in me, it were better for him that a millstone were hanged about his neck, and that he were drowned in the depth of the sea."[14]

Lesson: what you believe in, what you are taught, matters.

V

What do we make of it all?

Well, it's a very unhappy ending, isn't it? It reminds me again of *1984*, when, at the very end, it is said of Winston Smith that, "He loved Big Brother," called "one of the most heartbreaking lines in literature,"[15] and for good reason.

In watching "The Children's Story" today, you might think to yourself that this isn't a cautionary tale so much as it is a documentary. However, Clavell's warning about the future, which appears so prophetic in so many ways, got one detail wrong: the Marxist infiltration of the education system didn't require a war being lost or a nation being conquered; the abandonment of our children to this singular form of indoctrination happened without a shot being fired.

(It goes without saying, but I'll say it anyway, that not *all* teachers are like the New Teacher; there are exceptional teachers out there, including one who is a co-dedicatee of this book.)

You might also think the children in this story are very stupid, that all you have to do is say their name or know their birthday or give them a piece of candy, and they'll do anything you want. I don't know that I'd call them stupid, though—I'd call them human. We're all vulnerable to flattery, to bribery, to being made to feel important. It's like wearing a badge or a medal. It shows everyone else that I'm special. I'm *more* special than you. Of course, we're all special in the eyes of God. But I forgot—there's no God either, is there? After all, if He were there, He'd answer your prayers, wouldn't He? Praying to God or anyone for something is a waste of time, the New Teacher tells her students. You can pray if you want to, if it makes you feel better, but it won't do any good. Your parents want you to, "but we know, you and I, that it means nothing. That's our secret."

We're told how it's so very important that we protect people from wrong thoughts, from fake news, from "misinformation" and "harmful content." Those quotes are from

Facebook's "Community Standards and Protections Policy," by the way.[16]

Other forms of social media have similar policies, and most companies have Diversity, Equity, and Inclusion (DEI) policies with similar language. And if you violate those policies, you're subject to some kind of sensitivity training. It's just like going back to school, isn't it? And who decides what makes thoughts strange and content harmful? The people who make the policy, of course. As the New Teacher tells Johnny, "It's right to show grown-ups right thoughts when they're wrong." Kind of like the Hitler Youth, don't you think?

And what were those wrong thoughts? "Just some grown-up thoughts that are old-fashioned. We're going to learn all about them in class. Then we can share knowledge so I can learn from you as you can learn from me." Ah, yes, those old-fashioned thoughts are so gauche, aren't they? Ideas like religion, patriotism, American history, and the Founding Fathers. Actions like questioning the "experts" when it comes to COVID Theater, or insisting that you have the right not to be injected with an experimental, morally illicit drug against your will. They're just in the way, you know, preventing us from getting where we need to be. Anyway, "It's not right for others to believe wrong thoughts. Is it?"

This is the world in which we live today, the world we've been living in for some time now, and if you think this isn't already happening, no matter where you live, you haven't been paying attention. From Common Core to Critical Race Theory, public schools in America—and many private ones as well, including schools professing to be Christian—have become nothing more than indoctrination centers for the government, repositories of hate and division, of propagandizing and conditioning; institutions committed to undermining the authority of parents, the values of society, and the traditions of a nation, where even silence can be seen as dissent from this new Creed, the Creed of, as the New Teacher put it, "our new world."

A world where history is what we say it is. A world where the only thing that matters is what happens today. A world founded on slavery, on bigotry, where our homeland was never great, or perhaps even good. A world where error has no rights and wrong thoughts must be punished, where supposedly free citizens must have the proper papers to avoid being branded as a dissident, where there are no such things as second chances, where doubt can never be allowed, even for a moment, to darken the precepts of the new morality.

In such a world, who can you trust? Not history. Not God. Certainly not what you thought you knew, or what your parents or grandparents taught you. They're prisoners of the old way of thinking. They're trapped by wrong ideas.

No, the only thing that matters is having the right thoughts. The thoughts that you learn in your government school. That's what it is, you know, so we might as well call it that, the unholy alliance between the state and the education establishment.

"Freedom, however you conceive it, is such a fragile possession," Peter Ustinov says at the end of "The Children's Story." "It has to be worked at to be protected. So all of us have a part in this story. What's the value of your child's mind? Or your right to question?"

Yes, *this* children's story is most definitely not *just* for children.

All dialogue quoted is from "The Children's Story" (*Mobil Showcase*).
1. Lu, *Prodigy*, 125.
2. Clavell, "The Children's Story."

3. Higgins, "Hollywood Flashback," para. 2.
4. Clavell, afterward.
5. *Children's Story (1982)*, cast list.
6. *Television Academy*, "1984 Emmy Awards."
7. Maslin, "Children's Story," C21.
8. Triplett, "Chilling Parable."
9. Unger, "Horror Show," 18.
10. Lewis, *It Can't Happen Here*.
11. Plato, *Republic*, 485c–d
12. John 18:38 (*KJV*).
13. Haines, "Future of Truth," para. 2-3.
14. Matthew 18:6 (*KJV*).
15. Trombetta, "Last Line," para. 7.
16. Facebook. "Community Standards."

A Sound of Different Drummers

Written by Robert Allen Aurthur
Produced by Martin Manulis
Directed by John Frankenheimer
First broadcast on *Playhouse 90*, October 3, 1957

Liberal institutions cease to be liberal as soon as they are attained: later on, there are no worse and no more thorough injurers of freedom than liberal institutions. Their effects are known well enough: they undermine the will to power; they level mountain and valley, and call that morality; they make men small, cowardly, and hedonistic — every time it is the herd animal that triumphs with them. Liberalism: in other words, herd-animalization.

— Friedrich Nietzsche[1]

Welcome to the future, a liberal world governed by a World Union; a world in which people live in high-tech domed cities with controlled environments, where crime has been eliminated and lifespans lengthened, and where tranquilizers and computerized analysts take care of any concerns you might have. Books are banned in this future world, since independent thought is held to be a source of trouble, and books can only be a source of misinformation and worry. Those caught possessing books—"Readers"—are guilty of treason and executed by teams of "Bookmen," who then take the confiscated books to the "library," where technical and instructional books are catalogued; all others are destroyed.

Such is the price one pays for Utopia.

I

Gordon Miller (Sterling Hayden), a Bookman tasked with enforcing the ban on reading, is drawn to Susan (Diana Lynn), the new librarian. He flirts with her; her response is polite, yet guarded. Returning, he catches her hiding a book—a capital offense—but her uniqueness captivates him. Despite his role, Gordon begins seeing her regularly.

Gordon's partner, Ben (John Ireland), disapproves, hating Readers—those who defy the ban. When Gordon questions Ben's beliefs, asking if he ever thinks for himself, Ben snaps, "What is there to think about? I don't want to think. I hate Readers." Meanwhile, Gordon confides in his "analyst," a computerized voice that replaced human therapists to prevent self-censorship. He admits his feelings for Susan and her status as a Reader. The analyst warns that Readers are traitors, stating, "My answers are scientifically accurate. There is no deviation from the truth."

Undeterred, Gordon grows closer to Susan, secretly reading books himself. Torn between his Bookman duties and what he learns from her, he warns Susan of the risks of loving a Bookman. She insists life without him would be worse, and Gordon realizes he loves her. They plan to marry once the Department of Genetics approves their application.

Susan eventually invites Gordon to a secret Readers' meeting, where he meets their leader, Howard Ellis (David Opatoshu). Curious, Gordon asks how society reached this point. Ellis explains that individuals are now seen as criminals, quoting Thoreau's *Walden*: "If a man does not keep pace with his companions, perhaps it is because he hears a different drummer. Let him step to the music which he hears, however measured or far away." Readers, Ellis says, simply follow their own paths. When Ellis asks if Gordon is committed, Gordon agrees, learning that refusal would have meant death.

As Gordon bonds with the Readers, Ellis warns that it's too dangerous for him and Susan to stay. He proposes they escape to a free colony in South America while the Readers continue their fight. Gordon sees the need—Ben has noticed Gordon's absence from Bookman duties and urges him to abandon the Readers before it's too late.

When Ben insists Gordon join him on a Bookman call, Gordon is devastated to find the accused are George and Mildred, his surrogate parents. Unable to participate in their execution, he flees, vowing revenge against Ben. Rushing to Susan, he finds her apartment surrounded by Ben and other Bookmen. Gordon fights to buy her time to escape, killing two Bookmen before being captured.

In court, Gordon faces charges of treason and murder. Shockingly, the chief judge is Ellis. The prosecutor (Paul Lambert) offers leniency if Gordon names his co-conspirators, but he refuses. Returned to his cell, Gordon's analyst claims his silence defies survival instincts, suggesting he's unwell.

After weeks of interrogation, Ellis visits, urging Gordon to betray the Readers. He reveals his true motive: Gordon's death as a Bookman could martyr him, fueling the movement. Gordon refuses, unwilling to cause more deaths after years of killing as a Bookman. He accepts his fate on his own terms.

As Ellis leaves, guards throw Ben into Gordon's cell. Ben confesses that after Gordon's arrest, he read Gordon's books to understand him. Now a Reader himself, Ben believes the Union will fall. Finally embracing his role as a martyr, Gordon faces execution alongside Ben, defiant to the end.

II

Most discussions regarding "A Sound of Different Drummers" center on Ray Bradbury's plagiarism suit against Robert Alan Aurthur* for borrowing too heavily from Bradbury's *Fahrenheit 451*.[2] That's unfortunate, because such discussions tend to overshadow the power of this story: that of a nightmare world where everything is perfect—as long as you don't rock the boat.

Starring as the conflicted Bookman Gordon Miller was noir star Sterling Hayden; Diana Lynn, a frequent star on *Playhouse 90*, played his love interest, Susan, while John Ireland was properly threatening as Gordon's partner, Ben. Playing the leader of the Readers (and the secret trial judge) was David Opatoshu, and rounding out the compelling cast was Paul Lambert in an intriguing dual role, as both the prosecutor and the voice of the analyst.† The evocative incidental music was by Fred Steiner.

The director was 27-year-old John Frankenheimer, considered at the time one of the premier directors in live television; between 1954 and 1960 he'd direct 152 live dramas, an average of about one every two weeks, and was responsible for 27 of the 133 episodes of *Playhouse 90*, more than any other director. As was the case with many of the directors weaned on

---

* Aurthur married actress Bernice Frankel in 1944. When they divorced in 1950, she retained a variation of his last name, spelling it "Arthur," and adopted the stage name of—yes—Bea Arthur.
† Charlton Heston, in *The Ten Commandments* (1956), persuaded director Cecil B. DeMille to let him voice God in the Burning Bush scene, arguing that "any man hears the voice of God from inside himself." (Jon Simkins, "Charlton Heston Had a Heavenly Take on Voicing God in 'The Ten Commandments,'" *Showbiz Cheat Sheet*, October 10, 2020). Could this suggest a parallel to the Union acting as humanity's analyst, confidante, friend, or even God?

live television, Frankenheimer eventually transitioned to feature films, including the political thrillers *The Manchurian Candidate* and *Seven Days in May*.

Frankenheimer was known as a dynamic and creative stylist, both of which were on display here. Hayden, a newcomer to live television, freely admitted to being scared by Frankenheimer's creativity. "Frankenheimer loved to move the camera so fast... I went into one set to do a scene and there were no cameras! Then around the corner, like an old San Francisco fire truck, comes the camera on a dolly. And a guy comes along, puts up a light, and BANG, we go."[3]

The broadcast received generally favorable reviews from both critics and viewers (excepting Ray Bradbury, of course). *New York Times* TV critic Jack Gould called it "the boldest and most stimulating" play of the season, an "intellectually compelling narrative," and "a powerful drama protesting the disease of conformity"[4]; and the *St. Joseph News-Press* found it "a stimulating plea for intellectual freedom."[5] Hayden, who turned in a performance so intense that he appeared capable of bursting into flames at any moment, received what he would describe as "among my first good notices."[6]

One dissenting view came from Mary Wood, the radio and television critic for the *Cincinnati Post*, who, while finding the play "engrossing," also called it "far-fetched," and added that Aurthur might have made more of an impact had he "made his imaginary society more believable."[7] On the other hand, a viewer in Buckingham, Pennsylvania, writing in the *Philadelphia Inquirer*, said, "We are in that rut NOW! Anyone with different ideas is frowned upon and made to feel like a pariah. All we need to make it complete is to dress in uniforms and live under a glass dome, like waxed flowers."[8]

What's interesting in all these contemporary reviews is how people talk of "intellectual freedom" as if freedom is merely a topic for academic discussion, not practical at all. Aurthur raises this very point several times during the course of "Different Drummers." "Why do you want to change things?" someone asks one of the Readers; "We have everything so perfect." That attitude is mirrored in Gordon's illuminating rhetorical question:

> Who am I to tear up perfection? Look, we have World Union. There's not a man living who remembers war. We have no crime: no crimes of passion because tranquilizers and analysts have wiped them out; no crimes for gain because everyone over there has what he wants or needs materially.

But, Susan corrects him, "There *is* one crime." And there *should* be one crime, Gordon replies. This perfect world can be destroyed only by "sick people with sick ideas," and they get those ideas from books. If everyone read books, Gordon says, "we'd end up with a bunch of psychotics running around with destructive, non-conformist ideas." And "if a few psychotics have to die for the common good, then I have to do it in spite of the fact that I don't like it." In other words, Susan says, the end justifies the means. Yes, Gordon replies. "That's a good phrase. I'll have to remember it."

You might think we'd wised up since then, but have we? After all, Americans embraced the Patriot Act because it promised us safety from terrorists, and what's a little inconvenience in comparison to that? And when businesses were shut down during COVID Theater, when people were ordered to mask up, and those in hospitals and care facilities were isolated from their friends and loved ones? We were reminded that it was only a little disruption, and it was for the common good, and what's a little discomfort like wearing a mask when it comes to saving lives? Except when it comes to the loss of freedom, nothing is insignificant.

So was Mary Wood short-sighted in calling Aurthur's world "far-fetched"? Such critiques were common when it came to such gloomy dystopian presentations. Maybe she was speaking for many Americans for whom the prospect of such a totalitarian state was unthinkable.

Perhaps, then, it's not an issue of being short-sighted so much as it is an indication of how much and how quickly things have changed in the past decade or so.

III

The conversations between Gordon and Susan illustrate the different ways in which they see the world—for instance, their opinion of the city: Gordon sees it as perfect, safe, and secure; to Susan, it's a prison, where the people are kept in ignorance. "In the old days, people were afraid of the dark," she says. "Nowadays we live in darkness, so we're afraid of the light."

Susan also says that Gordon's observation about people not smiling very much is a dangerous one: "If you say that people don't smile, you might conclude that people aren't happy." And that simply wouldn't do in a perfect society, would it?

She explains to him that her unusual outlook on life came from a childhood spent with her parents—something strictly forbidden today. "The Union didn't catch up with us until I was eight." Gordon replies that it's no wonder they're so different. "That's a pretty unhealthy start. Before the Union took over the raising of infants, all neuroses in children were caused by parents. It's a scientific fact. A child raised by parents has to grow up disturbed."

That probably would have been a far-fetched idea for Mary Wood, that the State should be responsible for raising children. And yet today's discourse is dominated by debates on the role parents should play in the lives of their own children. To the left, parents are spreaders of hate and ignorance, teaching their children the "wrong" ideas, preventing them from getting a "complete education." Teachers' unions fight to prevent parents from having input in the school curriculum[9]; politicians claim that "school children don't belong to parents 'when they're in the classroom.'"[10]

In some states, minors can get an abortion without telling their parents. School districts seek to block parents from knowing "whether their child identifies as a different gender in the classroom,"[11] and organizations provide schools with training and materials on how to transition students without the approval of their parents. Meanwhile, federal agencies move to remove words like "mother" and "father" from childcare laws.[12]

As for those parents naïve enough to think that they, and not the schools, know what's best for their children, "The National Socialist state cannot allow the education of youth to be determined by the will of parents alone; it is the state's duty to ensure that all education serves the Führer and the Reich."[13]

That quote came from Bernhard Rust, the German Reich Minister of Education from 1933 to 1945. Unlike the politicians the left loves to attack, he actually *was* a Nazi.

IV

Many of the stories in this book are products of Cold War thinking, with the shadows of totalitarian governments—

German, Russian, Chinese, Korean—darkening the corners of their landscapes.

There is another Cold War theme running through many of these stories, including "A Sound of Different Drummers": McCarthyism, what Aurthur referred to as the "dark days of democracy," days in which "nobody spoke up because his head could come off for this kind of talk."[14] It was an era in which people were questioned about every association they've ever had, every organization they've ever belonged to, every person they've ever talked to, until the questioners could find a flaw in the façade, a weapon to use against the accused like a battering ram, until their reputation lies in tatters on the ground, and with it any semblance of whether or not the accusations were actually true.

Think of the questioning Gordon undergoes in court, and later with Ellis. It all sounds so reasonable: all he has to do is give them the names of the others in the cell. His own guilt will be wiped away—expunged from the record—and he and Susan will be free to go. (I don't think Gordon believes them for one second. Neither would I.)

Anyone watching this at the time would instantly have recognized this tactic from Senator Joseph McCarthy and his House Un-American Activities Committee hearings. They might also have remembered the fate of the so-called Hollywood Ten: movie producers, directors, and screenwriters who appeared before HUAC, refused to answer questions or name names, and ended up serving time for contempt of Congress, after which they were blacklisted.

Just tell us the names of your fellow Readers. The Union would have referred to this as being a "Friendly Witness."

Sterling Hayden had his own brush with the Blacklist, appearing before HUAC in 1951 due to his brief membership in the

Communist Party following the war. He wound up becoming a Friendly Witness, a decision he regretted for the rest of his life.

> If I have any excuse, and it's not a good reason, the FBI made it clear to me that if I became an "Unfriendly Witness" I could damn well forget the custody of my children. I didn't want to go to jail, that was the other thing. The FBI office promised that my testimony was confidential. And they were very pleasant. So I spilled my guts out, and the months went by, and I was on some shit-ass picture, and I got a subpoena. The next thing I knew I was flying to Washington to testify. The worst day of my life. They knew it already, and there is the savage irony.[15]

He was one of the most prominent namers of names in the industry; in his 1963 autobiography, he wrote, "I don't think you have the foggiest notion of the contempt I have had for myself since the day I did that thing."[16]

It seems unlikely, if not inconceivable, that this did not influence how Hayden played that scene, almost as if it were a do-over for him. As, maybe, it was.

A new McCarthy era exists today; once again, people fear the ramifications of anything they might have said or done in the past. The difference in the new McCarthyism, of course, is that it extends to what you've done on social media, what you've done in a video. It believes in guilt by association, guilt by insinuation, guilt by omission. It believes that those who voice dissent are in error, and that error has no rights.

Anyone doubting the existence of this new McCarthyism has only to look at the number of people who've been canceled in the last few years: shamed in their professions, ostracized by their colleagues, fired by their employers, canceled by their banks, silenced by social media, dropped by their friends, shunned by polite society.

If you're found guilty by the new McCarthyism, anything of merit that you might have said or done in the past will simply be forgotten. You'll find yourself removed from the picture, just as the Soviets used to do in the case of party functionaries who'd fallen into disgrace or disfavor. Only now it's even easier than it was then; you don't require any special photograph-editing skills, only a finger to press a button on a computer, and it's all over.

Back then, it was called "Blacklisting." Today, it's called "Cancel Culture."

Back then, the dreaded word was Communist. Today, it's "Nazi," "racist," "homophobe," "Islamophobe," "misogynist," "climate denier," "anti-vaxxer," "Christian."

V

One of the things about revolutionaries is that you can seldom trust them to remain true to their ideals once they've achieved their goals. To underline this, Gordon quotes Friedrich Nietzsche from one of the books he's reading: "Liberal institutions straightaway cease from being liberal the moment they are soundly established. Once this is obtained, no more grievous and more thorough enemy of freedom exists than liberal institutions."[17]

Gordon discovers the truth of this in his initial meeting with the other members of the Readers' cell. After Ellis explains the group's philosophy, talking about how extraordinary individualism is, he tells Gordon, "We think of ourselves not as criminals, but simply as people who hear different drummers. We'd like you to be with us, Gordon."

"Then there'd be no turning back," Gordon replies.

"*Can* you turn back now?" Ellis asks.

After Gordon tells Ellis he's with them, Ellis then reveals that, had Gordon said no, Ellis would have had to have Gordon shot. "We have to be a little ruthless, too, Gordon."

"How does that make you any different from them?" Gordon asks.

"That's one of those vast complications we'll discuss later," Ellis says.

From a purely tactical viewpoint, this makes perfect sense. In wartime, maintaining the integrity of an organization's security is paramount; the success of its mission and the very lives of its members depend on it. For Gordon, however, it exposes another side of the Readers: a willingness to use tactics similar to those of the State.

Ellis's "complications" become even more complicated after he is revealed as chief judge of the court. Yes, Ellis tells Gordon, Susan is safe—but the court still wants those names. "Gordon, they're very frightened men, don't you understand that? A society so rigid that when it goes, it goes smash. You confound them, Gordon, you confuse them. Tiny cracks. They must let you talk or kill you."

Gordon is shocked by Ellis's cavalier advice to give up the names, but Ellis provides him with a rationalization: "If you talk, twelve people will die, but they would eventually die anyway. What would they be? Victims of cruelty, certainly not the first and maybe not the last." And when Gordon wearily points out that as a Bookman, he's already killed over a hundred people, Ellis replies, "Twelve more. What difference would it make?"

Has Ellis been a wolf in sheep's clothing all along, trying to trick Gordon by giving him "permission" to name names? Or does he have something else in mind? Having presented Gordon with an option he must have known would be unacceptable, he offers an alternative: accepting martyrdom, a death that means something.

> Your death will widen the crack, maybe just enough that it will smash it. And when it falls, I will be there. Susan will be there. The twelve you don't name will be there. If not us, our children. Gordon, if you die silent, you will be the first the people will hear. I promise you that. They'll hear of the bookman reader who died for his ideals.

Gordon assures Ellis he'll remain silent, ensuring his death—but not for the reason Ellis hopes:

> You want me to believe my death will be something normal. You talk about ideals. You talk about people knowing. You want it to seem big and normal that I'd die for ideals. Howard, there's nothing big and noble about a man dying. I've seen over a hundred people die. A man dies alone, in the dark.

Before parting, Gordon asks Ellis one final question. "You used the word ruthless," he says, thinking back to when Ellis was prepared to kill him if he hadn't joined the Readers. "What *does* happen, Howard, when you are soundly established?"

"I don't know, Gordon," Ellis replies quietly.

It's a *tough* message.

VI

For all we know, Ellis is just another politician, the flip side of the very coin minted by the World Union. In a way, though, that uncertainty itself is the real weapon—the infiltration of organizations by officials of the government, the next-door neighbors and co-workers who may be on the spymaster's payroll, the endless question of who you can trust. That kind of mutual mistrust prevents people from getting together, from comparing notes, from taking action. As Gordon tells Susan:

> They've broken us down so that alone, we're afraid. Alone, we're helpless. You know, I hope we can exist because we're always in groups, we're never alone. The great crimes of history can only have been committed by groups. Whether they're people hiding under hoods or with swastikas on the arms or wearing Bookmen's uniforms.

Or governments isolating us from our loved ones, ordering us to hide our identities behind masks, making us suspect those standing next to us or living next door, people we thought were our friends.

You might remember, for instance, the story from a while back about the FBI attempting to infiltrate traditional Catholic organizations under the pretense of them being extremist groups? Or the COVID-snitches who ratted out those who violated the lockdown rules, who might—horrors—have invited some friends over without having them separated by the proper distance. "Get vaccinated for others," they said; "It's for the common good."[18]

I keep coming back to Mary Wood's review in the *Cincinnati Post* and her comments about Aurthur's "far-fetched" world. Would she have found my theory about Ellis a far-fetched one? Would she have been surprised to find out that much of it has since come true?

And the fact that it has—well, really, whose fault is that?

All dialogue quoted is from "A Sound of Different Drummers": (*Playhouse 90*).
1. Nietzsche, *Twilight of the Idols*, 78.
2. Beley, *Bradbury Uncensored*, 144-149.
3. Hayden, interview by Peary.
4. Gould, "Powerful Drama," 47.
5. *St. Joseph News-Press*, TVKey, 22.
6. Hayden, interview by Peary.
7. Wood, "A Contrast in Deejays," 22.
8. Spare, quoted in "Screening TV," *Philadelphia Inquirer*, 23.
9. Capital Research Center, "Schools Go Secret,".
10. Downey, "Biden Claims," para. 1.
11. Christensen, "Schools Hide," para. 1.
12. Russo, "Massachusetts Bill," para. 2
13. Pine, *Education*, 22.
14. Aurthur, quoted in Kaplan, "Television Drama," 553.
15. Hayden, interview by Peary.
16. Hayden, *Wanderer*, 378.
17. Nietzsche, *Twilight of the Idols*, 78.
18. Palmer, "FBI Targeting," para. 2.

One

Written by David Karp
Based on his novel of the same name
Produced by Fred Coe
Directed by George Roy Hill
First broadcast on *Kraft Television Theatre*, October 26, 1955

There is in this world no such force as the force of a person determined to rise. The human soul cannot be permanently chained.

—W.E.B. DuBois[1]

Plato believed the soul was the essence of a person, the source of life, the "bearer of moral properties."[2] Thomas Aquinas described the soul as "the first principle of life of those things which live,"[3] and that the body and soul together form one thing. Pope Pius XII stated that souls come not from our parents, nor from a variety of sources, but "are immediately created by God."[4] To be plain about it, the soul is the one, singular thing that determines human behavior, what makes you an individual, different from anyone else who ever has been or ever will be. Without the soul, the individual cannot exist.

The question arises: can the soul be separated from the individual? Can you destroy someone and then rebuild him, changing his very essence, remaking him in your own image—or will his soul always assert itself despite anyone's attempts, returning the individual to his natural state, unlike anyone who has ever been or ever will be?

We are about to discover the answer.

Darkness in Primetime

I

At Templar College, English professor Burden (Harry Townes) leads a double life as a "field agent" for the State, a role he's held for ten years. Weekly, he submits meticulous reports scrutinizing his colleagues for signs of disloyalty or freethinking—behaviors deemed threats in this authoritarian but "benevolent" regime. Burden takes pride in his work; "It's an honor," he tells his wife (Helen Shields), comparing his reports to "a son writing to his father about the other children." She recoils, asking if it's honorable to be a paid informant. Bristling, Burden warns her against such talk. "The State loves us, each of us," he insists. "There's no punishment, nothing to fear." After finalizing his latest report, he seals it in an envelope, drops it in a mailbox, and heads home, unaware of the storm awaiting him.

Randomly, his report catches the eye of Conger, a Special Service Detail Officer. Without opening it, Conger dictates a summons for Burden to appear at the Department. Puzzled but taking things in stride, Burden attends, half-expecting praise for his diligence. Instead, Conger probes sharply: Does Burden consider himself superior to other agents? He reveals that Burden's reports rank below average, shocking and offending him. Defiant, Burden insists his reports are thorough, crafted with care over an hour each, and even enjoyable. Conger twists every word: accusing him of omitting details, resenting the time spent, savoring a sense of power over others. When Burden voices frustration at Conger's tone, Conger schedules a formal hearing and dismisses him. In his report, Conger labels Burden a "major deviation" with "deep subconscious individualism," recommending "elimination"—a death sentence.

At home, Burden's wife begs him to flee, whispering rumors of people driven mad by the State. Burden, certain it's a

One

clerical error, takes her hand. "There's nothing to fear," he reassures her, reminding her that there is no longer such a thing as punishment: "The State *loves* us." Yet doubt gnaws at her as he prepares for the hearing, determined to clear his name.

The hearing unfolds before a review board, but the real power lies behind a one-way mirror, where Commissioner Lark (Laurence Hugo), his assistant Richard, Conger, and Dr. Wright (Barry Jones) observe. Wright, a celebrated physicist and known nonconformist, is spared elimination only for his value to the State. Silent but watchful, he studies Burden with empathy. Conger and Richard brand Burden an "irreconcilable nonconformist," urging his destruction. Wright counters, warning Lark that individuals like Burden are the State's Achilles' heel, and as long as that seed exists, "your Society is doomed." Lark, confident, wagers he can reshape Burden into a "humble, conforming citizen" within two weeks, stripped of ego. He invites Wright to witness, aiming to prove the State's invincibility.

Burden, told he passed the hearing, is escorted to a locked room for a "physical examination" to confirm that investigators used no violence. Grumbling but compliant, he reminds himself to stay reasonable. That night, he's roused and led down a dim corridor to an examination room. A nurse administers a sedative to "calm" him, but as it clouds his mind, Lark and Wright enter. The drug, far from benign, dismantles Burden's defenses, priming him for interrogation. Under its influence, he voices forbidden thoughts: "I'm the one and only Burden, unique in the world!" Lark, to Wright, marvels at his "ego, flaming like a sword." Wright, clinging to hope, wills Burden's spirit to resist.

Meanwhile, Mrs. Burden, frantic after days without word, visits the Department. Lark suavely assures her that Burden is fine, undergoing "special training" for a high-ranking role, which will be completed in two weeks. Skeptical, she leaves, unconvinced. Wright remarks, "That woman didn't believe you." Lark shrugs, "Perhaps not. But it will hold her for a time anyway." He then calls a mortuary to prepare a body resembling Burden's for a grim deception.

Lark confronts Burden, diagnosing him with a "psychiatric disease" of disloyal nonconformity. "You would like to conform if you could but you can't," Lark says, offering a "cure" that may take a lifetime. Horrified, Burden vows to cooperate, desperate to prove his loyalty. But the nightly interrogations intensify. Lark calls him a hypocritical teacher, feigning care for students he deems dull. Richard, seizing Burden's hair, brands him a cowardly informant whose sons will despise him as he must despise himself. Wright, observing, fears Burden's mind will shatter, but Lark dismisses it as "personality readjustment."

The final blow comes in the examination room. Lark unveils a covered body, declaring it Professor Burden, dead for burial. "You no longer exist," he intones, revealing the duplicate corpse. Burden, terrified, collapses, his identity crumbling. Lark renames him Frank Hughes, and Mrs. Burden is told her husband died in an accident, with the duplicate provided for burial. At the funeral, she harshly states to Wright, representing the State, that Burden was murdered. He replies cryptically, "Burden will live again."

"Hughes" is eventually released, believing himself a widower who suffered a breakdown after his wife's death in childbirth. Cumbers, Lark's agent posing as a friend, helps him settle into a boarding house and resume his old job. Unlike Burden's poise, Hughes is timid, eager to please, and curious about his forgotten past. Wright, defiant, tells Lark the soul can't be surgically erased. "It will assert itself," he warns.

One night, Hughes and Cumbers, along with their landlady, attend a meeting of the Moral Brotherhood—a State-sanctioned "social religion" where members deny selfhood, speaking in the third person to blend into the collective. Praising the State's gifts—friendship, safety, love—Cumbers feels moved, tempted to join for belonging. When he asks Hughes what he thinks, however, Hughes admits it wouldn't be for him; he seeks *the* Mr. Hughes, the unique Frank Hughes, "of which there's no other on Earth."

Alarmed, Cumbers reports this to Lark and Wright. Lark grows uneasy, but Wright knows what has happened: you've failed to eliminate the individual. If you kill Hughes now, he tells Lark, "it will be your final admission of failure," he'll have to kill *everyone* like him, and even then they'll keep coming. When Hughes enters, bolder and more like Burden, he mentions seeking a more stimulating job. Wright, laughing, suggests teaching. They exit together, Wright's laughter ringing as Lark, defeated, covers his ears, trying vainly to block out the sound of his failure.

II

Our first of two stories written by David Karp, "One" is an adaptation of his own novel, published in 1953; it was broadcast on October 26, 1955, as the fourth episode of the ninth season of *Kraft Television Theatre*,* one of the most prestigious drama anthologies of the 1950s.

Karp was already an accomplished writer for television, having worked in the medium since 1950; eventually, although he authored seven novels altogether, he would abandon that form to write exclusively for television. "One" was the first of

---

* *Kraft Television Theatre* aired Rod Serling's acclaimed "Patterns" in 1955, cementing his reputation. When it ended in 1958, it was the last 1940s-debuted TV show and the longest-running series to that point.

two teleplays he wrote for Kraft; he also provided scripts for several other dramatic and anthology series of the 1950s and 1960s, including *General Electric Theater*, *Playhouse 90*, *Studio One*, *The Untouchables*, *The Defenders* (for which he'd win an Emmy), and *Quincy, M.E.*; he also created the series *Men at Law* and *Hawkins*. A major theme of his writing was "the pressure on the individual to conform," whether that pressure is applied by the state (as in "One") or by society itself, in the sense of prestige and position.[5]

Upon publication, the novel drew immediate comparisons to the other great totalitarian-dystopian novels of the era. Cyril Connolly remarked that it had been billed as in the tradition of *Darkness at Noon*, *1984*, and *Brave New World*, "which I first thought presumptuous; but now, after reading it, I am inclined to agree,"[6] while *Saturday Review* thought it was "perhaps even more terrifying"[7] than *1984*; *The New York Times* added that by comparison, "most of the Utopian writing of this century ... is mere science fiction."[8]

There is, sadly, little written evidence remaining about the broadcast, even when it comes to the casting. British actor Barry Jones was singled out as Dr. Wright, the dissident within the ranks of the State and the moral conscience of the story; Jones considered the program important enough that he canceled a Broadway appearance to appear. Harry Townes, a marvelous chameleon of a character actor, excelled as Burden; he "carries off the major acting honors" due primarily to the transformation scene, becoming "an (almost) complete animated zero, a flawless, undeviating, amoebic cell in the body of the super-state." Helen Shields played his wife Emma, her apprehension matching that of Caesar's wife Calpurnia. Laurence Hugo likely took the role of the seductive, devilish Lark. As for the actors portraying Conger and Richard—well, as someone once said, not even artificial intelligence can find what isn't there.

There's no problem identifying the director, though: 33-year-old George Roy Hill, who had started on *Kraft* as both a writer and actor, was assigned to the production, one of a number of notable directing credits he accumulated in the Golden Age, including the famous live broadcast of "A Night to Remember" (the story of the sinking of the *Titanic*), and the original *Playhouse 90* production of "Judgment at Nuremberg." After working in theater, he moved to a highly-regarded career in feature films, including *Butch Cassidy and the Sundance Kid*, *Slaughterhouse-Five*, *The Sting* (for which he won the Best Director Oscar), and *Slap Shot*.

Contemporary accounts refer to "One," variously, as, "fantasy," "melodrama," or "satire." (It hadn't yet become fashionable to refer to such plays as "dystopian fiction.") What was agreed on, though, was that "One" provided a punch to the gut; Burton Rascoe, writing in the *Staten Island Advance*, called it "one of the most unforgettable and most talked-about dramas of the season," a "spine-chilling melodrama" that depicts what the United States might be like "if a Soviet world superstate should ever be realized." Karp would be given an Ohio State Award for the teleplay.[9]

"One" was performed again on February 7, 1957, as part of NBC's prestige daytime anthology series *Matinee Theatre*, based on Karp's original script, changed slightly for time and budget constraints. *The New York Times* critic Jack Gould praised this version, calling it "a bitter indictment of the credo of conformity." Gould also provided an excellent summary of the play's meaning, recognizing that Burden/Hughes's reversion provided evidence that a man's "search for an identity—for the unduplicated soul that is in every human being—reasserts itself. The master state cannot survive without killing everyone."¹⁰ The "TVKey Previews" section of the *Hackensack Record*, while warning of "some frightening scenes of brainwashing and deliberate mental torture" (unheard-of for daytime television of the era), applauded "One" as an "intriguing" and "chilling" psychological melodrama.*¹¹

As we'll see shortly, Karp's 1952 novel *The Brotherhood of Velvet* would also make it onto television, in not one, but two, adaptations—but that's another story.

III

In adapting "One" for *Kraft*, Karp made a major change to the story's conclusion, although its ultimate significance is a matter of interpretation. In the novel, there is no happy ending for Hughes; when Lark discovers that the conversion has failed, he realizes that he has no choice but to eliminate Hughes. The book's final scene has Hughes entering Lark's office with no idea of what lies ahead, but thinking he might be in line for a promotion.¹²

It's no surprise that this version failed to make it to the screen; although Karp's initial notes for the script suggest an ending more faithful to the novel, 1950s television could be reluctant to air stories that finished on such a downbeat note, sometimes because of the censors, sometimes due to complaints from the sponsors. CBS even figured out, once upon a time, a way to give "Heart of Darkness" a happy ending, or at least a reasonably optimistic one.¹³

But is this revised ending really all that big a change? Despite Hughes's death in the book, it is made clear that the State is doomed. When Lark tells Wright that they'll eventually

---

* Yet another version of "One" appeared on British television in 1956 on ITV's *Play of the Week*, in an adaptation by John Letts.

succeed in preventing future reversions, Wright responds, "You'll never have the answer, not if you have two hundred years. And you don't have that much time at all." Behind his bravado, Lark knows that Wright is correct, has been all along. Wright concludes by telling Lark that he's going to go back to church for one visit. "To thank God for whatever it was He gave us that can't be bullied out of us—not by torture, not by lies, not by threats, no, not even by kindness."[14]

I find this ending—the original one, I mean—kind of reassuring, to be honest. Perhaps it's that old every-cloud-has-a-silver-lining concept at work, but in the real world, it can be comforting to think that there is a consistency to goodness, a resilience: that in the struggle between good and evil, even when it seems as if good is down and out, it will eventually triumph.

IV

Marx famously remarked that religion was "the opium of the people,"[15] a metaphorical balm that helps soothe the pain that results from true suffering. In that sense, the Moral Brotherhood serves that function perfectly, preventing citizens from succumbing to the loneliness that leads to unhappiness, discontent, and, eventually, revolution.

Most religions are viewed by the State as rivals, which makes them enemies. The Brotherhood, though, poses no threat to the State. Their meetings are part charismatic revival meeting, part pep rally for the State. Their motto is, "Life—Love—Brotherhood!" They chant, "We were friendless, and now we are not... We were hungry and we were fed... Nature cast us into the world naked and helpless . . . Who is our friend?" No supernatural answer here; in this church, the answer each time is "The State!" Their "hymn" concludes with the verse, "Oh sing and proclaim us all,/In like one another,/In life one another,/In birth and death of all." Religion without God, then.

It would be interesting to know the origins of the Brotherhood: is it a remnant of traditional religion, corrupted and co-opted over time by the State until it evolved into some kind of New Age cult; or was it created by the State itself as a necessity, a means of pacification to keep the citizenry docile and dedicated to their overlords, the providers of the feast?

One thing is for certain: the Brotherhood ends up proving the exact opposite of that for which it was intended. When Cumbers asks Hughes for his opinion on the subject, Hughes replies that it has no appeal for him, that he has to discover himself. Don't you want to be "the Cumbers, the only one of your sort in the world"? Or do you want to be like all the others?

In the failure of Lark's grand experiment, the Brotherhood has inadvertently performed the very function for which all churches were intended: to save souls.

V

At the heart of "One" is a macabre version of "Pygmalion," with Lark and Wright as Professor Higgins and Colonel Pickering, in a zero-sum game for the highest possible stakes, a contest between the State and the Soul in which only one can emerge intact.

Lark talks of reclaiming Burden, and indeed, his actions are more in line with a warring nation seeking to reclaim lost territory, not a linguist's attempt to remake a Cockney flower girl into a duchess. "I'm going to pulverize this man's identity," Lark says of Burden. "I'm going to break his deviations one by one. I'm going to dig out his soul and squeeze it between my fingers. I'm going to reduce him to a cipher, from one to nothing." And when that time comes, the sheer brutality, the dehumanization, of Lark's language is breathtaking. "You have no identity. You have no privacy. You have nothing, because you are nothing." He even refers to his new creation as "it." Recall that in *The Prisoner*, Number Six declared that he was not a number, but a free man. Here, the State seeks to destroy even the number, to make sure that there is no "one" remaining.

To Lark, the human body is nothing more than an empty shell, the container of a computer that can be reprogrammed by the user to function anew. It is the antithesis of artificial intelligence, because in Lark's philosophy, the individual lacks the ability to evolve, to adapt and transform. Instead, his goal is obedience. The benevolent State decries things such as ambition, ego, and accomplishment, preferring to level society with fake egalitarianism and quota-based admissions. There is no punishment, only "therapy." There is no room for dissent, no place for disobedience, no tolerance for individual thought. How different is it, really, from the world of today?

David Seed, in his 2004 book *Brainwashing: The Fictions of Mind Control*, observes that "One" combines a "security-minded, cautious, and uncontroversial" Americanized society with the "totalitarian methods" used in communist countries. Or, to think of it another way, a cross between the Patriot Act security state of the right and the controlling, oppressive nanny state of the left. Both seek to eliminate risk, counting on the fear and anxiety of the public to be fine with the idea that it is in their best interests to accept repression (through the curtailment of personal freedom) in return for promises of "order, security, and protection from impending chaos."[16]

Indeed, the State—or the government, if you're more comfortable thinking about it that way—demands many things of us today. We are told not to question the official narrative in order to achieve "societal resilience." We are told that certain things are no longer acceptable in society—words we can't use, thoughts we can't express, feelings we can't have. To do otherwise, we are told, means we are victims of a phobia, filled with hate, that we must admit our shame and guilt and submit ourselves to re-education—or conversion, as Lark would brand it. In response, we become self-censoring, in order to avoid being censored; we cancel ourselves, to prevent being canceled; and eventually, all that self-governing will become unnecessary, because we will simply cease to have any thoughts at all.

But the soul, as Dr. Wright correctly posits, is the evidence that humanity exists—Lark may insist that human nature is a myth, but it is Lark's viewpoint that is the myth. Each created soul is unique—none like it before, none to be like it again. That soul is implanted in each one of us at the instant of our conception, stamping each of us as an individual. And no matter how hard he tries to grind it into the ground, it will keep on rising. Wright leaves Lark with this thought:

> The greatest butcher in ancient history, a Roman Emperor named Caligula, in his hatred and in his madness and in his frustration cried out one day: "I wish all the people had but one neck so that I could cut off all their heads at one time." But all the people don't have one neck, and you must murder every one of them one by one, and they will come up again, generation after generation, like so much green, green grass.

VI

Ronald Reagan once warned that "If fascism ever comes to America, it will come in the name of liberalism."[17]

One of the most disconcerting aspects of "One" is that the world in which it takes place is, in so many respects, so damned normal. We've become accustomed to the idea that a dystopian world is somehow readily identifiable: telescreens, advanced technologies, and futuristic cities on the one hand; battle-scarred landscapes, with the shattered remains of society ruled over by an iron-fisted dictator on the other.

Not so the world in which "One" takes place. Rather than posters warning that "Big Brother Is Watching," people are reminded that "The State Loves You" and only wants the best for you. We're constantly reminded of the nirvana that the State has created: no poverty, no crime, no war, no religious intolerance, no punishment. Those are all "words of the Dark Ages." It isn't that the State has provided a safety net for everyone; there's no need for safety, because there's nothing left that could threaten people. Isn't that what we're always demanding of our public officials at election time?

And being an individual, of course, necessitates adhering to certain responsibilities that come with rights; you can't have one without the other. Which has to account for much of the appeal of the Benevolent State; responsibility entails making decisions for yourself, thinking for yourself, instead of allowing someone else to do the thinking, to make the choices for you. Which is so much simpler.

Remember that at the very beginning, Burden uses an analogy in talking about his work as an informant: it was as if he were "a son writing to his father about the other children." Now that's an interesting word to use, isn't it? One big, happy family with the State as the father, hearing our needs and taking care of us because we don't know how to take care of ourselves. We only want what's best for you. The experts know best. The scientists know best. The government knows best. Not you peasants. Oh, and that bit about how the State loves its citizens? Of course! We only do this because we love you and care about you. They left out the part about how if you don't go along, you'll be destroyed; that must have been in the fine print.

As we saw during COVID Theater, there were a lot of people who had no problem with being told by the experts what they were supposed to do, especially if it meant that they were then allowed to tell others what to do. Many of the five-year retrospectives on the advent of those restrictions remarked on how unthinkable it was that people would submit to living in the kinds of conditions mandated by governments around the world. Things like that just aren't supposed to happen in liberal democracies, and isn't that what we live in?

We should be very frightened, I think, by a world like this, a world that so much resembles our own. The difference is all in the mind.

And the soul.

All dialogue quoted is from "One" (*Kraft Television Theatre*).
1. Du Bois, "Economic Aspects," 493.
2. Campbell, "Plato's Theory," 523.
3. *New Advent*, "Question 75," para. 7.
4. Pius XII, *Humani Generis*, para. 36.
5. Boakes, introduction to *One*, v.
6. Connolly, quoted by Boakes, v.
7. Quoted in *One*, back cover.
8. Mankiewicz, "Heretic in Utopia," BR-29.
9. Rascoe, "Spine-Chiller,"37.
10. Gould, "'Drama of Power,' on Matinee," 47;
11. *Hackensack Record*, "TVKey Previews," 44.
12. Karp, script notes for "One."
13. Stern, "Heart of Darkness."

14. Karp, *One*, 281.
15. Marx, *Critique of Hegel*, intro.
16. Seed, *Brainwashing*, 145.
17. Reagan, quoted in Thinking Conservative, "*60 Minutes.*"

**THREE
SHADOWS OF DOUBT**

The Monsters Are Due on Maple Street

Written by Rod Serling
Produced by Buck Houghton
Directed by Ronald Winston
First broadcast on *The Twilight Zone*, March 4, 1960

The community disintegrates because it has failed in one of its fundamental purposes: to make the members more free and safe together than they would be alone.

—Wendell Berry[1]

Maple Street, Anytown, U.S.A. A nice place to live, where the neighbors are friendly, where the children play in the street, where (this being the very beginning of the 1960s) you imagine nobody locks their doors at night. Jim and Betty Anderson might live next door, Donna and Alex Stone across the street, and the Cleavers just around the corner, right next to where Steve Douglas is raising his three sons. It's that kind of neighborhood.

Let's take a walk down Maple Street, shall we? It might not look terribly interesting to us right now, but in just a little while, everyone in this close-knit community will be trying to kill each other. And if you pay close attention, you'll have a how-to manual on how to destroy a civilization.

I

In a quaint neighborhood of front porches, barbecues, and children's laughter, a shadow sweeps overhead with a roar and

Darkness in Primetime

a flash of light. Residents dismiss it as a meteor, but unease lingers. Soon, they notice nothing works—not just electricity, but gas stoves, lawnmowers, phones, radios, even cars. No logical explanation fits. Gathering in the street, Steve Brand (Claude Akins) voices their confusion to Charlie (Jack Weston): "It's not just the power. If it was, we'd get a broadcast on the portable radio." Neighbor Pete Van Horn (Ben Elway) volunteers to check nearby Floral Street, cutting through backyards. With their cars useless, Steve and Charlie decide to walk downtown to the police.

Before they leave, young Tommy (Jan Handzlik), a teenager, warns, "They don't want us to leave. That's why they shut everything off." Asked who "they" are, he points skyward: "Whoever was in that thing that came by overhead." Scoffing, Steve tells him to go home, but Tommy persists, citing sci-fi stories: "Nobody could leave. Nobody except the people they'd sent down ahead of them. They looked just like humans." He adds, "They sent four people. A mother and a father and two kids who looked just like humans...but they weren't." Though dismissed as fantasy, his words rattle the group, sowing doubt.

Paranoia takes hold. Les Goodman's car suddenly starts, and a neighbor recalls seeing him stargazing late at night, "as if he were waiting for something." Les (Barry Atwater) defends himself, but suspicion shifts to Steve when Charlie questions the radio set he tinkers with in his basement. "What kind of 'radio set' you workin' on?" Charlie demands. "I never seen it. Neither has anyone else. Who you talk to on that radio set? And who talks to you?" Accusations fly back and forth—everyone is now seen as a potential traitor. Tension peaks as a figure approaches in the dark. Don aims a shotgun, but Charlie seizes it. "No more talk, Steve!" he yells. "You'd let whatever's out there walk right over us!" He fires, killing Pete Van Horn, returning from Floral Street.

The Monsters Are Due on Maple Street

Horror grips the group. Charlie stammers excuses, but when his house's lights flicker on, suspicion turns on him. "You were so quick to kill, Charlie, and you were so quick to tell us who we had to be careful of," Goodman snaps. "Well, maybe you had to kill. Maybe Peter there was trying to tell us something. Maybe he'd found out something and came back to tell us who there was amongst us we should watch out for." Panicked, Charlie flees, the mob chasing him home. Desperate, he accuses Tommy: "He's the one!" A woman eagerly adds, "He was the only one who knew! He told us all about it. Well, how did he know?" Lights flash erratically across the street—Bob Weaver's house, Don Martin's, others. "It's the kid!" Charlie insists. Overcome by fear, neighbors turn on each other, sparking a full-scale riot.

The camera pulls back, revealing a spacecraft hidden in the shadows, its alien occupants observing the chaos. "Understand the procedure now?" one asks. "Just stop a few of their machines and radios and telephones and lawn mowers. . . throw them into darkness for a few hours and then you just sit back and watch the pattern."

The other asks if it's always the same. "With few variations," the first replies. "They pick the most dangerous enemy they can find. . . and it's themselves. And all we need do is sit back. . . and watch.." And then? "Their world is full of Maple Streets. And we'll go from one to the other and let them destroy themselves. One to the other. . . one to the other. . ."

II

"The Monsters Are Due on Maple Street" was the twenty-second episode of *The Twilight Zone*, fondly remembered by the show's fans; in 2009, *Time* named it one of the ten best *Twilight Zone* episodes ever.[2] Even those who haven't watched the series may well have heard of it. A strong cast is led by Claude Akins, a voice of sanity until the very end, and it illustrates how even the most powerful voice can, when it's a lone voice, be shouted down by a multitude of lesser ones.

The script, not surprisingly, is by Rod Serling, and allegorical interpretations abound. Serling obviously intends this as one of his "message" scripts; his closing narration states that "thoughts, attitudes, prejudices" are weapons found only in our minds, and that "prejudices can kill. . . and suspicion can destroy. . . and a thoughtless, frightened search for a scapegoat has a fallout all of its own—for the children and the children yet unborn." It could be a treatise on McCarthyism and the Red Scare, or a warning about racism; both are causes that were close to Serling's heart.

But there's something timeless about this story, as there is about all great stories. One can watch it today, as I have, and find all kinds of meaning in it. It could be about terrorism, immigration—even COVID.

III

In 1787, following the end of Shays' Rebellion,* General Benjamin Lincoln, commander of the Massachusetts state militia that put down the rebellion, wrote a letter to George Washington. Lincoln was concerned about the harsh measures taken by the Massachusetts state government against the rebels, which included stripping them of the rights of citizenship, and took the opportunity to present his thoughts on the

---

* An armed uprising in Western Massachusetts in 1786-1787 against the state government's tax and debt policies, which was put down by state and private militias. It was influential in the call for a constitutional convention, which resulted in the United States Constitution.

relationship between a government and its citizens. There were, he wrote, two ways in which governments could use their authority to maintain civil order: through love, or through fear. He called love and fear "the bonds of civil Society."

> Love is the noblest incentive to obedience; a Government supported hereon is certainly the most desirable, and ensures the first degrees of happiness which can be derived from civil compact. Such a Government as this is always wounded, when any thing [sic] shall exist which makes it necessary to apply to the fears of the governed.

Ruling by fear, according to Lincoln, "never will be done by a wise administration" except in the most extreme of circumstances; even then, he concluded, "it will be removed the first moment it can be."

Lincoln believed the wisest course of government in the wake of Shays' Rebellion was for the government to "reclaim its citizens" through love; If not, future rebels will "come forth hereafter with redoubled vigor," and resist the government all the more.[3]

So what did state governments do when COVID restrictions first started? They set up snitch lines and encouraged people to rat on neighbors they saw violating the norms of "social distancing."[4] That's why, when COVID Theater became a thing, I immediately thought of "Monsters," and the picture it painted of people being turned against one another, of resentments coming to the surface.

We saw social media ridicule individuals who failed to join in nightly neighborhood celebrations of health workers. We read of businesses that discriminated against people based on their vaccination status. And we heard about families across America being torn apart along political and ideological lines.

We divided as we always do, whether liberal or conservative, Republican or Democrat, red state or blue, vaxxer or anti-vaxxer. We made claims, exchanged accusations, and hurled invective. Those who claimed to be protecting lives were called tyrants; those who claimed to be protecting jobs were called traitors. If we didn't close everything up, people would die. If we didn't open everything up, people would die. And, as is always the case, anyone who disagreed was a fool—or, worse, a "domestic violent extremist."[5]

IV

Maybe the residents of Maple Street always harbored dark thoughts about their neighbors. It would be strange if they didn't; what we say to our neighbors as we chat over the fence or across the street isn't always the same as what we say when we're in the privacy of our homes, with the doors and windows shut. There, beyond earshot of others, we experience a kind of domestic *in vino veritas*—"in wine, there is truth," only in this case it's what happens within the confines of our four walls. (*In domus veritas?*)

Some people think of this as hypocrisy, but others might use the word civilized. We know what is expected of us in public, or at least we used to know. You don't tell a new mother that her child is ugly. You don't tell people their clothes make them look fat. (Especially if you're married.) You know the routine. The withholding of your true opinion until you're safely behind closed doors—it's a basic kindness, but it's really more than that. It's one of the foundations of a civilized society. Without it, we'd find it impossible to have even the most basic of human interactions.

The Monsters Are Due on Maple Street

What happens when we weaponize those thoughts, though, when we use them against the subjects of those thoughts? When we share those thoughts with others, with friends or neighbors or acquaintances ("Did you hear what Ralph did last night?"), it's called gossip; it's a sin, and rightly so. And it results in a breakdown in trust, even if the subject of your whisperings never gets wind of it. After all, what do you think when someone shares gossip with you? If you really think about it, you'd wonder, "If this is what he says about Ralph when he's not around, what does he say about me when I'm not around?" And when you add fear to the equation, when you bring these whisperings out in the open so everyone can hear them, they become accusations, and those eccentricities and hobbies become traitorous efforts to communicate with aliens from another world. That was the goal of the aliens in "Monsters," and it worked wonderfully.

But what happens when you share them with, let's say, an agent of the government, or some other figure of authority? That's called being an informant, although there's a better, more descriptive word for it—snitch. Some people snitch for ideological reasons, some do it for profit, some to achieve a sort of protection by insinuating themselves with the government, some to curry favor with the authorities. And not only is it an effective way of gathering information, it creates a sense of fear and paranoia. Most importantly, the lack of trust creates an environment that makes it difficult, if not impossible, to form a cohesive opposition. That is the goal of a totalitarian government, and it often works wonderfully.

The COVID scare, like other scares of the past that were manipulated and used by the government to exercise a certain kind of power, brought out the worst in people, or at least brought it to the surface. It acted not as a unifier, a "We're all in this together" moment. It didn't create bonds, it ruptured them. Whatever the motives happened to be, for individuals and communities alike, the attempts to isolate and discriminate created that very sense of unease and mistrust that a totalitarian might well desire. And it's only gotten worse with time.

V

In 2003, there was a remake, of sorts, of "The Monsters Are Due on Maple Street." It was part of one of the periodic revivals of *The Twilight Zone*, and it was called "The Monsters Are on Maple Street" with a script by Erin Maher and Kay Reindl, and a "story by" credit to Serling; whether the new title is an improvement or not is up to you, based on whether you think external events can turn people into monsters, or whether they're already monsters to begin with.

In the 2003 "Monsters," the prime suspects are not aliens, but terrorists. As the panic and uncertainty caused by a mysterious power surge spread up and down Maple Street, hidden jealousies and simmering resentments come to the surface. Suspicion immediately falls on a family new to the neighborhood; they've put up a chain-link fence around their property, and they were the only ones not to fly a flag on Veterans' Day. The discovery of surveillance cameras around everyone's house convinces the neighbors that the new family are terrorists; the father works at an electrical firm (explaining the presence of the cameras), and their house is the only one on Maple Street that still has electricity. Instead of a full-scale riot, the neighbors invade the new family's home, leaving them fearing for their lives.

Meanwhile, in a truck parked on an isolated street (the classic "black van"?), two U.S. Army soldiers observe the ongoing attack on television monitors. It is the Army, not aliens or terrorists or the Boogeyman, that is responsible for the power surge. It's all part of an experiment on "isolated communities" to see "how people behave in times of crisis." The military's hope, apparently, is that such communities will band together under a common threat, but it's clear from the reaction of the two that Maple Street has failed miserably, taking only five hours to descend into chaos and violence. As the new family's house goes up in flames, one of the soldiers remarked, "If the other civilian security tests went like this, we're all in trouble."

In his closing voiceover, Forest Whitaker, host of this incarnation of *The Twilight Zone*, comments that in a time of uncertainty, "we're so sure that villains lurk around every corner that we will create them ourselves if we can't find them. For while fear may keep us vigilant, it's also fear that tears us apart." And America itself may be in jeopardy if Americans divide against one another so quickly.

The plot of this version resembles that of the 1963 *Outer Limits* episode "Nightmare," in which we are led to believe that aliens are holding prisoner and interrogating several soldiers from Earth, taken in an interplanetary war (although not explicitly stated, the "Unified Earth" forces presumably represent the United Nations). At the episode's conclusion, we find out that this is actually an experiment being conducted by the Earth's united military to see how men respond to interrogation and psychological stress. In both cases, we find out that the perpetrators of this cruel hoax are governments, which have no compunction about using their own citizens as guinea pigs. Which goes to show there's nothing new under the sun.

Of course, we know the stories of how the United States government, in the Tuskegee Syphilis Study, experimented on black men for 40 years in the mid-20th century[6]; or how we discovered the government had been spraying zinc cadmium sulfide, a toxic substance, in cities around the country as part of a military experiment. Nothing to fear, though, even though subsequent research suggests the government may have added a radioactive agent to the chemical compound. After all, they're from the government and they're here to help.[7]

VI

Someone once said that behind every act of violence, there's a desire for revenge. If this is true, and it doesn't occur to me to doubt it, then a story such as "The Monsters Are Due on Maple Street" should chill us to the marrow, as I'm sure Serling intended. We can understand the concept of revenge; most of us have, at one time or another, felt the desire to get even for something that's happened to us, and we've probably done things that have made others want to get even for what we've done to them. For some people, that desire metastasizes into a grudge, a lifelong attempt to even the score; the result is usually either a ruined life or the stuff of epic literature. A lot of the time, we're trying to get even for things that in retrospect might seem small: an insult, an injustice, a stolen girlfriend. Other times, we're confronted with something more serious: a murdered relative, an abused child, something so horrific that we not only understand the desire, we empathize with it, we defend it, we might even (if we have the opportunity) help facilitate it. These may be rarer, but they're also more visible.

However—

What about the idea of someone who reacts violently to us because of who we are, what we are, what we represent? What kind of a threat can we possibly pose to them? Why on earth are they trying to get even with us?

What did I ever do to you? you ask them. They reply: *You exist.*

They're driven by envy, jealousy, a feeling of inferiority, a simmering resentment. They feel as if life has dealt them a bad hand, that they haven't been treated the way they should be, that the world hasn't given them what they deserve. They resent your success, your happiness, your philosophy, your beliefs. They'll use terms like "unearned privilege" and "cultural appropriation" and various types of oppression, because you don't recognize them for what they are: the elites, the enlightened, the superior. You don't bow down to them, and they want to make sure you get the message. They're determined to take it out on you because somehow it's your fault. There are no longer two sides to every story; there's only one: theirs. Because error has no rights. And if you offer a differing opinion, they'll deny it, because they don't want to lose their influence, their leverage, their power.

And it really is all about that, isn't it? Power. The kind that thrives on fear and intimidation, that pits friends, neighbors, and countrymen against one another. Whether it's an alien force looking to conquer Earth, a government experimenting on its own citizens, or a regime willing to subvert and divide to remain in control.

On June 16, 1858, Abraham Lincoln delivered what came to be known as the "House Divided" speech, given before an assembly at the Illinois State Capitol in Springfield. Not only is it one of Lincoln's most famous speeches, it's one of the most cherished in American history; in the speech's money quote, the future president says that "A house divided against itself cannot stand."[8] It is a philosophy that resounds throughout American history; Benjamin Franklin, at the signing of the Declaration of Independence, is supposed to have said, "We must all hang together or we will all hang separately" (although he wasn't credited with it until 1840, making its origins somewhat suspect). Through wars and depressions and external threats, from Shays' Rebellion to the Civil War to Vietnam, some of the nation's greatest crises have come from times when "Neighbors turned against neighbors, [and] even fathers and sons turned against each other."[9] The Founding Fathers spoke of America as a great experiment, but reminded us that there were no guarantees of success.

Throughout history, civilizations have faced many threats, but it seems as if it's always the internal ones that are the most chilling, that cause the most damage and destruction. Those are the stakes, and in case there are any doubts, recall the words from which Lincoln drew his inspiration. For as Christ said, "Every kingdom divided against itself is brought to desolation; and every city or house divided against itself shall not stand."[10] It's a warning that has yet to be disproved. And then we will know the monsters are here, because we will have seen them. They are us.

All dialogue quoted is from "The Monsters Are Due on Maple Street": (*The Twilight Zone*).
1. Berry, *Unsettling of America*, 111.
2. *Time*, "Top 10 Twilight Zone," para. 2.
3. Lincoln to Washington, in *Papers of George Washington*, 5:45.
4. Schow, "COVID Hotline."
5. Koutsobinas, "Domestic Violent Extemists," para. 1.
6. Tuskegee University, "Syphilis Study."
7. National Academies, "Toxicologic Assessment."
8. Lincoln, "House Divided," in *Collected Works*, 2:461.
9. *America in Class*, "After Shays."
10. Matthew 12:25 (*KJV*).

The Brotherhood of the Bell

Written by David Karp
Based on his novel *The Brotherhood of Velvet*
Produced by Hugh Benson and David Karp
Directed by Paul Wendkos
First broadcast on September 17, 1970

The very word "secrecy" is repugnant in a free and open society; and we are as a people inherently and historically opposed to secret societies, to secret oaths and to secret proceedings. We decided long ago that the dangers of excessive and unwarranted concealment of pertinent facts far outweighed the dangers which are cited to justify it.

- John F. Kennedy[1]

You're a member of an organization—a society, let's call it. Membership in the society is exclusive, by invitation only, and its purpose is to place its members in positions of influence in business, politics, finance, and academia, so you were greatly honored when you were invited to join. To be a member is a privilege, but not one you can share with others; not only can you not tell your colleagues, your friends, your family, even the very existence of the society is a secret. Through the years, you've attained the wealth and power that were promised, but there's a catch: in return for the advantages you've been given, the society may call on you one day to return a favor, one consistent with the status you've attained. It's an offer you won't be able to refuse, and you know what that means, because once you become a member of this society, there's no backing down, no way out.

Is it the World Economic Forum, the Trilateral Commission, the Freemasons, the Illuminati?

Or is it the Brotherhood of the Bell?

I

In the hallowed halls of California's College of St. George, a solemn ritual unfolds: Philip Dunning (Robert Pine) is inducted into the Brotherhood of the Bell, a clandestine society of the institution's most exceptional graduates. Among the onlookers is Andrew Patterson (Glenn Ford), Dunning's mentor and sponsor, now a distinguished professor and head of the Institute for the Study of Western Civilization. Twenty-two years prior, financier Chad Harmon (Dean Jagger) sponsored Patterson into the same elite circle. Membership is no mere accolade—it's a golden ticket to unparalleled success. The Brotherhood's ranks include titans of business, finance, academia, and politics, not merely part of the Establishment but its very architects. For those chosen, the rewards are vast: professional triumphs, personal fulfillment, financial security, all but guaranteed.

Yet this privilege comes at a steep price. During the candlelit ceremony, inductees swear "absolute obedience and absolute secrecy," vowing to perform any "favor" the Brotherhood demands, no questions asked. For Patterson, who has basked in the group's largesse for over two decades, the bill comes due shortly after Dunning's induction. Harmon summons him with a chilling task: ensure Dr. Konstantin Horvathy (Eduard Franz), Patterson's close friend and colleague, declines a prestigious deanship at a college of linguistics—a post reserved for a Brotherhood member. To enforce compliance, the Brotherhood provides a list of agents who risked their lives to help Horvathy defect from behind the Iron Curtain years ago. Patterson is instructed to threaten Horvathy with exposing these names, a move that would almost certainly lead to their execution.

The assignment unsettles Patterson deeply. Horvathy, a political refugee and fierce anti-communist, is not just a colleague but a moral anchor. Patterson tries every angle to persuade him to withdraw without resorting to blackmail—offering vague warnings, appealing to their friendship—but Horvathy, principled and resolute, refuses to yield. Cornered by his oath, Patterson reluctantly presents the list, revealing the dire consequences of defiance. The betrayal shatters Horvathy. Unable to reconcile his friend's actions with his lifelong fight for freedom, he takes his own life, leaving Patterson reeling.

Horvathy's death has a profound effect on Patterson, who falls into a deep depression, overcome by self-loathing, suffocating guilt, and an overwhelming desire for justice. Realizing that he has willingly allowed himself to be used—to be stripped of his humanity—he becomes determined to redeem himself by bringing the Brotherhood down. He first confides in his wife, Vivian (Rosemary Forsyth), whose initial support wavers under the weight of his obsession. She urges him to seek advice from her father, Harry Masters (Maurice Evans), a real estate magnate known for his savvy. Masters listens gravely, then arranges a meeting with Burns, a federal agent purportedly probing the Brotherhood. Patterson, hopeful, hands Burns the incriminating list and instructions. But when he returns, the office is gone, and the agency denies any record of Burns. Masters, chillingly, claims no recollection of their discussion, suggesting Patterson's grief has unhinged him.

The Brotherhood's retaliation is swift and merciless. The foundation funding Patterson's Institute abruptly cuts support, dismantling his department and leaving colleagues jobless.

Desperate, he flies to San Francisco to confront Harmon. The financier's revelations are devastating: every milestone in Patterson's life—his academic posts, fellowships, even meeting Vivian—was orchestrated by the Brotherhood. Harmon taunts, "You have never competed for one thing in the 22 years since you took your oath at sunrise." Even his father's construction empire, now a millionaire's legacy, owed its success to Brotherhood contracts. Stunned, Patterson grapples with the truth: his life has been a carefully scripted illusion.

Undeterred, he fights on, but the world turns against him. The media paints him as a paranoid crank; the district attorney dismisses his claims as baseless. His father (Will Geer), a steadfast ally who believes him without question, faces an IRS audit on fabricated charges. The pressure triggers a stroke, and he dies, leaving Patterson bereft. At home, Vivian's fear peaks when she shoots a neighbor she mistakes for an intruder—possibly a Brotherhood setup to discredit her. Furious, she begs Patterson to abandon his crusade, assuring him that Masters can secure him a job. Seeing her allegiance to her father, Patterson realizes their marriage was another Brotherhood construct. Heartbroken yet furious, he tells her to leave.

Patterson's lowest point comes on a local talk show, where the host (William Conrad) mocks his allegations, goading him into a brawl that lands him in jail. His only supporters are fringe conspiracy theorists, their zeal underscoring his isolation. Salvation arrives unexpectedly when Jerry Fielder (William Smithers), his boss at the Institute, bails him out. Patterson had suspected Fielder of Brotherhood ties, but Fielder reveals he's been digging independently, alarmed by Patterson's blacklisting from academia. He now believes the Brotherhood exists but insists Patterson needs another member's testimony to prove it.

Patterson pleads with Dunning, his protégé, to join him. "You've either got to be at war with them or you're in their service!," he warns. Initially loyal to the Brotherhood, Dunning ultimately joins Patterson at the airport, signaling he will stand with him and fight.

II

In "One," David Karp presented a nightmarish vision of a State that rules with an iron fist wrapped in velvet; in *The Brotherhood of the Bell*, he offers up something equally dark: the puppet master, a secret organization that controls lives, controls businesses, controls governments, controls the world.

The Brotherhood of the Bell, based on Karp's 1952 novel *The Brotherhood of Velvet*, was adapted for television once before, appearing on CBS's *Studio One* on January 6, 1958, with a script by Dale Wasserman and Jack Baich.[*] It starred Cameron Mitchell as protagonist Jim Watterson, who "lead[s] a double life as government official and member of a secret order whose aim is the domination of the world."[2]

The original title—*The Brotherhood of Velvet*—was probably a non-starter, given the subtext of the novel, which involved Watterson blackmailing his close friend Clark Sherrell (Tom Drake), a State Department official, into resigning his office by confronting him with evidence of past homosexual behavior. (The somewhat lurid cover of the paperback edition, depicting a semi-clad young woman being confronted by a man wearing only a pajama bottom, with the phrase "They stripped him of EVERYTHING. . . EVEN HIS MANHOOD" prominently spread

---

[*] The script sets the story in the near future: 1976, the 200th anniversary of American independence—a reminder of the values behind the country's founding, perhaps?

across the top, probably didn't help matters.³) The premise was based on fact—using evidence of homosexual behavior for blackmail purposes was a favorite tactic by intelligence agencies around the world—but it probably would have been too spicy for 1950s TV. (Contemporary reviewers don't specify what replaced the gay angle; only that the alternative was "public disgrace and ruin for Sherell and his wife."⁴)

Despite a good amount of advance publicity—the broadcast represented the inaugural *Studio One* to originate from Hollywood rather than New York—the play apparently fell far short of its hoped-for results, at least according to AP television critic Charles Mercer, who called the adaptation of Karp's "novel of some substance" a "great disappointment."⁵ Arthur Grace, writing in the *Miami News*, concurred, finding the premise preposterous: "I've known many intellectuals and have never heard any of them express a desire to rule the world," he wrote.⁶ Trusting soul, isn't he?

The 1970 remake, although it retains the *Brotherhood of the Bell* title, differs in several significant respects from its predecessor. The location has been transferred from the halls of government to the ivy-covered walls of academia; the Brotherhood demands possession not of a position in the State Department, but a college deanship; the blackmail involves not homosexuality, but the revelation of names of U.S. intelligence agents working behind the Iron Curtain. Most significant, perhaps, is the presence of Karp himself as both producer and writer.

The essence of the story, however, remains the same: a decent man caught in a trap between his duty to an organization to which he has belonged for his entire adult life, an organization that has played a role in everything he has accomplished; and his duty to himself, his moral code, and his humanity.

Glenn Ford, making his TV-movie debut as professor Andrew Patterson, heads up a distinguished cast that includes

Oscar winner Dean Jagger as the exemplar of cold-blooded evil, Chad Harmon; Eduard Franz as Dr. Horvathy, the Eastern European refugee who refuses to sell out those responsible for getting him to the West; Rosemary Forsyth as Patterson's wife, who never really belonged to him at all; Maurice Evans as his father-in-law, smooth and calculating and untrustworthy; and William Conrad in a marvelously nasty turn as a smarmy talk-show host who's a cross between Morton Downey Jr. and Jerry Springer.

Reviews were generally positive; the *Youngstown Vindicator* called it an "excellent" production[7], while *The Warsaw Times-Union* described the premise as "astonishing."[8] The AP's Cynthia Lowry found it "handsome [and] slick," with a believable performance by Ford; however, she found the ambiguity of the ending unfair for viewers.[9] The *Deseret News*, on the other hand, called it "fairly routine."[10]

Meanwhile, Ford was enthusiastic about the experience. "Karp's script is a beauty," he told Cecil Smith; "a marvelous man named Paul Wendkos directed it, and the professionals on that set with Dean Jagger, Maurice Evans, Will Geer and others were remarkable. So was Rosemary Forsyth, the wife of the character I play."[11] His positive reaction encouraged him to take on series television, with *Cade's County*.

III

One of the most tender of all human vulnerabilities is the secret, and there is a reason why so many of us are so sensitive to it. Whether it be the diary of a teenage girl, the pseudonymous writings of a blogger, or the innermost confidences we share with a best friend, a secret exposes our most intimate thoughts and provides something of a window into the human soul: the hopes and fears and aspirations, but also the guilt and the wrongdoing and the unmasking of the truth. One of the reasons why the Catholic Church maintains the inviolability of the Seal of Confession is that reconciliation with God demands nothing less than complete, total honesty regarding sin, a candor that can be achieved only through its confidentiality.[12]

Is it any wonder, then, that the thought of having these secrets exposed in public, whether to anonymous strangers, co-workers, or our own family and friends, chills us to our bones and fills us with an inexplicable dread? Even reality stars, who seem to have no secrets whatsoever (nor any shame), use their shows at least partly to maintain control over the revelations of those secrets. Just look at what happens when some frenemy spills the beans: tears, screaming, and slap fights abound. And let's face it, they still have secrets. Listen to what they admit, and then ask yourself how embarrassing those things they won't admit must be. (And while you're at it, ask yourself whether you think they're capable of doing those very things.)

We've gotten used to losing privacy in the name of convenience; what's security when compared to being able to have Siri take care of your needs just by saying the word? But the thought of an organization that has a file on you, filled with those secrets that you'd rather never see the light of day—that seems to cross a line for people (unless, of course, you're the one gathering the information). We're outraged, offended, filled with rage. "*You have no right!*" we say.

But in the very next instant, fear overcomes rage. What if someone were to find out? The secrets could be trivial embarrassments, law-breaking admissions, or something in between; it might even be something that's not your fault, just difficult to explain. No matter: it's why blackmail never goes out of style, and private detectives never go out of business.

(It's also why so many blackmailers wind up being murdered, at least on television.) Many, perhaps most, would do anything to keep those secrets from becoming public.

There's one thing that we understand, though: there's something wrong about an organization that collects and uses this kind of information. It is itself a secretive organization: a government agency, a public safety department, a human resources department, a company hired to provide background checks. It's filled with nameless, faceless automatons, just doing their jobs, but the information they collect could cost you the chance at a job, a loan, a business transaction; they won't really tell you how it works, how it comes into play.

They use various rationales for what they do: national security, for instance, or public safety, or the promotion of diversity. They tell you their goals are noble ones: the public good, the survival of the planet, or cultural enrichment. Like your parents, they may say that it hurts them more than it does you.

And if you disagree with them, they'll start a whispering campaign against you, one that gets louder the more you resist. They'll accuse you of the worst possible mental illness known to man: being a conspiracy theorist. They'll turn it into a joke, tell you that you're wearing a tinfoil hat. Conspiracy becomes the dirty word of all dirty words, as if the mere suggestion means that nothing you say matters.

Understand, though, that there's nothing personal about it; they're only doing this in the name of a higher good, for you and for everyone. If you don't accept this, you're just being selfish. And the fact that they deal in secrets while remaining secret themselves is just the icing on the cake.

IV

At the time of *The Brotherhood of the Bell*, it was generally assumed that the Brotherhood was based on Yale's Skull and Bones society, an organization that has included many of the world's leaders in business, finance, academia, and politics. Its members have included U.S. presidents and presidential candidates, cabinet members and Supreme Court justices, publishers, corporate executives, and intelligence agents. Two of its members were George W. Bush and John Kerry, who faced each other in the 2004 presidential election; in his autobiography, Bush described Skull and Bones as "a secret society; so secret, I can't say anything more,"[13] a description that both Bush and Kerry reiterated when asked by Tim Russert on *Meet the Press*.[14]

Today, we might add to that various organizations, such as the World Economic Forum. If you look at its list of "Young Global Leaders" (they're quite up-front about it), you'll find members of Congress, prime ministers, business leaders, government officials, media personalities—quite a Who's Who of people in a position to *Make Things Happen*. Political and ideological affiliation doesn't matter, but, of course, it wouldn't in the era of the uniparty. Nor does location; members come from practically every part of the world. They seem to be interested in everything, from the air you breathe to the food you eat, the type of community you live in, the length of your commute, the job you work at, the climate in your country, the energy you consume, the amount of carbon emissions you're responsible for. And it's all led by the German businessman Klaus Schwab, who—if he weren't a real person—would most assuredly exist as a James Bond villain.[15]

There are others: the Trilateral Commission, although it may have been superseded by the WEF, has always been a favorite, as have ancient organizations such as the Freemasons and the Illuminati. There are individuals, Bill Gates and George Soros, among others. There's the military-industrial complex, Big Tech, Big Pharma, and Big Ag, controlling and listening to what we see, what we hear, and what we say; and others that make us wonder if we aren't living in a world we didn't bargain for, ruled by people we didn't vote for, making laws we didn't ask for.

They might tell us that they're Citizens of the World, but it feels more as if they're the Masters of the Universe. Which makes us, of course, their servants.

V

One reviewer, reviewing our version, suggested that, "apparently some idiot network executive made writer Karp tack on a schlocky hopeful ending"[16]; a reviewer of the novel suggests a certain ambiguity, asking, "Is it truly a plot or has Jim lost his mind and imagined it all as a result of paranoid schizophrenia?"[17] That wasn't an issue in the movie, but there's no doubt that *The Brotherhood of the Bell* is unsettling in the extreme.

It's difficult to know where paranoia begins and ends in a story like this, one that's equal parts Kafka and Koestler. (Critics have labeled it variously as anything from a political thriller to a horror story.) One way is to see it everywhere: Dunning only appears to join Patterson, but in reality, he's there to keep an eye on him, to eliminate him as a threat to the Brotherhood. But that's far too cynical for me, and besides, it's not consistent with the way the scene is played. Dunning has pledged himself to the Brotherhood; Patterson himself is the one who has brought him in. And now Patterson is telling him, in effect, that everything was a lie, that the Brotherhood is an evil organization determined to control the key sources of power in the world. That's a hell of a shock for anyone to have to absorb; under the circumstances, Dunning's hesitancy is all too real.

How would we react in such a situation, being asked to turn against an organization we've so recently joined, an organization that promises us everything, an organization that Patterson himself built up in prestige? Would we dismiss Patterson and his story as the ravings of a crazy man? Would we play it safe, not wanting to be ostracized by our family, our friends, our coworkers? Or would we consider the alternative, that everything Patterson says—about the Brotherhood and its control over us—is true?

Would we be afraid to join Patterson, or afraid *not* to join him?

It's that fear that organizations like the Brotherhood count on—and themselves fear.

We keep coming back to fear, don't we? Every. Damn. Time.

VI

One of the things that I think sets David Karp's stories apart is their timelessness, their ability to offer us a shadowy, shape-shifting antagonist able to adapt to any given period in history. The fear and paranoia, the mysterious masters pulling all the strings—contemporary critics have been quite right to liken it to the McCarthy blacklists and the Stalin purges, but we can also see it in the elite with their secret societies, the government infiltration of organizations deemed "threatening," the ever-expanding surveillance state, the suffocating conformity of the corporate workplace, the social-media censorship of those who question the official line. They are timeless because the desire for absolute power is timeless, and the determination of the powerful to do anything necessary to keep that power is timeless. They are timeless because evil is timeless, and it doesn't matter where you live, because evil recognizes no borders.

And yet we can't deny that times have changed. If evil has always been here, it's also true that over time, evil becomes less and less selective about those on whom its shadow falls. Perhaps the most frustrating aspect is that those who put this evil into motion don't even bother to hide their footprints anymore. They follow the plan so closely, so predictably, it's as if they don't *care* that you know what they're doing. When confronted with the evidence, they simply whisper a few well-chosen words in a few well-chosen ears—conspiracy—as if that's all that's needed to discredit you. Meanwhile, it's still sunny where we stand, and anyway, they didn't say anything on the morning news about clouds, and you can take it to the bank. Right?

Then night falls, and everyone is quiet as a church mouse.

All dialogue quoted is from *The Brotherhood of the Bell*.
1. Kennedy, Address to Publishers, in *Public Papers*, 335.
2. *TV Guide*, "Brotherhood of the Bell" (New England edition), A-26.
3. Karp, *Brotherhood of Velvet*, cover.
4. *The Atlanta Journal*, "Gripping Drama," B-1.
5. Mercer, "Studio 1 Fades."
6. Grace, "Studio One Clinker," 4B
7. *Youngstown Vindicator*, "TV Time Previews," 25.
8. *Warsaw Times-Union*, "Tonight's Television," 7.
9. Lowry, "TV Star," 11.
10. Pearson, "Type Cast," 4B.
11. Smith, "Views on Television," 11.

12. *Code of Canon Law*, Canon 983 §1.
13. Bush, *Charge to Keep*, 55.
14. *Meet the Press*, NBC, February 8, 2004.
15. *World Economic Forum*, "Young Global Leaders," para. 2.
16. Chatterbox, "Skulls (and Bones)," para. 13.
17. Norris, "Brotherhood of Velvet," para. 8.

They

Written by Marya Mannes and Charles LeMay
Based on the novel by Marya Mannes
Produced by Jac Venza
Directed by Marc Daniels
First broadcast on *NET Playhouse*, April 17, 1970
Part 8 of "A Generation of Leaves"

And the people shall be oppressed, every one by another, and every one by his neighbor: the child shall behave himself proudly against the ancient, and the base against the honorable.

—Isaiah 3:5[1]

We're viewing a documentary being shown to us in the present time—that is, 1990. The presenter (Linda Decoff), an icy young woman speaking with the cold precision of one convinced of the truth of her words, explains that what we are about to see is based on "an old-style written report" describing "an outmoded culture." The purpose of the presentation is to counteract the rising influence of this "report," which is being spread by the underground press, especially affecting "those now reaching 40." It is important to counteract this propaganda now, before it can destabilize the new society and the technological rationality that has made it what it is today; before it can lead to the return of love, compassion, and similar feelings—feelings that cannot be permitted to rise again under the appearance of "humanity."

What follows, except for an occasional interjection from the presenter, is the story They don't want you to see.

Darkness in Primetime

I

In a weathered beachfront house on a desolate stretch of the Northeastern U.S. coast, five aging artists endure exile: Barney (Gary Merrill), a painter and the group's eldest at 62; his wife Annie (Carmen Mathews), the nurturing "earth mother" who anchors them emotionally; Joey (Jack Gilford), a once-celebrated musical-comedy songwriter; Lev (Joseph Wiseman), a meticulous orchestra conductor; and Kate (Cornelia Otis Skinner), a novelist chronicling their isolation in a "report" that serves as the foundation for this documentary narrative.

Twenty years ago, a radical youth movement—the self-styled "now" generation—seized control through an electoral landslide, exploiting widespread discontent with the Vietnam War, urban violence, racial tensions, and economic inequality. They didn't stage a revolution; they manipulated the system to rewrite it. Blaming the older generation for society's failures, they deemed anyone over 50 an obstacle to progress. A new constitution established the Age Agency, enforcing mandatory retirement at 50. Those past that age were severed from society, including their own families, and banished to remote "communities" far from the young.

These enclaves offered no radio, no television, and no real mobility—only small electric cars, capped at 25 miles per hour, for trips to computerized service centers providing groceries and basic medical care. The young saw the old as a drain, subjecting them to regular computerized health exams. When illness struck or they reached 65, they faced a stark choice: "self-disposal" or "compulsory liquidation." Kate, with biting irony, calls this "liberal," noting that each year of their continued existence burdens the state with costs and administrative oversight. A vast computer system, cold and infallible, governed every aspect of this new order.

Many elders broke under the weight of shock, denial giving way to numbness and resignation. The state supplied unlimited drugs, cigarettes, and alcohol, a cynical nudge toward self-destruction—an "easeful death," as it was euphemistically termed. But not these five. The house, once Kate's summer retreat with her husband Jeff, became their refuge after Jeff's suicide. The others, renowned in their artistic fields, were permitted to join her—a gesture less kind than pragmatic, clearing space in overcrowded camps. Together, they reject the label of "outmoded culture," finding purpose in their shared defiance.

They sustain themselves through creativity and camaraderie. Barney tends a modest garden, coaxing life from barren soil. Joey and Lev duet at the piano, reviving old melodies. Annie pours her care into cooking, her kitchen a haven of warmth. Kate writes tirelessly, weaving their discussions into a manifesto—a testament to their values for a future that might one day care. Their conversations, rich with memory, revolve around the world they lost and the principles they still hold dear.

Each recalls the cultural decay that preceded the takeover. Barney scorns the modern art movement, where "fakers" abandoned humility for navel-gazing chaos: "Paint what you feel, not what you see." Joey laments his songs twisted into commercial jingles and the rise of crude performers hailed as "significant" overnight. Lev mourns the "barbarians" who amplified music to insanity, stripping it of warmth—a "rape of the ear." Kate remembers the universities' collapse, overrun by hostile youth demanding control over curricula and faculty, their force a tool of the "spiritually illiterate." Annie recalls her growing fear of the young—tough, profane, alien. "They erased the past to charge forward," she says. Lev nods: "To them, history's just ten seconds old." Kate sighs, "We should've seen it coming, but who believes disaster until it strikes?"

One stormy day, they discover a young man (Robert McLane) washed ashore, emaciated, bearded, and mute. Near death, he's revived with care and named Michael. His presence violates isolation rules, so they hide him during patrols. He draws intricate line sketches, often of television sets, sparking debate: Is this skill learned or innate? Does he grasp their words, their world? His silence deepens their curiosity about the society beyond. Have fractures—Black/White, Rich/Poor, Old/Young—widened? The young had despised the old, blaming them for every ill, stripping their dignity. Barney calls it worse than hate: "We were ghosts before we died."

Time erodes their resilience. Creative rituals wane, and Barney's health crumbles—a persistent cough, growing frailty, and labored speech suggest cancer. Annie, heartbroken, knows he'll fail his next exam, triggering the Agency's death sentence. The group faces an unbearable truth. Long ago, they vowed to die together, refusing to let the system pick them off one by one. Waiting would be surrender. They choose drugged whiskey—"pills and liquor"—as their means of exit, a final act of control.

The final night becomes part wake, part elegy. Kate sums it up for the rest when they discuss the kind of message they want to leave if They ever read it. "That you fight for your humanity and dignity. That you refuse to be bent, folded, spindled, or mutilated by any machine. That you perceive and love the nature of the universe inside and outside of yourself." They say their toasts and drink their poison—and then, as they had wished, after they have lost consciousness, Michael sets fire to the house and flees with the manuscript, delivering it to the underground. He had understood after all.

The presenter reveals that this manuscript inspired the documentary—a record of courage against erasure. Yet a final, wrenching twist awaits. Weeks before their deaths, the government, under pressure from those nearing 50 and perhaps glimpsing their own mortality, repealed the age-segregation laws. The news never reached the isolated exiles. Their noble sacrifice, their act of defiance, was unnecessary.

II

"They," based on Marya Mannes' controversial 1968 novel, originally aired on *NET Playhouse* on April 17, 1970, the final episode in an eight-part series of plays titled "A Generation of Leaves," dealing with what was popularly known at the time as the Generation Gap. Jac Venza, executive producer of *NET Playhouse*, described the central theme of all eight episodes as "the seemingly world-wide breach between youth and elders." "The younger generation questions its inheritance," said Venza, "the older generation questions the values of the younger generation and herein lies the communications gap. Which is, by the way, nothing new."[2]

Mannes, with collaborator Charles Lemaire, adapted her own novel for the script; the director was Marc Daniels, who, among his many television credits, directed the first season of *I Love Lucy* and, along with his wife, Emily, and cinematographer Karl Freund, pioneered the three-camera technique of filming. Appropriately, the drama was blessed with a superlative cast of stage and film veterans: Cornelia Otis Skinner as Kate, Gary Merrill as Barney, Carmen Mathews as Annie, Jack Gilford as Joey, and Joseph Wiseman as Lev.* Taping was done

---

* Joseph Wiseman was best known to viewers as the supervillain Dr. No in the James Bond movie of the same name. Maureen O'Sullivan was originally scheduled to play Annie, but was replaced by Mathews due to illness. Some program listings continued to include O'Sullivan in the cast, even on the day of the broadcast.

on location at Bridgehampton, New York; the cast was said to have worked "around the clock, from 5 a.m. to 5 a.m."[3]

The reaction to what critic Howard Pearson called "one of the strangest shows of the season"[4] was interesting. Reviews were mostly favorable; Donald Kirkley of the *Baltimore Sun* called it "a plight to remember,"[5] and *The Houston Post*'s Millie Budd referred to it as "a real horror story."[6] *The New York Times* described it as "hauntingly effective and heartrending," and praised director Daniels, who "effortlessly moved his company about the stage and through deft psychedelic electronics achieved the desired quality of eeriness to complement the human element." As for the cast, the *Times* pronounced it "so excellent that it would be unfair to pick out one member over another."[7]

The *Times* wasn't alone in its praise for the cast; *The St. Petersburg Independent* said that "listening to Cornelia Otis Skinner, Carmen Mathews, Jack Gilford, Joseph Wiseman, and Gary Merrill project their love of life and art to the willing ears of a wide-eyed young man washed up on the beach, is a memorable experience indeed."[8] and the *Pittsburgh Post-Gazette* called it an "enchanted visit with a group of veteran characters, played with taste and sensitivity by an eloquent cast of actors."[9]

The story also hit home with viewers, some of whom were left shaken by what they'd seen. Mary Ann Lee from the *Memphis Press-Scimitar* reported receiving a letter from a viewer comparing "They" to "a bad dream," saying, "Such a world in 1990 would be worse than anything that comparative Pollyanna, H.G. Wells, ever dreamed up."[10]

Percy Shain of the *Boston Globe* was less enthusiastic, finding that it was "chilling and well put, but failed to provide the dramatic tension necessary for a compelling experience." However, Shain may have inadvertently touched on the real message of the story when he wrote that "the concluding suicides were almost welcome."[11] For in the world that Mannes had constructed, there could have been no other way; the lack of drama itself emphasizes the lack of options—the tragedy.

Shain remarked that "They" "had some telling things to say about the consequences of rudeness in the young and permissiveness by their elders—and about the new outlook that comes to a youthful rebel of 20 when he reaches 40."[12] This is a perceptive comment as far as it goes, but it would seem that Their homicidal madness extends much farther than simple "rudeness."

One of the more negative assessments of the show, in fact, came from one of its stars, Jack Gilford, who played the songwriter, Joey. "Marya Mannes never mentions the word 'fascist,' but that's what she means," Gilford said when asked about the story. "She depicts this future society in frightening terms with youth at the helm. I think she's wrong in many aspects." Even though Gilford thought Mannes went too far, however, "he agrees the possibilities of 'They' exist."[13]

The most ironic comment, however, came from Mary Ann Lee, who commented in her reply to her letter writer that, ". . . if taken to an ultimate, ugly extreme, the society of 'They' would not be impossible. I doubt, however, that even Miss Mannes believes it is probable."[14]

You know, I wouldn't be so sure about that today.

III

Mannes's didactic story of a man-made post-apocalyptic society run by the computerized "now" generation is both simple and complex, and despite what some might think, it defies pigeonholing into an easy category.

Mannes denied that "They" was inherently anti-youth; in fact, she agreed with the younger generation's attitude on issues such as the war, abortion, and women's rights. And she refused to spare the older generation their share of responsibility for creating the environment that made it possible for They to take over. Kate speaks of how their generation had failed in their duty: cities turned into centers of poverty, crime, and racial strife; continued military adventures in Vietnam and elsewhere; the private gain triumphing over the public need.

The young had been coddled, indulged, even encouraged: "Don't forget that a lot of this sort of crap was pushed on the public by people old enough to know better," Kate says. "Don't blame Them if Their mini-talents were blown up out of all proportion. The cultural elite was so goddamn scared of missing the boat they'd ride on junk."

Most of all, the adults had refused to act like adults when they had the chance, and the youth had seen through them, lost respect for them, hated them for it. Rather than standing up like adults, they tried to reason with them, to be one of them. Instead of accepting the responsibility for being the grown-ups in the room, they had chosen to dine at the kids' table.

That didn't mean she was letting the kids off the hook, though. Interviewed by Hugh Downs and Barbara Walters on the *Today* show the day before the broadcast, Mannes told them, "To destroy the past is to cripple the future. I don't believe in an autocracy of the old any more than I do in one by the young. The seniority rule in Congress, for example, must be changed. But the division between the old and young is deeper now than ever before, and I'm on the wrong end of it. But I'm a fighter, and I'm not going to sit back and be liquidated."[15]

"I am violently against the concept of a generation gap," she told another interviewer. "It is a losing game—everybody loses." (As, indeed, happens in "They.")

"What upsets me the most," she continued,

> is the assumption that the world started in 1970, that there was nothing before. That one generation, the young, have a monopoly on religion, truth, courage... I think they've made it hard for themselves by deliberately antagonizing all others except themselves, by making of themselves a self-conscious, almost conformist power group. They talk about love a great deal, and it's true among themselves, but they have very little love or tolerance not only to those older but to those who don't go along with them.[16]

Several times Mannes returns to the idea of the new generation as "barbarians": "Barbarians are essentially people without a past or a future, living entirely for the gratification of their immediate desires. They're an aggressor, against language, sex, nature, love, art, life. The barbarian is a violator: the agent of violence."

And in perhaps the most pertinent, most timeless comment of all, one that could be applied to contemporary issues—forced equality, fraudulent egalitarianism, demanding an equality of results rather than opportunity, the culture of victimhood—she reminds us that "Democracy cannot survive without individual responsibility, and equality has never existed in the first place. Certain people are better than others and always will be, and it is only the barbarians who do not know this."

IV

At the conclusion of "They," we learn the irony of ironies, that They, finally understanding that the death sentences They passed will eventually apply to Them as well, repeal the age-segregation laws—too late for our protagonists, to be sure, but in time for future generations.

This seems to be something that happens with an alarming frequency in totalitarian governments. Perhaps it's the shock of discovering that the laws you pass to oppress the masses can also be used against *you*; the truth is that what seemed like a good idea when it applied to the other guy frequently doesn't look so good when the shoe's on the other foot.

I wonder if that will turn out to be the case with one of the most prophetic aspects of "They." When Great Britain passed the euphemistically-named "assisted dying" bill to permit physician-assisted suicide for the terminally ill, one of the strongest arguments against the law (aside from its basic immorality) was that it wouldn't take long for the proverbial slippery slope to appear. Soon, it will evolve from elective suicide to the denial of medical care for the terminally ill, whether or not they'd chosen suicide; after that, those who aren't terminally ill, just depressed or maybe lonely.[17]

After all, there's that whole "Quality of Life" thing where if you can't do the things you did when you were young, your life isn't *really* worth living, right? Eventually, that slope trickles down to those considered a drain on society's limited resources. The problem, you see, is that there are too many parasites around: people who don't contribute, people who are, when you come right down to it, just too expensive to take care of. Of course, we'd never actually call them that, parasites; it wouldn't be polite, and we always have to take pains not to offend; but that's what they amount to, in our eyes: they take more and more, and contribute less and less, and it produces a model that's simply unsustainable for the future. We hardly have enough food and clean water and land to go around now; what about all the stress that people put on the planet, things like climate change and global warming and overpopulation and running out of clean energy alternatives?

And think about your loved ones. According to one estimate, "terminally ill pensioners could end their lives earlier to spare loved ones six-figure tax bills under assisted dying legislation." Under current rules, pensions "are passed on free of income tax if the person dies before 75 years old."[18] Who knew you needed to include your doctor in your financial planning?

Therefore, assisted dying is not only an act of mercy, it's really the only sensible thing for a responsible person, someone who cares about the next generation, to do, *n'est-ce pas?* A Final Solution, you might even say, for the mentally ill, the infirm, and the aged.

But as those responsible for that bill in Great Britain age, as their time invariably draws nearer, one can't help but wonder if they'll start to have second thoughts about the whole thing. Perhaps it will occur to them that this whole "assisted dying" thing wasn't a good idea after all, and amend the law. By then, however, things might have changed. There might be another, younger generation in charge, one that figures it can do quite well without that older generation, the one responsible for making assisted dying legal in the first place. Why should we change the laws for Them, they'll ask.

And there might not be a good answer left for Them.

V

"They" is set in the near future, only 20 years from the time the story was written, which made it 1990. But the fact that 1990 came and passed without Marya Mannes' predictions coming to fruition—well, that really isn't important. We'd already come to see the aged as a drain on society long before then, thanks to the breakdown in the family structure and the explosion in retirement communities, where Grandma and Grandpa could be shuffled off without too much thought. We stopped caring about them a long time ago.

And as our economies continued to hemorrhage, and our foreign adventures became more frequent and more costly, we looked at how much it cost to take care of those who, if you're being honest, contribute very little, at least as far as productivity was concerned. Social Security always seemed to be getting in the way of balancing the budget, and it was obvious that healthcare was one of those resources that was simply going to have to be rationed, and we had to make sure, after all, that the most productive members of society could continue to function, in order to create a new society, a pragmatic society, one built to meet the needs and withstand the pressures of a modern world.

We created the computers that became part of our everyday life, and we dreamed about the day when they could think for themselves; "Artificial Intelligence," we called it.

> We were told, of course, that the machine was still the servant of the man: that what you put into it determined what came out of it. And the simple fact was that when the programmers, in their new, special, and to us, totally incomprehensible language, fed their machines the plethora of data available on the old, out came the one recurrent and irrefutable answer: dispensable.

And when enough people tell you that, you "become what others believe."

So here we are today. They were late. Big deal.

At one point, Lev remarks, "People do not really want change. They are told by a minority that they must have it, and then a minority fights for it—and the majority are changed."[19]

Maybe, then, we don't need to wait for Them to take over. Maybe They already have.

All dialogue quoted is from "They" (*NET Playhouse*). Supplemented by quotations from Mannes, *They*.
1. Isaiah 3:5 (*KJV*).
2. American Archive of Public Broadcasting, "NET Playhouse; They."
3. Lyons, "Lyons Den," 32
4. Pearson, "TV Highlights 'Documentaries for Utah'," 4D.
5. Kirkley, "Look and Listen," B-5.
6. Budd, "The Happy Ending," 4-9.
7. *New York Times*, "'They' Adapted," 59.
8. *St. Petersburg Independent*, "Eloquent Cast," 15B.
9. *Pittsburgh Post-Gazette*, "TV Key Previews," 16.
10. Lee, "TV News," 34.
11. Shain, "Concluding suicides," 38.
12. Ibid.
13. Williams, "Actor Finds," 56.
14. Lee, "TV News."
15. Murphy, "Behind the Mike," 7.
16. Frymer, "Dialogue With Marya Mannes," 4-A.
17. Brodsky, "Consider Suicide," para. 2.
18. Gorner, "Assisted Dying."
19. Mannes, *They*, 215.

The Invasion of Kevin Ireland

Written by Jack B. Sowards
Story by Bret Huggins
Produced by Steve Heilpern
Directed by Alexander Singer
First broadcast on *The Bold Ones: The Lawyers*, September 26, 1971

Civilization is the progress toward a society of privacy. The savage's whole existence is public, ruled by the laws of his tribe. Civilization is the process of setting man free from men.

—Ayn Rand[1]

Philosophers since Aristotle have struggled to define privacy as it applies to the individual; even today, there is no clear-cut answer when it comes to the distinction between information that the individual has the right to keep private and that, when disclosed, serves the public interest.

Edwin Lawrence Godkin, founder of *The Nation*, wrote in the late 19th century that "nothing is better worthy of legal protection than private life, or, in other words, the right of every man to keep his affairs to himself, and to decide for himself to what extent they shall be the subject of public observation and discussion." It is expressed today in the concept of "limited access," in other words, an individual's ability to participate in society without having other individuals and organizations collect information about them.

Limited access is, by definition, *limited* rather than absolute, implying a tension between the right to privacy and the right to information. And when that tension involves you on the one hand, and your government, your employer, or your community on the other, and when that information is both more extensive and more accessible than ever, then the question of where that line is drawn between the public sphere and the private sphere becomes a very important one.

I

In a courtroom, Kevin Ireland (Darren McGavin) stands trial for breaking into and vandalizing the office of Corporate Research Associates (CRA), causing extensive damage. Flashbacks show him, one dark night, smashing computers before a security guard apprehends him. His guilt is undeniable, as his attorney, Walt Nichols (Burl Ives), admits, but Nichols argues mitigating circumstances regarding Ireland's state of mind, which the judge allows. Ireland takes the stand, his story unfolding through flashbacks.

Ireland, a skilled international marketing expert, lost his job due to a merger. Despite months of applications and his qualifications, he found no work, while less experienced colleagues succeeded. The stress forced him to sell his house, shattered his marriage, and eroded his self-respect. Two years later, a former co-worker tipped him off about a job, but he was rejected. When pressed, the friend revealed CRA's background check flagged Ireland negatively, but refused to elaborate; he said he'd even gotten in trouble for recommending him.

Desperate, Ireland hired Nichols and his partners, Brian and Neil Darrell (Joseph Campanella and James Farentino), to obtain CRA's dossier. To Ireland's shock, it was filled with falsehoods: he was labeled a wild partier (based on a neighbor's baseless complaints against everyone), accused of violence (for escorting that neighbor off his property during a shrub dispute), linked to a suspicious death (the same neighbor's heart attack), and tied to a hit-and-run (a dismissed claim). Ireland insists an investigation would have debunked these lies.

Neil confronts CRA's representative, Mr. Gale (Dana Elcar), who callously admits they don't verify reports, relying on "reliable citizens." Fact-checking, Gale claims, is "economically unfeasible." Neil retorts, "So that's the answer. Destroy a man's life but don't bother to double check the facts because it's 'economically unfeasible.'"

On the stand, Ireland recounts his futile attempts to correct CRA's errors. With his life in ruins, he snapped, breaking into CRA's office. "I don't remember planning it," he tells Nichols. "I don't recall how I got there or intending to destroy anything."

In closing, Nichols argues Ireland's actions stemmed from desperation. "Could it happen to you?" he asks the jury. Ireland played by the rules, yet his life was destroyed through no fault of his own. Unlike CRA's negligence, he urges, "You are required to seek justice. . . what happened to Kevin Ireland could happen to any of us." The jury returns a not-guilty verdict.

Weeks later, Nichols calls Ireland, who hesitantly admits he still hasn't found work. Alarmed, Nichols and Brian confront Gale, learning that CRA updated Ireland's file with his unemployment and arrest, dooming his job prospects. Nichols, furious, declares, "You told our colleague that you couldn't be sued for libel by us because we couldn't prove malice. You were right," Nichols says. "Now it's a vendetta, and a vendetta, Mr. Gale, means malice. We are going to sue you and that's not a threat. It is a fact." When Gale defiantly tells them to go ahead and try—"You don't frighten me"—Nichols coldly replies, "No? Well, I'll try to rectify that in court."

When they visit Ireland, however, they find that the stress has broken him—he has retreated into a world of unreality, convinced that his next job offer is just around the corner.

II

"The Invasion of Kevin Ireland" opened the third season of *The Bold Ones*, NBC's "wheel" series that rotated between episodes of *The New Doctors*, *The Senator*, and, in this case, *The Lawyers*. Burl Ives stars as Walter Nichols, a prominent and respected attorney who has taken two brothers, Brian and Neil Darrell (Joseph Campanella and James Farentino), into practice with him. The series established its bona fides as relevant and topical from the start (a must in the shifting world of drama in the early 1970s) in the pilot, the made-for-TV movie, *The Whole World Is Watching*, which involved the killing of a university policeman during a campus protest.

Eschewing the conventional murder cases central to the tradition of television courtroom dramas, *The Lawyers* continued to pursue controversial social issues—miseries rather than mysteries—throughout its three-season run, in this case setting its sights on the relatively new practice of computerized background checks. Central to the episode's impact is Darren McGavin's performance as Ireland, a masterful display of human tragedy. He is the average American: proud, accomplished, with a nice home and family; successful but not exceptionally so; a man who has lived his life playing by the rules, and in return has been rewarded with his portion of the American dream. And then, out of nowhere, he is blindsided by a Sisyphean nightmare beyond his comprehension, overwhelmed by a nameless, faceless phantom from which there is no escape.

His slow descent into madness is difficult to watch; it is, in all respects, superb.

Complementing McGavin's performance are those of the episode's secondary characters: series star Burl Ives and guest star Dana Elcar. Elcar, playing Gale, the smarmy Corporate Research Associates representative (who doesn't even rate a first name), is a malignant cancer, a man stripped of all humanity, someone who might well have been right at home at Auschwitz, claiming there was nothing personal in it all, that he was just following orders.

For all the physical violence that explodes on the screen at the start of the episode, the most dangerous man on the screen might be Ives's Walt Nichols, a man who didn't reach the heights of the legal profession without an eye for the jugular. Throughout the episode, he simmers with a below-the-surface menace; in the final confrontation with Gale, he goes into full Big Daddy mode, informing him in icy tones that his behavior has crossed the line into the legal definition of malice, which Nichols can, and will, prove. It may end up being a Pyrrhic victory, considering Ireland's mental state at the end of the episode, but one gets the feeling that Gale will be a man destroyed when it's all over, with the additional irony that all this will go in his background report.

The power of "The Invasion of Kevin Ireland" did not go unnoticed at awards time. Director Alexander Singer took home an Emmy for Outstanding Directorial Achievement in Drama, and Jack Sowards was nominated for Best Episodic Drama by the Writers Guild. The most significant honor, though, came from U.S. Senator William Proxmire, a crusader for consumer rights, who took to the floor of the Senate nine days after the episode's airing to commend the network, Sowards, producer Steve Heilpern, show creator Roy Huggins, and the show's sponsors (like any good politician, he made sure to mention all the constituencies) for "giving the viewing public a chance to see the human side of the law"; he also had the script inserted into the *Congressional Record*.*²

III

At the close of "The Invasion of Kevin Ireland," the following statement appears on-screen:

> On April 25, 1971, Congress enacted legislation which gives every American the right to know the nature and substance of all personal information concerning him that has been compiled by a private company and to contest and correct any errors he might find in that information. These companies, however, retain the right to investigate any area of a person's private life, relevant to their purposes or not.

Limited access, indeed.

IV

There's something meaningful about the use of the word "invasion" in the title of this episode. One of the several definitions of the word is "the incoming or first attack of anything hurtful or pernicious,"³ and that's exactly what the actions of Corporate Research Associates amount to; consequently, we see

---

* The episode resembles "Epitaph on a Computer Card" from *Judd for the Defense* (Jan 1969), where William Daniels' character, Harry Straton, loses his job and reputation due to a computer error. Attorney Clinton Judd (Carl Betz) sues the company, but Straton suffers a mental breakdown. Proxmire praised this episode as well for exposing invasive credit and investigative practices.

what happens to Kevin Ireland as a gross injustice, an invasion of his privacy.

In the case of Kevin Ireland, the invasion is twofold. Not only has his private life been violated by this gathering of information, but much of that information turns out to be either incorrect, incomplete, or misleading. Remember that Corporate Research Associates, by Gale's own admission, had neither the time nor the budget to authenticate the information in its reports. That didn't stop CRA from making that information available to their clients—information that could be used to damage or destroy someone, with the result that anyone with access to his dossier receives a profile that, at best, is inaccurate; at worst, it creates a totally false impression of him. Anyone acting on the basis of that information does a grave disservice, not only to Ireland personally, but to the company that is deprived of an employee who could prove to be an asset to the business.

As we discover, inaccurate information is not, in and of itself, grounds for successful legal action. The organization gathering such information could be acting in good faith, or that information could be presented in such a way that a reasonable person would arrive at a similar conclusion. That is why it's so important, at the end of the episode, that Nichols can demonstrate malice on the part of CRA, and Gale specifically. Ireland's acquittal in the trial was based on what could loosely be construed as a type of temporary insanity—not in the legal sense of the word, of course, but in the sense that the jurors decided they couldn't blame Ireland for reacting the way he did. A civil suit, which is what Nichols is proposing to file, would be more problematic without evidence of malice.

Legal niceties aside, there's something deeply troubling in this invasion, because it demonstrates just how easily something like this can happen—to you, to me, to anyone. There but for the grace of God, and if you think you're somehow immune from this happening, you've got another think coming. It may be more or less likely in your case, but that isn't going to keep you from developing a fine sense of paranoia anytime you consider the incredible amount of information about you that exists in the digital world, and how vulnerable to manipulation and falsification that data is.

Consider the importance of your credit score. It's hard not to; everything from getting a credit card to buying a car to renting an apartment to purchasing a home depends on that score. In case you haven't noticed that, you're reminded of it every few hours by commercials on television, by ads on the internet.

A national investment firm offers this description of how your credit score is calculated: "The personal data used in your credit score is provided by 3 primary credit reporting bureaus — Equifax, Experian, and TransUnion — which is where lenders report debt repayment information. Because different lenders may use different formulas and reporting agencies, your credit score may vary depending on where you check it."[4]

Consider China's Social Credit System, or SoCS. It "tracks financial transactions and encourages ethical behavior. It assesses individuals, businesses, and government agencies' economic, legal, and social performance... Unlike Western credit systems, SoCS does not just track monetary transactions; it also tracks legal and ethical behavior. The authorities use government records, surveillance, and AI inputs for this. Authorities can impose travel restrictions or social shaming penalties on those who go astray."[5]

Assesses individuals, businesses, and government agencies' economic, legal, and social performance. Tracks legal and ethical behavior. Can impose travel restrictions or social shaming penalties on those who go astray. The obvious question here is: who decides?

Who decides what "ethical behavior" constitutes? Who decides what it means when someone goes "astray"?

Consider debanking, the relatively recent phenomenon in which individuals and nonprofits find their accounts suddenly closed by their bank, without a reason being given or an appeal being possible. The practice was originally instituted to protect financial institutions from liabilities incurred by account holders perceived as financially risky; it has now spread to include those who fail to align their political or religious philosophies with those dictated by the institution.[6]

The National Committee for Religious Freedom, a nonpartisan, interfaith nonprofit, saw their account with JPMorgan Chase closed in the spring of 2022; when they requested information as to why the action was being taken, "they received a list of demands from the financial institution. They were told their account would be reinstated if they provided a list of their large donors, political candidates they support, and an explanation of how the NCRF determines what candidates they support."[7] Similar incidents abound, with numerous examples of institutions (often pressured by activist groups) "blacklisting" organizations that don't align with their viewpoints.

Consider the phenomenon of fake news. One of the things we deplore about it is its ability to damage or destroy one's reputation over allegations that prove to be either false or misleading. The stories are calculated to appeal to emotions and existing prejudices, and they prey on the unaware, the ignorant, those who buy into them because they want to believe them. Their propagation is due to those who don't stop to ask questions, to check their sources, to verify their information. In the rush to be first, to get the most clicks, they just pass it on. And if mistakes are made, well, that's too bad (they say), it wasn't intentional (they say), it could happen to *anyone*.

Which is rather the point, isn't it?

It's easy to see how "The Invasion of Kevin Ireland" portends all this. It didn't predict each and every example of it, but it presented viewers with a vision of the future, one that combined an alarming invasion of privacy with a computerized method of data storage. This episode showed us the tip of the iceberg, and you know what that did to the *Titanic*.

Look at what happened to Kevin Ireland, and then apply that to every aspect of your life. That's where we'll be. The best-case scenario is that we'll be victimized by "honest" mistakes, errors, incomplete information. At worst? Well, imagine if someone were to act with malice. How easy would it be for them to press a few keys, massage a line or two of text, fabricate a few incidents from your past, include an altered image that puts you in the picture, or removes you from it? It leaves us at the mercy of those who have no mercy, those who attempt to rule over every aspect of our lives. Punishing us for supporting the wrong causes, purchasing the wrong kinds of food, saying the wrong words in public, reading the wrong books, traveling beyond where we're permitted to go.

There's virtually no part of your life that isn't being tracked somewhere by someone. Computers record every website we visit, every video we watch or upload, every email and text we send. Phones track every call we make, and their GPS systems can trace our locations, no matter where we might be. Voice-activated systems listen in, even when turned off, and the next thing we know, something from that conversation last night is turning up as an ad while we're scrolling on our phones. Credit cards keep track of all our purchases, and where they come from. Closed-circuit cameras and facial recognition systems trade one kind of security for another, while creating a database of images of you.

But what happens if those records wind up in the hands of someone who, say, wants to check and see if you've had your

COVID vaccine, if you have a condition that might be too expensive for your insurance company to cover, if you've told your therapist something that you thought was confidential? Are you comfortable with that? What happens if your financial information indicates you have a gambling habit, if the GPS reveals you've been cheating on your spouse, if your phone makes a record of what you tell your priest in the confessional?

Are you comfortable with all that? Maybe you are.

If this was an isolated risk in 1971, when "The Invasion of Kevin Ireland" was telecast, it's everywhere today, part of the technological tyranny that rules over us all and makes us prisoners of our electronic dossiers. And where does the greatest repository of such information reside? With those who already have the most authority over you, of course.

V

What really gets me—I suppose it shouldn't, after all these years, but it still does—is how cavalierly we've given up our privacy. Why why are we so willing to sacrifice our privacy? Why are we so willing to live our lives in public? Andy Rooney astutely observed that "[w]e're all torn between the desire for privacy and the fear of loneliness,"[8] which I think strikes at the heart of what plagues us in these schizophrenic times, when people complain about the very things they enable.

The youngest generations have no real concept of privacy, nor even much of an interest in it, while the rest of us have surrendered it blithely, all in the name of convenience. And let's admit it: all these things do make life more convenient. That's a major part of what technology was supposed to accomplish, back in the halcyon days of The World of Tomorrow. But how often do we think of the side effects that come with these little helpers? True, there are those who talk about going off the grid, and some have done so, but for many, it's not an option; while others, conceding the threat, nonetheless seem resigned to the thought that things are too far gone already, that it's too late to do anything now, and anyway, if they really want your information, they will figure out a way to get it. Former Supreme Court Justice William O. Douglas once warned that "We are rapidly entering the age of no privacy, where everyone is open to surveillance at all times; where there are no secrets from government." That was back in 1966.[9]

Think of how many of us live our entire lives on social media, sharing pictures, texts, messages on Facebook and X. When we live online, our souls live there as well; it becomes a part of our permanent record. In the Freudian quest to rid the world of shame, we seem to live in an era of compulsory shamelessness; our internal filters seem to have become one more piece of baggage to be jettisoned; nothing is too extreme, nothing is so private that it cannot be shared with the world.

Women with OnlyFans accounts boast of how many men they've slept with in one day, and if they feel any shame over this—and I think they do, down deep—they try to hide it from the public. (Odd that shame is the one thing they'd choose to keep private, isn't it?) They don't do this in a vacuum, of course; their male partners seem only too willing to participate in these public exhibitions.

These things don't go away, you know: that is, if you've been canceled for something you said or did when you were in high school, if you're persecuted for a political opinion you expressed, or if one day you're living an exceptionally average life and the next day you're labeled an extremist, a racist, or a Nazi. You don't think about those kinds of consequences when you're in the moment, acting out of anger or joy or just plain stupidity.

And as Kevin Ireland discovered, there's no room for explanation, no opportunity for the rest of the story. They can arrange the story however they want, to tell whatever it is they want, and there's not a damn thing you can do about it; it'll haunt you for the rest of your life.

Where does it all end? For that, perhaps, we have to look to where it all started, and I think the novelist Milan Kundera understood that when he said, "A man who loses his privacy loses everything. And a man who gives it up of his own free will is a monster."[10]

All dialogue quoted is from "The Invasion of Kevin Ireland" (*The Bold Ones: The Lawyers*). NBC.
1. Rand, *Fountainhead*, 715.
2. U.S. Congress, "Invasion," 35005.
3. *Merriam-Webster's Dictionary*, s.v. "invasion."
4. *Fidelity Investments*, "Credit Score," para. 2.
5. Dockrill, "Social Credit System," para. 3.
6. Berlau, "Debanking," para. 4.
7. Coffey, "What is Debanking?" para. 2.
8. Rooney, *60 Years*, 129.
9. *Osborn v. United States*, 385 U.S. 323 (1966) (Douglas, J., dissenting).
10. Kundera, *Unbearable Lightness*, 109.

**FOUR
SCALES OF JUSTICE**

The Investigation

Adapted by Ulu Grosbard from the play by Peter Weiss
Produced by Ulu Grosbard, Alan King, Walter A. Hyman, Eugene V. Wolsk, and Emanuel Azenberg
Directed by Ulu Grosbard and Larry Ellikan
First broadcast on April 14, 1967

Once you foul clean water, you'll never draw it pure again.

—Aeschylus[1]

In December 1963, a trial was convened in Frankfurt, West Germany. The accused were 25 defendants, mid- and low-level functionaries, accused of taking part in murders committed on their own initiative in the Auschwitz-Birkenau concentration camp during World War II. The trial would last until August 1965, when guilty verdicts were returned against all but two of the defendants. The question hanging over the trial, then and to this day: were the German officials involved in the Holocaust animals, brutes, savage freaks, abnormal monsters of some kind, involved in something that was an accident in history? Or is the answer to be found, not inside a courtroom, but much deeper, inside each one of us?

I

The Attorneys are seated at one table, the Accused at another. Before them, seated all in a row, are the Witnesses. The Judge speaks. The trial has begun—and with it, the horrors of

Auschwitz unfold, through cold, methodical recitations recounted with the precision of a timetable, stark and antiseptic.

It begins at the train platform, where cattle cars disgorge their human cargo. Families, dazed and clutching meager belongings, are met by barking guards. The Accused, former camp personnel, describe their roles with detachment. "All I had to do," says Accused #15, "was to organize prisoners into groups. I never did any shooting." The sorting is brutal: healthy men and women are deemed fit for labor; the elderly, infirm, and women with children—most of the arrivals—are herded toward "showers," a euphemism for gas chambers. Some of the guards, unwilling to face "Platform Duty," feign illness to escape the grim task, leaving colleagues to decide who lives or dies.

Those selected for work face immediate dehumanization. Guards strip them of watches, rings, photos—any link to their past. Numbers are tattooed onto left forearms, branding them as statistics. They're then issued threadbare undergarments, torn jackets, mismatched pants, a cap, and wooden shoes that blister their feet, and marched to barracks. Designed for 500, these buildings cram 1,000, forcing six to share a single straw mattress. A Witness shares the camp's unwritten code: "I knew that what mattered here was to look out for yourself, to try to work your way up, to make a good impression and to keep away from anything that might drag you down." Survival demands ruthlessness—stealing rations from the sick, claiming warmer bunks from the dying. "It was normal that everything had been stolen from us," another Witness says, "it was normal that we stole too."

The camp rewards strength and cunning. Skilled prisoners claw their way to "special-duty" roles—Barrack-Elders, clerks, or assistants—gaining access to food, clothes, even contraband. Barrack-Elders, prisoners overseeing others, mete

The Investigation

out cruelty, knowing guards punish them for any lapse. Survival hinges on health; the weakest vanish. Punishments are inventive and lethal. "The Swing," dubbed the "talking machine," suspends prisoners on a pole frame, beaten as special-duty workers swing them like pendulums. A stolen crust of bread or a sluggish response to orders invites such torture. Informant boxes, scattered across the camp, encourage betrayal—accuse a fellow prisoner, and they're as good as dead. "If they weren't dead then," a Witness recalls, "they seldom lived much longer." When one testifies to enduring The Swing, the Defense Attorney attempts to discredit him: "Then it was possible to survive it after all."

The Accused—doctors, teachers, clerks, soldiers in their pre-war lives—held godlike power. "They were free, each one of them, to kill or to save," a Witness says. Over time, prisoners, too, melded into the system, from privileged elders to those teetering on death. "The difference between us and the camp personnel," one notes, "was smaller than between us and the outside world."

Medical experiments pushed cruelty further. Doctors, some under Dr. Mengele, conducted horrors: mutilating genitals, injecting infections into wombs, burning ovaries with X-rays. The Defense objects: "The mere fact that our clients were in the vicinity when these events occurred by no means implicates them as accessories." An Accused, asked about prisoners' conditions, shrugs: "It was a penal camp. People weren't there for their health."

Testimony unveils execution sites. The Black Wall claimed 20,000, shot point-blank—men, women, children. Phenol injections killed 30,000, including children silenced with lies of "vaccination." The Bunker Block's standing cells, barely a foot square, trapped prisoners post-labor, fed sporadically or not at all. Zyklon B, the gas of choice, ended countless lives in chambers. "They went quietly," an Accused recalls, as if describing a routine. Crowds of 150 or 200 were processed in 20 minutes, their gold fillings harvested, bodies fed to crematoriums. Special Commandos, prisoners forced to assist, faced their own doom every few months, replaced by fresh crews. "I only followed instructions," an Accused insists when tied to the crematoriums.

The Accused meet charges with deflection or derision. Laughter—mocking or dismissive—punctuates their responses. "That's news to me," one says of guard brutalities. "Not within my jurisdiction," claims another. An officer cites the "military penal code." Accused of leading a "uniformed Murder Commando," one bristles: "You are attacking my honor."

The play concludes without a verdict rendered. The last word goes to an Accused, who says, "All of us, I want to make that very clear, did nothing but our duty, even when that duty was hard, and even when it grieved us to do it." He suggests that it is better to look to the future than to reflect on the past.

II

I heard a guard talking through the barbed wire to a nine-year-old boy. "You know a lot for a boy your age," he said. The boy answered, "I know that I know a lot, and I also know I'm not going to learn any more."

"Several years ago," *Newsday*'s Barbara Delatiner recalled, "mention of a crematorium was omitted from a teleplay because it might offend a gas company advertiser."[2] How far things had come on television in the years since could be seen by NBC's decision to devote 90 minutes in prime time to "The Investigation," Peter Weiss' controversial account of the

Auschwitz war crimes trial, which *The San Francisco Examiner*'s Dwight Newton would describe as "the most jolting, vivid essay on human cruelty and horrors ever dramatized for the living room audience."³

Weiss, who rose to prominence through his 1965 play about the French Revolution, "Marat/Sade,"* had attended the Auschwitz War Crimes Trials, held in Frankfurt between 1963 and 1965, with an eye toward making it part of a "World-Theater Project" modeled on the structure of Dante's *Divine Comedy*, but abandoned the idea due to the historical significance of the trial, and published "The Investigation" separately. The play, derived from transcripts of the trial, opened simultaneously on October 19, 1965, in fourteen West and East German cities, as well as with the Royal Shakespeare Company in London; its Broadway debut came a year later at the Ambassador Theatre.⁴

Weiss, in the foreword to the play, gave specific instructions for the actors to deliver their lines in a dry, matter-of-fact manner, devoid of all emotion. The play, he wrote, contains "nothing but facts. Personal experience and confrontations must be steeped in anonymity. Inasmuch as the witnesses in the play lose their names, they become mere speaking tubes... The variety of experiences can, at most, be indicated by a change of voice or bearing."⁵ Thus stripped of all but the bare minimum, Weiss felt that the play could more accurately explore what he felt was the central question: whether the Holocaust was an isolated phenomenon, a unique moment in time and history, or if the atrocities could have happened anywhere and at any time in society. In announcing the network's plan for the broadcast, NBC president John Durgin said, "It is our belief and expectation that the decision to put television

---

* Winner of the Tony Award for Best Play in 1965.

cameras on what will surely be one of [the] most shattering dramas ever brought to the American stage represents a major step forward in the use of the television medium."[6] When it was pointed out that Jewish viewers might not be able to watch the Friday night broadcast because of the Sabbath, NBC scheduled an additional showing on Sunday afternoon, April 16. The special would air without commercial interruption, save one break for local stations.

Resisting the temptation to cast well-known actors in the principal roles, the network employed the original Broadway cast, including Ward Costello, Alice Hirson, Vivian Nathan, Graham Jarvis, and John Marley as witnesses, Paul Lason, Peter Brandon, and Gordon Clarke as defendants, Will Hussung as the judge, Franklin Cover as the prosecutor, and Leon B. Stevens as the defense attorney. They were joined by the director of the Broadway production, Ulu Grosbard,* who had originally done the English translation of the play and then had adapted it to fit the 90-minute running time on television (the play ran for about two hours in the theater), while leaving intact the often graphic language.[7]

The major change between the stage and television versions was in the set; although Weiss had stated that "no attempt should be made" to replicate the look of a courtroom (instructions to which the Broadway production was faithful), the television staging, designed by Kert Lundell, was slightly adapted to present something more familiar to viewers. The broadcast was introduced by actor Alexander Scourby and taped in the NBC studios in Brooklyn.

Reaction from the critics was high praise mixed with an equal dose of shock. Stewart Allen of the *Arizona Republic* wrote that, "Without compromise or commercials, NBC-TV splashed

---

* Grosbard, a Broadway veteran who hadn't previously worked in television, was assisted on the broadcast by Larry Ellikan as co-director.

blood and horror across American living rooms last night. The nightmare's name was 'The Investigation,' its author Peter Weiss, its duration 90 minutes and its purpose to make us feel the drama, emotion and tragedy of Nazi atrocities by eliminating drama, emotion and tragedy from the presentation."[8] Rick DuBrow, writing for UPI, called the program "shattering," and an "extraordinary emotional experience,"[9] and Harriet Van Horne, in the *Knoxville News Sentinel*, found herself overwhelmed by the experience: "Watching it, I was not only in tears, my hands trembled too much to take notes.... The agony, the fury, the aching pity that rose from every sense were simply too much."[10] Sylvie Reice, too, was brought to the verge of tears; in the *Syracuse Herald Journal*, she called it "more terrifying than *Psycho*, more fantastic than *Frankenstein*."[11] *Variety* said that "The NBC presentation deserves all the recognition it may get as one of the outstanding programs of the season," and that "If to forget history is to be compelled to relive it, this dramatized presentation could not be aired often enough."[12]

The *Pittsburgh Post-Gazette*, in its preview, called it "a milestone for network TV" that puts "not only the Germans but humanity itself on trial."[13] Lou Cedrone of the *Baltimore Evening Sun* found the telecast superior to the stage production. "Recorded as it now is, it can be held for future exposure as an occasional reminder that mass killing is no stranger to man and could easily happen again—which is Weiss' message. It is also a recording that will increase in worth as it ages." He added that while the Holocaust might still be too recent in some people's minds, "A decade or two from now, when the deaths of 6,000,000 recede farther into history, 'The Investigation,' either on stage or on television (preferably the latter) will be a necessary reminder, a documentary of an age when madness prevailed."[14]

Many of the critics pointed out the stark difference in substance between "The Investigation" and what television normally offered. Joan Crosby, in the *Pittsburgh Press*, promised that viewers "will find [themselves] more tightly held, more emotionally possessed than by the vast majority of television's standard dramatic efforts."[15] The *Miami Herald*'s Jack E. Anderson said it was "an enormously interesting intrusion into the never-never land of fantasy and non-think."[16] Richard K. Shull, in *The Indianapolis News*, called it "something more than 325 colored dots per microsecond pinging off the brain." "Many things can be interpreted from Weiss' play, but regardless of what you find in it, it's certain Weiss won't leave you where he found you."[17]

III

They did not kill out of hatred or conviction. They killed only because they had to and there was no point in discussing that.

And yet there's something difficult to explain about "The Investigation." Consider that the special was previewed in newspapers and magazines nationwide, merited a Close-Up in TV Guide (as well as an interview of Weiss conducted by Walter Wager), was aired twice in a span of three days, and was almost unanimously praised by critics.

But have you ever heard of it? The television production, I mean? Does it ring a bell with you?

Phil Gries, founder and owner of Archival Television Audio, Inc., which has the premier collection of audio soundtracks from television programs dating back to the first years of the medium—programs that have since been erased, discarded, destroyed, or lost—notes that the broadcast of "The Investigation"

The Investigation

is not extant IN ANY FORM, VIDEO, AUDIO (with the exception of the master 1/4" reel to reel recording archived by Archival Television Audio, Inc.), or TRANSCRIPT. It was not archived by NBC or archived by the major museums in the USA (Paley Center for Media, UCLA Film & TV Archive, Library of Congress, Museum of Broadcasting).

Furthermore, and perhaps even more inexplicable, "there is NO REFERENCE to this broadcast title on the internet, or listed as an IMDb entry. The one listing of this title can be found in The Library of Congress as a rare theater program Playbill, ONLY (found in the Richard L. Coe Theater Programs Collection)." [Emphasis in the original.][18]

An internet search turns up an IMDb entry for ITV's *Play of the Week* production of "The Investigation," which appeared on British television in 1967, with a completely different cast and crew—but nothing for the NBC version. The Wikipedia entry for "The Investigation," in fact, fails to mention either television adaptation. Virtually all of the information included in this essay comes from primary sources found on Newspapers.com, the Internet Archive, and Google News Archives. Other than that? Good luck.

Now, how does something like this happen? Granted, it's not unusual for television broadcasts from this era to "disappear," and while this makes the job of a television historian much more frustrating, it's at least understandable; few industries have ever been more careless in preserving their heritage than television. Nor would it be terribly surprising for people, even those with a pretty extensive grasp of television history, to be unfamiliar with "The Investigation." It isn't the only (undeservedly) obscure program included in the book you're reading.

Still and all, it seems almost incomprehensible that the program has disappeared, leaving practically no trace of its existence, particularly when one considers *Variety*'s comment that it "could not be aired often enough." It really does make you wonder, doesn't it?

Or maybe not. John Marley, who would be so memorable in *The Godfather* and who played one of the prosecution witnesses, called "The Investigation" "the single most important show to be put on television," but at the same time, he doubted it would make much of a difference. "I'd like to think 'The Investigation' telecast would help, but I doubt it. People will watch and 10 minutes later forget it."[19]

IV

Every third word we heard, even back in grammar school, was about how they were to blame for everything, and how they ought to be weeded out. It was hammered into us that this would only be for the good of our people.

Without question, the most controversial aspect of "The Investigation" was Weiss's choice to see the play not just as a historical event, but as a metaphor, an indictment of crimes against humanity everywhere. "The word Auschwitz never gets mentioned, and not the word Jew either," Weiss said in a *TV Guide* interview published the week of the broadcast. "So it's not entirely a play about the extermination of the Jews in the special Auschwitz camp, but it's a play about suppression of people because of another race or another political view."[20]

Harriet Van Horne, in her *Knoxville News Sentinel* review, had wondered if he wasn't, whether intentionally or not, letting the Germans off the hook, "blurring a hard, essential fact of history."[21] That viewpoint was echoed by *Newsday*'s Barbara

Delatiner, who wrote that "While Weiss's basic philosophy—that only fate determines the oppressors and the oppressed—may be sound, surely the 4,000,000 who perished at Auschwitz and the men who fired the ovens cannot be dismissed merely as veiled statistics in man's continuous inhumanity to his fellow man."[22]

Whether or not Delatiner's criticism was accurate, it was the case that Weiss seemed focused on what Richard Shull, in his *Indianapolis News* review, referred to as "The Eichmann Impulse."* The play, Shull wrote, "emphasized the ease with which the human can become uncivilized." Many of the Auschwitz guards "had led normal lives in average jobs until circumstances put them in duty at the death camp, [and] after the war reverted to their old ways with hardly a backward glance." It was, many of them would claim, simply a case of trying to stay alive, of following orders because of the consequences they would suffer if they didn't.[23]

The same could be said to apply to those prisoners "who killed one another on orders from their masters, who stole food from their own weak and dying, were forced to give up their membership in the human race along with all their other possessions when they entered the camp." It was the basic instinct for self-preservation at work; no different, Weiss seemed to argue, from what motivated their captors: "I think it is a human psychological thing which develops under special circumstances where the ordinary values disappear, so the negative values will grow in certain people."[24] As one witness testified, "Those who were designated prisoners could have as easily been guards."

In the *TV Guide* interview, Weiss elaborated on the role that he felt chance had played in the Holocaust. Speaking in halting

---

* Adolf Eichmann, the architect of the "Final Solution," who had been tried and executed in Israel in 1962.

English, he acknowledged to Walter Wager that the play contained

> a suggestion that there are some of them [Jews] who could even become, would even have the possibility of sitting on the side of the accused because there were German Jews who were Nationalists. They were for Germany and they should have joined Hitler—many of them—if they weren't Jews, because Hitler was making up some "progress" for their society. And they looked down on the Jews from the Eastern countries.[25]

Fate, however, had said otherwise, and, therefore, the Jews had no option other than to accept the role they had been dealt:

> But, of course, they were chosen to be the victims and they just had to follow. And most of them did in a very passive way. That's a great tragedy—that they didn't find any possibility of fighting against the sort of pressure which was put.[26]

Interesting how he buries the lede there, slipping that little tidbit in at the end. But I find this idea of being a passive participant in your own persecution to be a terribly interesting one. Throughout "The Investigation," witnesses are asked if the prisoners ever offered any resistance—for instance, at the train station, where they vastly outnumbered the guards. No, one witness replied; "How could they foresee that, practically speaking, they had ceased to exist? Each one of them still believed he could survive." At another point, one of the accused volunteers that, "There wasn't any need to rough anybody up. They all took it very well. They didn't resist, since they could see resistance would have been pointless."

We've all heard the saying that "you can't fight City Hall," meaning that there are some things you just can't go up against because the other guys are bigger than you, richer than you, more powerful than you. That mentality still exists today, although I think fewer people are inclined to accept it at face value than they used to. They've been empowered, by the examples of others, to stand up for what they believe in: their values, their politics, their way of life. They're much less passive than they used to be. But, when all is said and done, how many people actually feel that way? How many will defer to authority, will accept the judgments of experts, will remain silent rather than risk their jobs, their incomes, their reputations, their lives? Will enough people have the courage to act to create real change, or will the status quo ultimately prevail?

There is, I suppose, only one way to find out, and that is a test we should all hope we never have to face.

V

Once when I was home on leave, I told my mother about it. She wouldn't believe it. That's impossible, she said. Anyway, people don't burn because you can't burn flesh.

Of all the many things that make the Holocaust difficult to understand, perhaps nothing approaches the defense offered by so many of the defendants, both in the Frankfurt Auschwitz trial and in other trials and other settings throughout the world: I was just following orders.

"I personally didn't have anything against those people," said Accused #8. "I always behaved decently. Anyway, what could I do? Orders are orders. And now, just because I obeyed, I've got this trial hung on my neck." Accused #6 said a lawyer told him that "illegal orders need not be obeyed, but that this should not be carried to the extreme where one's own life might be endangered. We were at war and all sorts of things were going on." "I came to the camp under protest," claimed Accused #5. Accused #12 admitted to taking part in "four or five" executions; when asked if he ever tried to get out of taking part, he replied, "But it was an order. It was my duty as a soldier." Summing it up for them all, he said, "Your Honor, we weren't supposed to think for ourselves. There were others around to do our thinking for us."

Certainly, there's nothing new in this defense; this was neither the first nor the last time it would be offered. Nor is it limited to war crimes. As The Libertarian Institute's Peter R. Quiñones wrote, "From the day they're born, the overwhelming majority of people are raised in environments that teach them to obey 'authority' and never question it." It applies to the military, but also to any organization or group built on any kind of hierarchy, as something of a one-stop defense no matter what the charge may be.[27]

And that's what we need to be worried about today. We may have found ways to penetrate the "just following orders" defense, to hold people accountable for their own actions, but that's a kind of *post-facto* justice, one that can be applied only after all is said and done. When a people are at the mercy of an authority that can simply justify their actions as having followed orders, without ever having to consider the legitimacy of that authority, the morality of that order, the consequences of that action, only bad things can result.

Just as we must develop the moral courage to stand up and refuse to be a victim, to cooperate in our own persecution, we must also deny illegitimate authority control over our lives. It becomes particularly important in the case of totalitarian governance, especially with the rise of militarized police departments, both in the United States and elsewhere. We've seen video of police officers assaulting peaceful protesters, arresting people for "silent prayer" in front of abortion mills, and for enforcing absurd (and likely unconstitutional) laws during the farce of COVID Theater. Not only do they follow orders, they seem to do so with relish. In some quarters, their actions have been referred to as "Gestapo-like," an interesting comparison given the context in which we're considering this.

What will happen if the day comes when soldiers and police officers are ordered to fire on demonstrators, to carry out "enhanced" interrogation techniques, or to prevent the exercise of free speech, on the grounds that such actions are necessary to prevent a "coup"? What happens if, in the case of another pandemic, they are ordered to sequester people in internment camps for refusing to take a vaccine? Ordered, in some cases, under threat of death. Would they choose to be a live coward, or a dead hero? Would they respond as Accused #12 did, "It was an order. It was my duty"?

VI

Today, the outside world wonders how they could have let themselves be destroyed that way. We who still live with these pictures know that millions could stand again, waiting to be destroyed, and that the new destruction will be far more efficient than the old one.

So here we are, and if we have come to know the horror that forms the basis of "The Investigation," if we have seen Peter Weiss's motivation in writing it, and if we appreciate the details of the television adaptation, the question that remains for us is this: how does this account of a historical event come to interest us as a television prophecy of the future? Is it not, in fact, a story that belongs to the past?

Weiss obviously didn't think so. "The Investigation," he said, was about "a human tragedy," about "the possibilities of what human beings are capable of, both in the good and the bad way," and this in no way ended with the Holocaust; Weiss felt it could be found "[in] what has happened in the French War in Algeria and in Vietnam, and even what happens in Vietnam now. I think they are psychological realities which are not only special German qualities. You find it everywhere. You find them in the Soviet concentration camps and you found them even in Norway among the quislings." He said that blacks in South Africa were in a similar situation, "[living] in a sort of concentration camp. . . . They're not massacred, but if one imagines a revolution there, they would be massacred there the same way."*28

A film version of "The Investigation" premiered in theaters in Israel and Germany in January 2025. Director R.P. Kahl, in discussing his motivation for making the film, said, "The audience needs to grasp the systemic factors that made Auschwitz possible: The totalitarian system, the terror, the erosion of humanity, and the promotion of opportunism. This active engagement allows for deeper understanding and reflection."[29]

The *totalitarian system*, the *terror*, the *erosion of humanity*, the *promotion of opportunism*. These are themes that will continue to run throughout this book, for they are the tools that have been, and continue to be, used by governments against their people, against freedom.

Yes, we know that another Holocaust can happen, as we've been told for as long as I can remember. Terrible things are

---

* Interestingly enough, earlier in the very evening that "The Investigation" was broadcast, *NET Playhouse* aired "Sponono," Alan Paton's drama about a young black inmate of a South African reformatory and his relationship with the white principal. Also on TV earlier that night: CBS's World War II POW comedy, *Hogan's Heroes*. Quite a night! (TV Guide, April 8, 1967.)

happening in the world, as we're reminded by events in Gaza. Longstanding prejudices continue, as we're reminded every time we hear a group of protesters chanting, "From the river to the sea."[30] Massacres of Christians take place worldwide on a weekly basis, although we seldom hear anything about them in the media. And none of these are possible without governments that employ, condone, or turn a blind eye, to terrorism. Totalitarian governments exist, even in countries that once fought against totalitarianism. The world is, if nothing else, an ironic place.

That is why the horrors of the past are not merely history; they can also serve as a prophecy of the future to come, a reminder that what happened then can happen to others as well. Those who don't know. Those who don't pay attention. Those who don't resist.

"I came out of the camp, yes, but the camp is still there."

All dialogue quoted is from the play *The Investigation* by Peter Weiss (New York: Atheneum, 1966.)
1. Aeschylus, *Oresteia*, 159.
2. Delatiner, "Horror Study," 69.
3. Newton, "Murder Was My Duty," 11.
4. Internet Broadway Database, "The Investigation."
5. Weiss, *The Investigation*, x.
6. Durgin, quoted in "'Boldest' New Venture."
7. Kirkley, "'Boldest' New Venture."
8. Allen, "'Investigation,' Nightmarish," 92.
9. Du Brow, "Awesome Description," 4.
10. Van Horne, "'Investigation' Painful," 17.
11. Reice, "Swinging Set," 14.
12. Gries, *Archival Television Audio*.
13. *Pittsburgh Post-Gazette*, "TV Key Previews," 39.

14. Cedrone, "Better on TV," 44.
15. Crosby, "'Investigation' Compelling," 55.
16. Anderson, "'Investigation' Provocative," G-5.
17. Shull, "An Investigation," 11.
18. Gries, *Archival Television Audio*.
19. Marley, quoted in Kleiner, "Hollywood Shrug," 36.
20. Wager, "Investigation Playwright Notes," 8.
21. Van Horne, "'Investigation'" Painful," C-4.
22. Delatiner, "Horror Study."
23. Shull, "An Investigation," 11.
24. Wager, "Investigation Playwright Notes," 8.
25. Ibid., 7.
26. Ibid.
27. Quiñones, "They Want You Dead," para. 3.
28. Weiss, interview by Wager, 8.
29. Kahl, quoted in "80 Years After," para. 10.
30. ADL, "From the River to the Sea," para. 1.

Darkness at Noon

Written by Robert Alan Aurthur
Based on the stage play by Sidney Kingsley, after the novel by
 Arthur Koestler
Produced by Fred Coe
Directed by Delbert Mann
First broadcast on *Producers' Showcase*, May 2, 1955

They meet with darkness in the day time, and grope in the noonday as in the night.

—Job 5:14[1]

The definition of insanity is doing the same thing over and over again and expecting a different result.[2]

—Anonymous

The year is 1937. Russia trembles under Stalin's Great Purge, a relentless campaign of show trials targeting Old Bolsheviks and Trotskyists who once fueled the Revolution. Now, there's no room for them, only for the dictator's iron will. As Greta Garbo quips in *Ninotchka*, the result is "fewer but better Russians." In the meantime, nobody is immune from the terror, no matter who you are, no matter how important you are—or *were*. It is the fear that comes from men who, not believing in God, feel free to make themselves gods. And as that tool of fear, the glare of the interrogator's spotlight, blinds us to the blackness of midnight, the darkness from its shadow eclipses the noonday light of the sun.

I

In a dim prison cell, Rubashov (Lee J. Cobb), once a towering "Old Bolshevik" and Party official, paces under the weight of his arrest for "straying from the Party line." The walls hum with tapped messages, a clandestine language among inmates. News of his fall spreads swiftly, each tap a ripple of shock. Alone, Rubashov's mind drifts to "walking, waking dreams"—vivid flashbacks that pull him into his past, as if stepping through time itself.

In one memory, he's Commissar of the Iron Works, dictating a speech to his secretary, Luba (Ruth Roman). His voice is firm: "To build our Communist state, one rule reigns—the end justifies the means. Those who are wrong will pay." Luba, new to his staff, transcribes without flinching, her beauty and quiet strength catching his eye. Over weeks, his admiration for her turns to love , though for him duty will always come first. Back in his cell, he whispers, "Yes, Luba, I will pay. I will pay my debt to you, above all." His reverie breaks as Prisoner 402 (Joseph Wiseman) taps from next door, cursing Rubashov and his ilk for ruling through terror and violence. Yet, bound by shared captivity, they exchange messages, comrades despite the rift.

Gletkin (David Wayne), a young guard with eyes like flint, embodies the Party's new breed—unyielding, contemptuous of Rubashov's intellectualism. "Your time's up," he sneers, dismissing the old revolutionary as a relic. Rubashov's mind escapes again, this time to Leipzig, where Nazis hunt communists. He meets Richard, a young pamphleteer who admits doubting the Party line. "I write what I must, because I must," Richard tells him. "Even if I'm wrong, I must write what I believe. That's how we arrive at the truth." Rubashov's response is icy: the individual is nothing, the Party everything. "The 'I' is a grammatical fiction." He'd betray Richard to the Nazis if his doubts endangered their cause. "Those who are not with us are against us."

The cell door clangs, and a guard leads Rubashov to interrogation. His questioner is Ivanov, an old comrade whose familiarity masks menace. Rubashov accuses Ivanov and the new guard of twisting the revolution's tools—terror, purges—against the people. Ivanov offers a lifeline: confess publicly to a fabricated "deviation," claiming repentance for joining an opposition plot. The scripted confession means a few years' imprisonment, sparing his life for future Party work. Refusal invites a secret trial and a bullet to the skull, erasing him without martyrdom. Rubashov defiantly rejects the deal, but Ivanov smiles thinly: "When you are ready to confess, send me a note. You will. I'm sure you will." Back in his cell, Rubashov taps his vow to 402: no confession, ever. Gletkin, observing Rubashov's resolve, clashes with Ivanov, advocating force over persuasion to break the prisoner.

Five weeks crawl by, Rubashov's resolve tested by isolation. Another flashback surfaces: the Iron Works, plagued by unmet quotas, with overwork leading to breakdowns of both men and machines. Rubashov, ever pragmatic, prepares to pin the blame on a subordinate, shielding himself. He recalls Luba's interrogation in Moscow over the failures; he had urged her to cooperate, rather than using his influence to intervene. withholding his influence, bound by Party loyalty over love. The memory causes him to realize that he no longer believes in his own infallibility.

The prison stirs with grim news: Bogrov, Rubashov's friend, is to be executed. The act, orchestrated by Gletkin, aims to crack Rubashov's spirit. Ivanov enters, pressing once again for Rubashov's confession, and revealing to him that Luba had been executed nine months prior—a wound Rubashov hadn't known. Gletkin has no past, only the present," Ivanov warns.

"He doesn't approve of us old apes in general, and of *you* in particular." Rubashov retorts that he and Ivanov *created* people like Gletkin. Ivanov insists Rubashov could still serve, if only he would bend. The offer remains, unanswered.

Days later, Gletkin conducts the third interrogation; Ivanov has now been executed for his failure. They debate the meaning of the revolution—Rubashov sees its betrayal in Gletkin's savagery. Gletkin reads Rubashov's own words back to him: *With us the objective result is everything. Those who prove wrong will pay!* Rubashov notes the irony; his own ideals birthed this merciless present. Gletkin reveals Luba's interrogation transcript—she refused to implicate him, loyal to the end. In a haunting vision, Luba appears: "You've made a prison of our country," she says. The trees wither, the people have been made miserable and fearful, and everything the Party says is a lie. Her words unravel him. He sees his guilt—not in the Party's charges, but in its crimes, enabled by his own hand. As he's led to die, 402 taps, "I envy you—it's over." On the way to be shot, Rubashov calls Gletkin his spiritual son. The means have become the end, and darkness has covered the land.

II

Producers' Showcase was another of NBC's most prestigious anthologies of the mid-1950s, an attempt to replicate the quality and impact of a television spectacular on a regularly scheduled basis. For three seasons, on the fourth Monday of every month, *Producers' Showcase* presented Broadway productions, original musicals and dramas, and concerts, all live and in color. Over the course of 37 episodes, the series won seven Emmys, including for the iconic "Peter Pan" with Mary Martin.

On May 2, 1955, two months after "Peter Pan," *Showcase* turned to a more chilling story: "Darkness at Noon," an adaptation of the 1940 novel by Arthur Koestler that had become a landmark critique of totalitarianism.

Arthur Koestler, born in Hungary, had become a communist in 1931, but by 1939, he had quit the party, disillusioned by what had become of the Bolshevik revolution. The following year, he wrote *Darkness at Noon*, and it became a literary and political triumph. Orwell considered the novel "brilliant," valuable as an exposé of the Moscow show trials "by someone with an inner knowledge of totalitarian methods."[3] Koestler's success at dealing with totalitarianism through fiction inspired Orwell to do the same with *Animal Farm* and *1984*.

It was adapted for the stage in 1951 by Sidney Kingsley, where it again won praise, and Kingsley's play was the basis for the teleplay by Robert Alan Aurthur. Claude Rains, who'd won Broadway's Tony Award for his portrayal of Rubashov, was originally scheduled to reprise the role for television; however, less than a month before the broadcast, NBC announced that Lee J. Cobb had been cast as Rubashov instead. (No official reason was ever provided for the switch, but rumor had it that Kingsley vetoed Rains's casting, suggesting he wanted "a younger-looking man" for the part.)[4]

Cobb was no slouch, having demonstrated his ability early on in Arthur Miller's "Death of a Salesman," a performance which prompted Miller to call him "the greatest dramatic actor I ever saw."[5] Already in 1955, he'd been nominated for an *Oscar for On the Waterfront*; he'd later portray one of the angriest of the jurors in *12 Angry Men*. Among his many television roles, he co-starred in *The Virginian*, and reprised his "Death of a Salesman" role, achieving a goal he'd long sought. His long and successful career would continue until he died in 1976.

The supporting cast included Ruth Roman as Luba, the secretary whom Rubashov loved and lost, Joseph Wiseman as a fellow prisoner, Oscar Homolka as an old colleague who places duty to the party above truth, Nehemiah Persoff and Henry Silva as prison officials, and David Wayne—who had starred in the family sitcom *Norby* earlier in 1955—as the cold, ruthless interrogator Gletkin, a role played on Broadway by Jack Palance.

Veteran director Delbert Mann—one attained veteran status quickly in the world of live television, and the 37-year-old Mann had already directed over 100 live dramas by this time—was known for being cool and calm under pressure, which proved necessary considering "Darkness at Noon"'s nonlinear storyline, alternating between Rubashov in his prison cell and flashbacks to earlier events:

> A whole, solid cell block was set up. Clever camera work got Cobb from the block into a single, backless cell. Then, while one camera was trained on him, another from another angle would pick him up, with the background of a past scene in the picture. A switch to the second camera would leave him in the flashback. He would leave a scene early, so that he could be back in his cell for the next prison scene.[6]*

Like all *Producers' Showcase* presentations, "Darkness at Noon" was broadcast in color, although only a black and white kinescope exists.† Even though relatively few homes had color sets, NBC banked on color broadcasts of prestige programming

---

* Mann would go on to motion pictures, winning a Best Director Oscar for his first movie, *Marty*, which he concluded just prior to "Darkness at Noon." Unlike many of his contemporaries, though, he never stopped working in television.
† The first national broadcast in color, the Tournament of Roses Parade, had occurred only four months earlier.

as an inducement for consumers to buy new color ones, made, not coincidentally, by NBC's parent company, RCA.

III

Reviews were effusive in their praise, describing it as "excellent," "a TV triumph," a technical "miracle," and an indication of television's "maturity in the field of drama." Writing in *The New York Times*, Jack Gould credited its "provocative power" and Lee J. Cobb's "most impressive performance,"[7] and the *Pittsburgh Post-Gazette*'s Win Fanning called it "an honest and devastating exposé of the Communist myth, both valid and harrowing."[8] Bernard Dube, in the *Montreal Gazette*, saw the play as "a grim denunciation of the human mess which the fanatic generation that followed the old revolutionaries made of that grand idealistic adventure—Communism," and summed it up by writing that, "The setting and staging conjured up more terror than has ever visited a TV screen."[9]

Cobb's performance was singled out: *Broadcasting* magazine said he "fully measured up" to previous stage performances by Rains and Edward G. Robinson, and in some respects surpassed them." Ray Oviatt of the *Toledo Blade* described his performance as "a wonderful piece of acting,"[10] and AP's Wayne Oliver said he "dominated the part with force and professional polish."[11]

Mann's creativity was lauded; Fanning wrote, "I have never seen a more effective TV adaptation of a Broadway play," and singled out Mann's use of multiple sets and his ability to shuttle Cobb between sets "with hardly a pause between scenes." "I have producer Fred Coe's word for it that there was not an inch of film used," he marveled.[12] And although relatively few were able to watch in color, Wayne Oliver suggested that might not be a bad thing: "The gray and black tones with the color control turned off seemed more in keeping with the brooding, melancholy mood of the drama than the color version that was mostly in pastels."¹³ The commercials, he noted dryly, benefited from color the most.

IV

Although the book never refers to the Soviet Union by name, there was little question, either in the United States or Europe, that "Darkness at Noon" was an attack on both the USSR and Stalin. The broadcast concluded with a brief film message from Vice President Richard Nixon, who commended the network for having aired the program.

> NBC, the television industry, and Producers' Showcase are to be congratulated for presenting this program to the American people, because in these times it is essential that we know our potential enemies, and the great moral of this play which you have had the opportunity to see is that we in the free nations must be eternally vigilant against the enemies from abroad and those from within.¹⁴

Koestler, Nixon said, had helped provide the answer to "one of the most intriguing questions which confronts the free world today": what makes a Communist tick?¹⁵ The actress and television interviewer Faye Emerson, reviewing the broadcast in her syndicated column, noted much the same thing: "[it] goes into the 'why' of Marxism, rather than the 'what.'"¹⁶

The communists considered *Darkness at Noon* to be important enough, and dangerous enough, that they worked to prevent it from being adapted for movies; the screenwriter (and

Blacklist member) Dalton Trumbo once boasted of using his influence to keep any adaptation from being made.[17]

Interestingly, Lee J. Cobb too had once been threatened with the Blacklist, having run afoul of the House Un-American Activities Committee in 1953; faced with the prospect of losing his livelihood, and with his wife having suffered a breakdown due to the stress, he chose to provide the committee with names. "I was pretty much worn down," he remembered years later. "I had no money. I couldn't borrow. I had the expenses of taking care of the children. Why am I subjecting my loved ones to this? . . . I decided it wasn't worth dying for, and if this gesture was the way of getting out of the penitentiary I'd do it. I had to be employable again.*"[18]

V

For Koestler, one of the questions at the heart of *Darkness at Noon* was why so many victims of the Great Purge, like Rubashov, had refused to defend themselves against these fabricated charges. Had they simply been worn down by the constant interrogation and torture they faced in the Gulag? Were they worried about the safety of family members who faced retribution at the hands of Stalin? Or was there something more to it, something dark and sinister, as Adam Kirsch described in a 2019 *New Yorker* article, that "in some obscure way, they deserved punishment for crimes they hadn't committed?"[19]

Central to the understanding of communist philosophy is what Karl Marx and Friedrich Engels saw as the "historical imperative," socialism's inevitable triumph. Any action that served to bring about this inevitability, no matter how ruthless,

---

* While working on *On the Waterfront*, Cobb worked with two other HUAC "friendly witnesses," writer Budd Schulberg and director Elia Kazan.

could be excused on such grounds. As Koestler put it, the member of such a movement [communist] "is forever damned to do what he loathes the most: become a butcher in order to stamp out butchery, sacrifice lambs so lambs will no longer be sacrificed." As Rubashov says at one point, "Whoever proves right in the end must first be and do wrong."

Koestler believed, in Kirsch's words, that "every political creed must eventually face the question of whether noble ends can justify evil means." Communism's stated goal was "the permanent abolition of social injustice throughout the world." Would any price be too high for such a goal? "Maybe a million or ten million people would die today," Kirsch writes, "but if billions would be happy tomorrow wasn't that worth it?"[20]

This is the language of what philosopher Eric Hoffer called the "True Believer," one for whom dogma is elevated above reason, replacing everything else in life.[21] Hoffer was fascinated by the propensity of mass movements to promote such single-mindedness, which served to foster, perfect, and perpetuate a facility for promoting power, unity, and self-sacrifice.[22] There is no such thing as the individual, they preach, only the overall good of the whole.* As Rubashov tells Luba, the very concept of the individual was a way of thinking "that had to be overcome in order to achieve justice for the many." The very terms "I" and "me" were, he said, nothing more than a "grammatical fiction."

Mass movements start with what Hoffer termed "men of words" who identify a need to reform the social order. As such movements grow, however, these reformers are crowded out by fanatics, those who, initially attracted by "doctrines and slogans of the new faith", eventually evolve into "an extremism against the social order." Hoffer distinguished the fanatic as

---

* Now you can see where Lark got his philosophy in "One."

one driven "to dominate and oppress each other,"[23] reflecting a philosophy known as "currentism," whose leaders "arrogantly believe they have the keys to the perfect society; they regard as evil only those thoughts or things which impede their will."[24] As Dr. James Toner astutely noted, "Such leaders are, they think, gods; but they are, in fact, mountebanks who, directly or indirectly, mutilate and murder, paying homage to the ubiquitous idols of the day."[25]

As the movement becomes institutionalized, "the focus shifts from immediate demands for revolution to establishing the mass movement as a social institution where the ambitious can find influence and fame." The movement develops a hierarchy of classes, a bureaucracy, a structure of leaders and followers, and the consolidation of power in the hands of a select few at the top—in other words, it becomes the very thing it sought to overthrow. When true believers fall victim to a party purge, they accept their unjust punishment as a necessary act, believing to the end that it somehow confirms the authority of the movement's cause and the advancement of the cause. They die *because* of a lie, which ultimately means they die *for* a lie.

VI

Revolutions, as Jacques Mallet du Pan warned, devour their own.[26] This is best illustrated in the final scene, as Gletkin leads Rubashov to his execution. The younger man represents the second generation of revolutionaries, fanatics who've come of age nourished by the blood of those who died at the hands of the Old Bolsheviks, whom they dismiss as counter-revolutionaries—"corrupt, like so many of your old guard," Gletkin says, "scum on the flood of the people's uprising." Rubashov, at last, sees himself for what he truly is: a man who believed that the end justifies the means until he learns the bitter lesson—that "the means have become the end, and darkness has come over the land."

"You don't build a paradise out of concrete, my son," he says to Gletkin.

"I am not your son," Gletkin interrupts.

"Oh, but you are," Rubashov replies. "*That* is the horror."

The sun didn't suddenly reappear at the end of the Cold War. We see its shadows spreading across our world even as we speak of it. We read about it every day: in silencing dissent, censoring content, monitoring opponents, talking about reeducation, spreading fear, all in the name of the cause. Sounds familiar, doesn't it? As is so often the case, the present is simply the past, returning in new guises. To those who point out such similarities, the response may be that today's ideas have never really been tried before, that what one thinks he saw in the past was in fact something else, something that people weren't quite ready for back then. *This time* things will be different. *This time*, the purity of the cause will not be diluted; ideas will be fully formed, plans will be fully implemented. Whether it's the French Revolution, Stalin's Great Purge, Mao's Cultural Revolution, the Cambodian Genocide, or the Great Reset, revolutionaries insist, "This time is different."

This time. *This time*.

No matter what time it is, it's always "this time." Same as the last time, same as the next time. It never works, and they never stop trying. Because even if you aren't interested in the revolution, rest assured that the revolution is interested in *you*.

All dialogue quoted is from "Darkness at Noon" (*Producers' Showcase*), based on the play by Sidney Kingley (New York, Random House, 1950).

1. Job 5:14 (*KJV*).
2. Unsourced—often tied to Alcoholics Anonymous or misattributed to Albert Einstein.
3. Orwell, "For What," para. 4.
4. *New York Daily News*, "Cancels Raines," 146.
5. Miller, quoted in McQuiston, "Lee J. Cobb, the Actor, is Dead," 33.
6. Craig, "'Darkness' Shows," 46.
7. Gould, "TV: 'Darkness at Noon' Impresses," 40.
8. Fanning, "'Showcase' Achieves," 14.
9. Dube, "Tviewing," 17.
10. Oviatt, "On the Beam."
11. Oliver, "'Darkness at Noon' Marks," 12.
12. Fanning, "'Showcase' Achieves," 14.
13. Oliver, "'Darkness at Noon' Marks." 12.
14. NBC, "Nixon Commends NBC."
15. Ibid.
16. Emerson, "Big Step," 11.
17. Billingsley, "Missing Movies."
18. Cobb, quoted in Navasky, *Naming Names*, 268-73.
19. Kirsch, "Desperate Plight," para. 6.
20. Ibid., para. 15.
21. Hoffer, *The True Believer*, 128.
22. Hoffer, *The True Believer*, n13.
23. Hoffer, *The True Believer*, 71.
24. Toner, "Currentism," para. 1.
25. Ibid.
26. du Pan, *Considérations*, 80.

A Taste of Armageddon

Written by Robert Hamner and Gene L. Coon
Produced Gene L. Coon
Directed by Joseph Pevney
First broadcast on *Star Trek*, February 23, 1967

It is well that war is so terrible. We should grow too fond of it.

—Robert E. Lee[1]

Hindsight is 20/20, the humorist Richard Armour tells us. That may not always be the case, but part of being a cultural archaeologist involves sifting through the detritus left by the past, searching for the clues that give us an idea of how the present came to be. Think of it as operating in the same way that an arson investigator goes about looking for evidence—always asking the question, "What happened here? And how?"

It's especially true when it comes to the wreckage of a civilization. How could such a thing happen? We wonder. It's an especially unsettling time, and try as we might to remain dispassionate, we can't help phrasing the question in the first person, as if we're looking in the mirror.

How did we allow this to happen?

I

Aboard the Enterprise, Captain James T. Kirk (William Shatner) navigates a delicate mission to Eminiar VII, escorting Federation Ambassador Robert Fox (Gene Lyons) to forge diplomatic ties. As the starship nears the planet, a stern transmission crackles through: "Stay away." Fox, brimming with bureaucratic confidence, dismisses the warning as posturing, urging Kirk to press on. Against his better judgment, Kirk complies, leading a landing party—Spock (Leonard Nimoy), two security officers, and a yeoman—to the surface, beaming down into a world both serene and unnervingly sterile. They're met by Mea 3 (Barbara Babcock), a poised emissary who escorts them to Anan 7 (David Opatoshu), leader of Eminiar's High Council. His calm demeanor belies a chilling truth about the planet's fate.

Anan explains that Eminiar has been locked in war with its neighbor, Vendikar, for five centuries. The conflict has claimed millions, a relentless cycle of devastation. Yet, as the landing party stands in the council chamber, an alert sounds: a "fusion bomb" attack from Vendikar has struck, killing thousands. Kirk and Spock exchange glances—no tremors, no smoke, no cries echo outside. The city remains pristine, its people unshaken. Suspicion deepens when Anan, with measured menace, unveils the war's surreal reality. Long ago, real battles ravaged both planets, threatening collapse. To preserve their societies while perpetuating their irreconcilable feud, Eminiar and Vendikar devised a grotesque solution: a computer-simulated war. Attacks are launched in code, casualties are calculated statistically, and destruction is confined to numbers on a screen.

The horror lies in the aftermath. Those designated "killed" in these virtual strikes—ordinary citizens, chosen by algorithm—have 24 hours to report to disintegrator chambers, where they are painlessly erased to uphold the treaty. Failure to comply allows the opposing planet to unleash a real attack, with all the carnage both sides dread. Anan's voice hardens as he delivers a bombshell: the Enterprise, orbiting above, and Kirk's landing party were "hit" in the latest simulation. They,

A Taste of Armageddon

too, are now casualties, expected to surrender to disintegration. Refusal endangers the treaty, risking annihilation for Eminiar. To enforce compliance, Anan attempts a ruse, using a voice duplicator to mimic Kirk and order the Enterprise crew to beam down. On the ship, Scott (James Doohan), acting in Kirk's absence, is suspicious; the message's cadence feels off. A quick scan by the ship's computer confirms it's a fake, and Scott holds his position, shields raised.

Kirk, no stranger to defying fate, rejects Anan's demand. Trapped in a guarded chamber, the landing party faces grim odds, but Spock's Vulcan ingenuity shifts the balance. With a subtle telepathic nudge, he plants doubt in their guard's mind, creating an opening for escape. As they slip through Eminiar's sleek corridors, Kirk's mind races: saving his crew means ending this war. Mea 3, torn by loyalty to her people yet haunted by the system's cold logic, becomes an unlikely ally, guiding them toward the war computer's core. Meanwhile, Ambassador Fox, insulated by diplomatic arrogance, decides to beam down, believing he can negotiate peace. Unaware of the trap, he materializes only to be seized by Anan's forces, slated for disintegration like the rest. Spock, tracking Fox's signal, intervenes, freeing him. Chastened, Fox sheds his clichés of useless diplomacy, joining Kirk's desperate bid to upend Eminiar's order.

The crisis peaks as Anan, increasingly desperate, confronts Kirk in the council chamber. Vendikar has noted Eminiar's failure to meet its casualty quota—a breach that could trigger real war, dooming both worlds. He pleads for Kirk to order the Enterprise crew down, framing disintegration as a noble sacrifice. Kirk, unyielding, sees through the sanitized horror. In a moment of calculated brinkmanship, he invokes General Order 24: unless he and his team are released within two hours, Scott will unleash Starfleet's wrath, reducing Eminiar to rubble. Anan blanches at the prospect, his society's obsession with "clean" war crumbling when faced by the threat of raw destruction. Seizing the moment, Kirk overpowers a guard, and the landing party storms the war room. Spock, with surgical precision, sabotages the computer system. Kirk says the two sides will now be forced to negotiate to avoid catastrophic bloodshed. Ambassador Fox offers his services to help mediate between the two planets, offering the possibility of peace for the region.

II

"A Taste of Armageddon" is unquestionably a blunt denunciation of war. And given that it was a product of the Vietnam era—written, produced, and telecast at a time when images of the war, briefings by Pentagon generals, and weekly casualty reports were an all-too-familiar aspect of the television experience—it is clear what conclusions we are to reach, what analogies we are to draw, what morals of the story we are to come away with.[*]

There is an unconscionable horror about the bland recitation of deaths in the episode, the reduction of life to a mere statistic, that is antithetical to what it means to be human. While not negating the unhappy reality that war is sometimes inevitable, it emphasizes the necessity of striving for peace, even if such attempts may prove ultimately unsuccessful. This is the power behind Kirk's threat to "finish" the conflict between the two planets. "Clean" warfare, such as that conducted between Eminiar and Vendikar—the very thought of it should

---

[*] The episode posits warfare as a treatable sickness, with Kirk's line, "We're killers, but we won't kill today," echoing Alcoholics Anonymous' one-day-at-a-time philosophy. It may also reflect the 1960s-1970s XYY "Criminal Chromosome" theory, which linked an extra chromosome to violence and suggested potential treatment, aligning with Kirk's stance and the era's scientific context.

be an abomination to sane men. Kirk intends to see to it that death is no longer so clean—that, as David Gerrold writes in *The World of Star Trek*, "if people were going to die, they were also going to have to see the blood and broken bodies."*²

(The very fact that the two planets negotiated a war that relied on computers and voluntary death rather than actual armed conflict suggests that some kind of military-industrial complex survives into the 22nd century, albeit one that preserves buildings and infrastructure. One can't help but wonder if constant war and death somehow supports these planets' economies. Or, even darker, that it serves as a type of population control. But that's another issue entirely.)

That Kirk can fulfill this promise, that he brings home to the leaders of Eminiar and Vendikar the truth of Robert E. Lee's horrible words, is intended to provide us with a happy ending, or at least a hopeful one (if Fox doesn't sabotage the negotiations through his own incompetence).

III

There is, though, something more to this story, something that allows us to come full circle to the observation that we started with. Namely, the apparent acquiescence of the people to go willingly, even unquestioningly, to their death—just because the government says so.

Yes, Vietnam is part of the storytelling. But isn't there another meaning to be drawn from this episode, one even deeper and darker, one which doesn't come up in discussions of "A

---

* Indeed, throughout the series (and subsequent movies), Kirk has repeatedly stressed the importance of pain and suffering, as well as the need to confront fear and uncertainty, as essential to the human experience. (He makes the point again in the very next *Star Trek* episode, "This Side of Paradise.")

Taste of Armageddon": its resemblance to Nazi concentration camps? At one point, Kirk and Spock find themselves walking down a corridor, past one of the disintegration stations. Watching as a young woman and a guard go in, Spock's description reduces "A Taste of Armageddon" to the bare essentials: "An entrance, Captain, but no exit. They go in, but they do not come out." It finds its echo in the testimony of a witness in the Auschwitz trials, revealing what really went on in the "showers" into which the prisoners were herded: "They entered, but they did not return."[3]

For what are the disintegration stations if not high-tech versions of gas chambers and cremation ovens? After all, one reason the gas chambers were implemented was to prevent mass executions from destroying the morale of German soldiers repulsed by such atrocities. The chambers and the ovens were cleaner, more sanitary, more socially acceptable.[4]

Author Stephen Green, author of *The Reluctant Meister: How Germany's Past Is Shaping Its European Future*, describes a Germany at the end of the 19th century marked by "an almost unquestioning commitment to obedience, a sense of duty that was very deeply ingrained."[5] Remember how, in discussing "The Investigation," Peter Weiss mentions that many of the Jews accepted their fate in "a very passive way."[6]

And then look at Anan's explanation of how the people of Eminiar accept their fate willingly because they have "a high consciousness of duty"? We've seen previously how the will to live is something deeply ingrained in humans; how, then, do we contrast this with the apparent mass insanity that would compel people to meekly accept their deaths out of a sense of duty?

Mea, one of those slated to die in the disintegrator, tries to explain it to Kirk from the standpoint of her people:

MEA: Don't you understand? Our duty—

KIRK: Your duty doesn't include stepping into a disintegrator and disappearing.

MEA: I'm afraid mine does, Captain. I, too, have been declared a casualty. I must report to a disintegrator by noon tomorrow.

KIRK: Is that all it means to you? To report and die?

MEA: My life is as dear to me as yours is to you, Captain.

KIRK: Then how can you stand—

MEA: Don't you see? If I refuse to report, and others refuse, then Vendikar would have no choice but to launch real weapons. We would have to do the same to defend ourselves. More than people would die then. A whole civilization would be destroyed. Surely you can see that ours is a better way.

On the planets of Eminiar and Vendikar, this "duty" means being complicit in one's own death. But how can this be? Has freedom of thought long since been eliminated in favor of obedience to their leaders, to the point that they don't fight for their own lives or those of others?

We are told that the computer war is necessary to preserve the civilizations of the two planets, but at this point, can they truly be called "civilized"?

IV

We aren't told much about the histories of Eminiar and Vendikar, other than that they've been at war for five hundred years, but what we know of German history can tell us a great deal.

The Germans have this saying, *Ordnung muss sein*: "There must be order." This mentality—the emphasis on order—dates back to the time of Martin Luther, and has become so much a part of German society that someone remarked it must be "in the water supply."[7] This aspect of the German psyche played a significant role in World War II (as it does in all of German history), especially in creating the mentality that prioritizes "following orders."

That phrase—"I was only following orders"—has become something of a grim punchline over the decades, a mocking of the defense offered by those who sought to explain away or excuse their actions in wartime atrocities.

But it's a mistake to think that "following orders" only applies to the business of concentration camps and gas chambers and disintegration stations. This may be where it ends, but it's not where it begins. It begins, as it always does, with the little things. A German remembers his early days in the Hitler Youth:

> I still recall with wonder that [the commander] once marched all 160 of us in his Fahnlein [unit] into an ice-cold river in November because our singing had displeased him. We cursed him bitterly under our breath, but not one of us refused. That would have been the unthinkable crime of disobeying a "direct order." During the war, such a refusal could be used—and frequently was—to put the offender before a firing squad.[8]

Ah, you say, but this is hardly a prophecy, is it? More like a reminiscence, a looking back at a time, long past, not our past, when civilization ceased to be, when orders were followed, and obedience was a given. An allegory set in the future, but surely not our future.

Perhaps.

And yet what does one make of the rise in anti-Semitism: the discrimination, the assaults, and violent protests, the chants of "From the river to the sea"?[9] Are these people who have forgotten the past, and the lessons to be learned from it? Or do they simply want to try it over again, to see if they can get it right this time?

V

How did we allow this to happen?
Some people think there's an element of betrayal in that question, that we have somehow been betrayed by those in charge of preventing "this," whatever it might be, from happening. And I'd agree with that. Those people in charge—and we're talking about authority figures, whether they're accountants, ministers, teachers, government leaders, even the president—they're put in a position of trust. We trust them to do the right thing by and for us, to protect our interests, to do what is best for the common welfare. We trust that the barber or the beautician is going to cut our hair in such a way that small children aren't going to run screaming when they see us coming.

And when they don't—when the accountant embezzles from our retirement plan, when our children come home from school unable to read, when the government treats us like the enemy—then we feel betrayed by them. We trusted you, we say, and you didn't do what you were supposed to do. Not only do we say it, but in this day and age, we say it loudly and we say it publicly.

But—and there's *always* a but . . .

Even the most trusted servant isn't given free rein over the household. You check up on him or her, make sure the bank account balances, count the silverware once in a while. It's nothing personal, it's just something you do. You have an *obligation* to do it. And if that servant takes advantage of you because you didn't keep proper tabs—well, there's a segment of the population, and maybe there's a part of you as well, that's thinking, "You invited all this." Remember the saying, "Fool me once, shame on you. Fool me twice, shame on me."

How did we allow this to happen?

Those trusted authority figures I mentioned—well, they are servants of a sort. They work on our behalf. And therefore, they require some kind of oversight. From us. And if we allow them to run free, if we refuse to follow through on our obligation, then some of that blame falls on us.

That can be an uncomfortable truth. It requires us to look in the mirror and to study what we see. A lot of people would rather not do that. They'd prefer to pass the buck, to put the blame squarely on those authority figures, to say they're one hundred percent responsible for letting it happen.

After all, it's much easier to ask how they let it happen than how we let it happen. Much easier, and much less guilt involved.

VI

There was no sense in fighting back, survivors remembered. The Germans sowed division in the camps, pitting inmates against each other by granting extra food and certain privileges to those whom they designated leaders. Divide and conquer, the old tactic worked.

Perhaps the Jews didn't accept their deaths in such a passive way, then. Perhaps they were just worn down, at a point where they knew resistance was useless. And wasn't that what the Germans wanted?

Isn't that what they always want, those in power who are determined to stay in power? And what better way to make sure than to set neighbor against neighbor, family members against each other, law enforcement authorities against the public?

Plato observed that, "Each form of government enacts the laws with a view to its own advantage, a democracy democratic laws and tyranny autocratic and the others likewise, and by so legislating they proclaim that the just for their subjects is that which is for their—the rulers'—advantage and the man who deviates from this law they chastise as a law-breaker and a wrongdoer."[10]

VII

How did we allow this to happen?

It can seem like a psychosis, a mass movement taking over supposedly normal people. We've even developed a word to describe them: sheeple, which Wiktionary colorfully defines as "people who unquestioningly accept as true whatever their political leaders say or who adopt popular opinion as their own without scrutiny."[11] They're docile, meekly submissive, easily swayed.

The people of Eminiar and Vendikar surely qualify as sheeple. As far as we can tell, based on the examples we see in "A Taste of Armageddon," they accepted their fate without question; after all, their leaders knew what was best, and their arguments about how it would create a stable society for each planet must have seemed convincing. If you're willing to pay the price for it.

People were told to go to a disintegrator chamber. And the sheeple went along.

How did we allow this to happen?

Someone more perceptive than I compared this to Hans Christian Andersen's fable of "The Emperor's New Clothes." You know how that works: the emperor striding through his kingdom in a suit made of material so fine that only the very smart or very competent can see it. None of his subjects wants to be thought a fool, and so they all keep their mouths shut, even though they all know how ridiculous it is, until a child blurts out that this guy's only wearing his skivvies. Well, the Good Book does say that we must have the faith of a child, and that includes the faith to state the truth.

Thing is, there's that uncomfortable truth we talked about. And that keeps some people from speaking up about the emperor.

Some people think it's easier to just ignore what's going on, and maybe it won't affect them.

Some people prefer to keep their mouths shut and not get involved, in hopes that it just goes away. Remember this, when someone suggests to you that it's best to go along to get along.

Some people believe the emperor must be right, because he is, after all, the emperor, and he knows best.

And some people like the idea that they're part of the elite, that they possess the intellect required to see the emperor's clothes. They're better than the peasants; they're among the privileged few. They get to tell everyone else what to do.

Surely, you're thinking, we can't draw a parallel between the Holocaust and the response to COVID, between what happened in Nazi Germany and what happened around the world in 2020. Well, that's *exactly* what I'm saying.

This is the truth of what happened:

People were told they couldn't go out in public, and the sheeple went along. People were told they couldn't visit sick or dying relatives, and the sheeple went along. People were told to take an unproven vaccine, to violate the beliefs of their religion, and the sheeple went along.

Those who asked questions, who dared to disagree, were threatened with having their bank accounts seized, their employment terminated, their children taken away, all for speaking their minds.

They were mocked by others, and they were arrested by police, and their places of business were closed down, and they became targets of the last prejudice.

Contrary opinions are not allowed, they were told. Resistance is unpatriotic, they were told. They're selfish, they're insurrectionists, they don't deserve to live, they were told. They're garbage, they were told.

And when confronted with the evidence they didn't want to hear, the differing opinions they didn't want to acknowledge, the independent thought they didn't want to allow, they replied, "These are the orders. This is what we must do."

People are told to go to a disintegrator chamber. And the sheeple go along.

They're the ones who know how we got to this point, how we allowed this to happen.

And unless there's a Captain Kirk out there, there's no going back.

All dialogue quoted is from "A Taste of Armageddon"(*Star Trek*).
1. Lee, Battle of Fredericksburg.
2. Gerrold, *World of Star Trek*, 252.
3. Wager, "Playwright's Program Notes," 7.
4. Llewellyn and Thompson, "*The Einsatzgruppen.*"
5. Green, quoted in Rösler, "Germany and Germans,"
6. Wager, "Playwright's Program Notes," 7.

7. Baur, "What Makes Germans."
8. Heck, *Child of Hitler*, 33–34.
9. ADL, "From the River to the Sea," para. 1.
10. Plato, *Republic*, 1.338e.
11. *Wictionary*, s.v. "sheeple."

The Year of the Sex Olympics

Written by Nigel Kneale
Produced by Ronald Travers
Directed by Michael Elliott
First broadcast on *Theatre 625*, July 29, 1968

[W]hen a population becomes distracted by trivia, when cultural life is redefined as a perpetual round of entertainments, ... then a nation finds itself at risk; the death of culture is a real possibility.

—Neil Postman[1]

In the future, there will be two classes: the High-Drives, an elite few who control the government and media; and the Low-Drives, the masses who comprise an overwhelming majority of the population. This is a stark future; fears of overpopulation abound, nourishment comes from protein sticks, the population lives in sterile accommodations isolated from nature, and while those things that bring pain and unhappiness have been eliminated, so have those that produce joy and pleasure. People speak a form of Pidgin English stripped to its bare essentials—perhaps from a lifetime of texting?—and many words no longer exist. To keep the Low-Drives pacified, they are fed a mind-numbing diet of banal television with the emphasis on pornography, brought to them by a sole network known only as Output.

The time, we are told in an onscreen graphic, is "sooner than you think." But we know what year it is. It is "The Year of the Sex Olympics."

I

In a neon-lit studio, a young couple's entangled limbs ignite the screen, their passion a prelude to *Sportsex*, a nightly spectacle feeding into the Sex Olympics. The camera pulls back to Control, where High-Drive executives Nat Mender (Tony Vogel), Lasar Opie (a pre-*Succession* Brian Cox), and Ugo Priest (a pre-*Reginald Perrin* Leonard Rossiter) oversee a world enslaved by "reality" TV. Below them, the Low-Drives— the placid, emotionless masses—lounge before screens, devouring shows designed to dull their minds. Television, under High-Drive rule, churns out endless drivel, crafting what Ugo calls a "vicarious society." Low-Drives, stripped of anger or ambition, live through what they watch, their lives a flicker of others' pain and pleasure. Success hinges on the Audience Sampler, a real-time gauge of reactions. Laughter or engagement spells triumph; boredom or apathy signals failure. Suffering—accidents, anguish—sends ratings soaring, as viewers sigh in relief: "Better them than us."

Nat, a cog in this machine, grapples with cracks in his High-Drive life. Unlike Low-Drives, barred from intimacy, High-Drives can indulge, but attachments are forbidden. Nat clings to Deanie Webb (Suzanne Neve), his former lover and *Artsex* colleague, and their daughter, Keten (Lesley Roach). Deanie drops a bombshell: Keten's metabolic test hints she's Low-Drive, a stigma that could derail their careers. Meanwhile, Kin Hodder (Martin Potter), Deanie's current lover and an *Artsex* "drape artist," chafes against the system. His side projects—raw, visceral artworks—aim to jolt viewers. "I want them to hurt, to see!" he declares. Deanie, loyal to High-Drive calm, asks Nat to rein him in. Nat hesitates, Kin's defiance appealing to his own buried doubts.

The Year of the Sex Olympics

Kin's rebellion sparks chaos. During a broadcast, he hijacks the feed, flashing a stark portrait that jolts the Audience Sampler into disarray—viewers wince, unsettled. Ugo fumes, condemning the tension it breeds, while Nat, denying involvement, admits fascination. Kin escalates, infiltrating a *Sportsex* taping. Suspended from studio rafters, he unfurls his art, shouting, "They hurt—you've gotta see them!" His grip fails, and he plummets, body crumpled on the stage. Blood seeps from his mouth as cameras zoom in. The audience roars with laughter, tears streaming, enthralled by death's spectacle. Apathy Control erupts in glee—"Look at those ratings! Toughest in six months!"—but Nat sees, beyond the numbers, a flicker of an idea.

Seizing the moment, Nat pitches a radical show: *The Live-Life Show*. Strand people on an island, self-reliant, their struggles—hunger, sickness, death—broadcast raw. "Nobody knows what'll happen," he says. "That suspense will hook them." Deanie, reeling from Kin's death and Keten's test, volunteers, craving escape. Nat, drawn by her resolve and his own unrest, joins her. Keten balks, estranged from Nat and fearing Low-Drive banishment, but Deanie soothes her: "We'll be a family." Lasar, now producer, selects a rugged island*—arable, fish-rich, neither too harsh nor forgiving. Supplies are minimal: seeds, clothes, a wired cabin pulsing with cameras. "Non-stop," Lasar grins. Ugo warns, "You'll face new problems, not flee old ones."

The Live-Life Show launches with fanfare, a helicopter sweeping over the island for viewers' delight. Nat, Deanie, and Keten step into their new world, awestruck by nature's vastness. Keten, raised on screens, mistakes a window for a TV screen, her disorientation poignant. Recorded instructions guide them—light a fire, sow crops. Deanie, touching flame,

---

* The real-life Isle of Man, though it's not identified as such.

flinches but smiles, masking pain. In Control, Lasar nods: "Ratings jumped when she burned." Days unfold with wonder—ocean breezes, soil underfoot—but disruption looms. Two strangers appear: Grels (George Murcell), sly and shadowed, and Betty (Hira Talfrey), his quiet companion. They claim to live across the island, spotting the newcomers' arrival. Grels offers help—gull eggs, crabs—but Nat's unease grows. In Control, Ugo's baffled; Lasar smirks, admitting he planted them for "scene setting." Worse, he reveals Grels is an exiled murderer, a "super king" twist kept from all.

Tension festers. Betty vanishes, and while Grels claims she fell, Nat and Deanie suspect murder. Keten, meanwhile, develops an infection, her fever climbing. Deanie's remedies fail, and Keten dies, her small body laid to rest. Ratings skyrocket, Lasar's gamble paying off. Nat's grief hardens into rage, aimed at unseen cameras. Grels, lurking, attacks Deanie in their cabin. Nat bursts in, pummeling Grels to death, but Deanie's wounds are fatal. He cradles her, screaming, his anguish raw. In Apathy Control, the audience howls, clapping wildly. As Lasar accepts the plaudits of the crowd, Ugo—broken by Lasar, broken by what has happened—looks on in horror. "Look at him!" he shouts into the din, unheard by the others. "He's alive! *He's alive!*" Despite Lasar's attempts to manipulate things, Nat has managed to survive.

II

Nigel Kneale was already one of British television's most prolific writers when he wrote "The Year of the Sex Olympics." His best-known works, popular to this day, are probably his science fiction serials featuring the heroic scientist Professor Bernard Quatermass, who helped save Earth from various alien threats. In his obituary of Kneale, the writer and actor Mark Gatiss described him as "the man who saw tomorrow," while Hammer Film Productions, for which Kneale worked several times, called him "one of the most influential writers of the 20th century."[2]

This wasn't Kneale's first go-around with dystopia: back in 1954, he had written the teleplay for the BBC's adaptation of Orwell's "1984". As one critic noted, there is an obvious direct line of descent from "1984" to "The Year of the Sex Olympics."[3] (I'd like to think that, privately, Kneale thought of "Sex Olympics" as taking place in 1984; that was, after all, an Olympic year.) He'd also done (never-produced) adaptations of Aldous Huxley's *Brave New World* and William Golding's *Lord of the Flies*, so temperamentally, he was well-suited to write a story like this.

Kneale had an animus for aspects of the counterculture that makes "The Year of the Sex Olympics" a good match with Marya Mannes' "They." "I didn't like the Sixties at all because of the whole thing of 'let it all hang out' and let's stop thinking, which was the all-too-frequent theme of the Sixties which I hated." Of the permissive, taboo-free hippy subculture, he said, "Inhibitions are like the bones in a creature. You pull all the bones out and you get a floppy jelly." He envisioned a society that "wouldn't be really a verbal society any more," using a vocabulary that had been eroded "through exposure to advertising slogans, mediaspeak, and predominantly visual media."[4]

He also laced the script with moments of dark humor that teeter between savage and pathetic, such as Keten's confusion about finding herself outside for the first time; she thinks the snow is grass, and that the window is a television screen. "Look at the screen. Mini screen. They all funny." Nat explains to her that it's not a screen; that everything she's seeing out there is real. But he doesn't have the words to tell her what to call them. "Sort of holes to look out. They called—I don't know."

"The Year of the Sex Olympics" aired on BBC2 on July 29, 1968. Although reviews were favorable—Sean Day-Lewis,* writing in the *Daily Telegraph*, praised "Sex Olympics" as "A highly original play written with great force and making as many valid points about the dangers of the future as any science fiction I can remember—including 1984!"—it was less successful with the 1.5 million viewers who watched it that night, many of whom found it "impenetrable."[5]

Impenetrable—that's an interesting word to use when describing "Sex Olympics," don't you think? (Like an electronic chastity belt, perhaps.) It must be far less impenetrable to us today, for we live in the future that it foretold; we're more likely to think of it as "far-reaching" or "prophetic." Pornography is widely available and widely consumed. People have created a kind of pidgin English when texting, not unlike the "reduced language" that Kneale anticipated. And we don't have to expand on the role reality television (or "Unscripted TV," as they euphemistically describe it) plays in today's culture.

But can you actually appreciate something as truly prophetic while you're watching it, or does it only attain that status after history has proven it right? Kneale himself, appearing on the program *Late Nite Line Up* after the broadcast, said, "You can't write about the future. One can play with the processes that might occur in the future, but one is really always writing about the present because that is what we know."[6] And if that is the case, then how could it not be impenetrable to most viewers? As Bishop Fulton Sheen once said, "men do not want to believe their own times are wicked." In their willful ignorance, they reject the clouds signaling the coming storm; they are

---

* Daniel Day-Lewis's father.

"unconscious of the destructive processes going on."[7] The shock of "Sex Olympics" on first viewing is that it presents such a grotesque vision of the future as to be unthinkable; the shock of viewing it today is that it's all come true.

There's one moment in particular, though, that stands out for its poignancy as much as its prophecy. It occurs as Ugo is warning Nat and Deanie that they may not be prepared for the challenges they'll face. "Listen," he abruptly says to Nat. "You hear?" When Nat tells him he doesn't hear anything, Ugo tells him that's the point. "You don't hear it because you never not heard it, and the standard smell you don't smell it, but out there it's terrible. Know what I did? I cried. Sat and cried for that smell and noise from the shelter."

How many of us, surrounded by our electronic devices, plugged into a constant stream of noise, our senses assaulted in our cars, in our stores, in our homes, how many of us have failed to hear the silence?

III

Despite the provocative title, there's really not much sex in "The Year of the Sex Olympics," aside from one tasteful nude (and seen from the side, at that). It *is* 1968, after all, even on British television.

Speaking of sex, though, worrying about overpopulation was quite the fad in the mid-60s (and continues to this day), thanks in part to the book *The Population Bomb*, published in 1968—the same year as "The Year of the Sex Olympics"—by Paul Ehrlich (a perennial doomsayer; besides overpopulation, he's also issued apocalyptic warnings about environmentalism, climate change, disease, and, for all I know, Girl Scout cookies, none of which have come true) and Anne H. Ehrlich.[8] While the use of pornography as a form of both birth control and dehumanization was not, at least as far as I know, one of Ehrlich's suggestions, it was, in fact, another prescient warning in "Sex Olympics."

For some time, researchers have linked pornography consumption to decreased sex drive. A particularly appalling study by the Naval Medical Center of San Diego finds disturbing, if unsurprising, correlations between Internet pornography and low sexual desire. "When a user has conditioned his sexual arousal to Internet pornography," the report states, "sex with desired real partners may register as 'not meeting expectations'." The study goes on to suggest that "the younger the age at which men first began regular use of Internet pornography, and the greater their preference for it over partnered sex, the less enjoyment they report from partnered sex, and the higher their current Internet pornography use."[9]

The key word here is "conditioned," for just as the subjects of the NMC study had conditioned their sexual arousal to porn, the world of "Sex Olympics" has conditioned viewers to prefer porn to actual sex. When Ugo uses the word "pornography" in conversation, Nat doesn't even know what the word means. And why should he? Pornography denotes an abnormality, a taboo, a negative connotation. And in a world without taboos, without restrictions, what does one need with such a word? It is, after all, just sex—no differentiation required.

The author Emile Cammaerts said that, "The first effect of not believing in God is to believe in anything."[10]* And so it is here. Anything goes—as long as it keeps the audience's interest. It is, as Ugo says, "the sheer power of watching."

---

* Cammaerts, in *The Laughing Prophet,* attributed the quote to G.K. Chesterton's famous Father Brown, but there's no actual evidence that the good father, or Chesterton for that matter, actually said it.

IV

When Mark Gatiss saw the reality show *Big Brother* for the first time, he shouted, "Don't they know what they're doing? It's 'The Year of the Sex Olympics'!" He meant it as a takedown of *Big Brother*, while praising Kneale for his foresight; in doing so, Gatiss pointed out the obvious: "Yesterday's satire is today's reality. Or today's reality TV."[11]

In Kneale's vision, reality television is the ultimate form of Lowest Common Denominator programming, intended to pacify the population, to provide them with a "vicarious society"— one in which, in Ugo's words, "the audience would make do with that in place of the real thing, take all experiences secondhand, just sit watching calmly and quietly." They would derive their amusement, their entertainment, from the foibles and troubles of others, taking satisfaction that it wasn't happening to them, debasing themselves through their passive acceptance of the humiliation of others.

Now, the idea of using mass media to keep the populace distracted and submissive isn't a new one; Juvenal used the phrase "bread and circuses" in 100 B.C.[12] As Neil Postman notes in *Amusing Ourselves to Death*, "Tyrants of all varieties have always known about the value of providing the masses with amusements as a means of pacifying discontent. But most of them could not have even hoped for a situation in which the Masses would ignore that which does not amuse."[13]

In "Sex Olympics," the vehicle used to measure such amusement is Apathy Control, and one of the most powerful moments occurs when the artist Kin Hodder falls to his death near the end of part one. The image of Hodder's twisted, bleeding body, juxtaposed with the laughter from the audience, is striking. Ugo immediately understands this as another breakthrough, the "fruit slip" moment they needed to engage the audience. "You heard it. The classic laugh. The fruit skin. Did not expect it. It happened. I'm glad it's not them. Jumbo relief. Jumbo laugh in all areas."

In other words, it's the horror of cashing in on other people's misery, whether it be the Audience Sampler howling with delight, or the mercenary High-Drives willing to exploit that misery to further pacify the masses. But what does it say about the masses who so willingly accept this form of entertainment, who find their pleasure in the pain of others? What does it say about us?

First, and most obviously, it says that we can be a cruel and heartless bunch. As Lasar Opie notes, the audience enjoys pain and suffering because "it not happen to them." We hardly need to be reminded of that, though; most of us experience it often enough every day. There's something else, though, something more subtle and more sinister: the complacency that results from such pacification. "A really efficient totalitarian state," Aldous Huxley wrote in 1947, "would be one in which the all-powerful executive of political bosses and their army of managers control a population of slaves who do not have to be coerced, because they love their servitude."[14]

V

How did this world come to pass? As Ugo explains it, the world had been overcome by a continuous and growing tension: war and riots and other kinds of crises, causing food shortages, riots, wars, and restless, rebellious masses. And then came the discovery that the masses could be controlled through a steady diet of programming appealing to the lowest common denominator. Apathy Control, they call it, a continuous diet of programming, particularly pornography, that conditions them to "make do with that in place of the real thing, take all experiences secondhand, just sit watching calmly and quietly." "Sex is not to do," Nat says. "Sex is to watch." Similarly, food competitions are designed to gross out viewers and turn them away from food, so they won't complain about the shortages.

How many times in this series have we encountered the word, and how much trouble have we seen as a result of it? Fear of invasion from outer space ("The Architects of Fear"), fear of the unknown ("The Monsters Are Due on Maple Street"), fear of individuality ("Number 12 Looks Just Like You"), fear of free thinking ("One"). Who knows if any of the fears in "The Year of the Sex Olympics" are genuine, or if they're all part of some gigantic PSYOP being perpetrated by someone pulling all the strings, something to distract you from what's really going on, while the powerful get more powerful. What we do know is that fear is at the heart of everything that happens; it motivates every action, drives every response, and can be summed up with one word: *tension*.

Kin Hodder strives to reach people through his pictures, to make them think, "make them hurt." But that can't be allowed; it would cause tension, and we all know what that means. Nat struggles to find the words to explain to Ugo what he sees in Kin's pictures. "Where they go, coordinator? Why they go, all those words?" And Ugo tells him where they went. "People didn't need them, Nat. They got out of having the thoughts and the words went too." Bad thoughts, don't you see? *Tension.*

We know that wars no longer exist in this world; Nat doesn't even know what the word means, and Ugo has to explain it to him. "A war is a kind of tension," like riots and other crises. But now things are different, Ugo says with satisfaction. "Everything got tried then, bombs and books and prayers, and love, the last of the politics. It all added up to tension." And so the tension had to be diffused, the audience needed to be cooled. "No more tensions, nothing, just cool," Ugo says.

> It's what the world needed. Just to call a big halt. No more progress. It was done kindly, not by lasering fetuses, chemical conditioning, electrodes, no, none of that. It was no threats. No, no, just by gentle discouragement. It's meant to cancel. Another world, having a rest, Nat. All of them out there waiting. You know what they are? A huge reservoir of genes. Huge genetic stockpile just waiting until it's safe to go on again.

Just waiting until it's safe again, to "give humanity a chance to survive a million years, to draw level with the least successful dinosaurs." But who decides such things? The experts, the Centers for Disease Control, the World Health Organization, the World Economic Forum? The presidents, the prime ministers, the governors? The billionaires, the corporate leaders of Big Business, Big Pharma, Big Media, Big Tech, deciding what you see and hear and consume? For they are the ones who are today's High-Drives, and let's be honest: what motive do they have to ease up on the fear, to tell us it's safe again?

And what do the High-Drives fear? The ultimate: the loss of power. It's never specified what percentage of the population consists of High-Drives, but we can tell it's a fairly small number. Let's say—just for the sake of argument, you understand—that the High-Drives make up one percent. Easy enough to remember. That leaves 99 percent of the population, and it's easy enough to keep them pacified with their television, right? After all, the Low-Drives don't make the rules, don't change things, don't decide what's what. The very meaning of the word prohibits it.

"The Year of the Sex Olympics" is a horrifying vision of the future, and a depressing one; depressing because so much of it has already come true. If you need further evidence, look at the passivity with which we accepted the restrictions on freedom in 2021 and 2022. Hell, some of us even wanted to go further! And yet we gave in, without a fight. We were too busy sitting "calmly and quietly," enjoying our screen addictions, investing in our reality television, monitoring what other people could or could not say, dehumanizing ourselves without their doing it to us.

Huxley understood that slavery is the very essence of passivity. And pacified people don't create problems, do they?

All dialogue quoted is from "The Year of the Sex Olympics": (*Theatre 625*).
1. Postman, *Amusing Ourselves*, 155–56.
2. Simpson, "Tribute to Nigel Kneale," para. 5.
3. BFI, "The Year of the Sex Olympics."
4. Pixley, "The Year of the Sex Olympics," 46–51.
5. Day-Lewis, quoted in Fulton, *TV Science Fiction*, 580.
6. Pixley, "The Year of the Sex Olympics," 51..
7. Sheen, "Signs of Our Times."
8. Ehrlich and Ehrlich, *Population Bomb*.
9. *Naval Medical Center*, "Internet Pornography," 3.4.3.
10. Cammaerts, *The Laughing Prophet*, 211.
11. Gatiss, "Man Who Saw Tomorrow."
12. Juvenal, *Satires*, 10.81.
13. Postman, *Amusing Ourselves*, 141.
14. Huxley, *Brave New World*, xviii.

FIVE
THE BLOOD OF THE MARTYRS

The Obsolete Man

Written by Rod Serling
Produced by Buck Houghton
Directed by Elliot Silverstein
First broadcast on *The Twilight Zone*, June 2, 1961

Avoiding danger is no safer in the long run than outright exposure. The fearful are caught as often as the bold.

—Helen Keller[1]

What makes Romney Wordsworth, the protagonist of "The Obsolete Man," stand out from some of the other characters we've studied here? It is, I think, his humanity. Many of these stories are contests of ideas and ideologies, and while the human toll can't be ignored, one still comes to the end of each story experiencing a sense of futility, of the individual being crushed.

Not so with Rod Serling's disturbing *Twilight Zone* episode, which originally aired on June 2, 1961. Now, it's true that Wordsworth, like so many of the figures we see here, is ultimately executed by the masters of the totalitarian government that rule over his society. Wordsworth, however, meets his fate with glorious, even joyful, defiance. It's not that he yearns for death; I think he appreciates life as much as anyone. The difference, though, is that he doesn't *fear* death; and, as the Chancellor will discover, that makes a huge difference.

I

In the bleak future, a librarian named Romney Wordsworth (Burgess Meredith) stands defiant in a cavernous courtroom, its stark angles dwarfing the humans inside. The Chancellor (Fritz Weaver), perched behind a towering podium, presides over a society that has outlawed books and religion, erasing the past to cement control. The subaltern reads the charges: Wordsworth, by clinging to his role as a librarian and professing belief in God, is an anachronism—an "obsolete man." The verdict is swift: death. Yet the State, cloaking its brutality in magnanimity, grants him a choice in how he will die, a gesture meant to underscore its dominance.*

Wordsworth, his eyes steady, selects his fate: execution in his library, surrounded by the forbidden tomes he's guarded, to be broadcast on live television across the nation. "It has an educative effect on the population," the Chancellor says approvingly, savoring the propaganda. The method—known only to Wordsworth and his executioner—remains a mystery, a detail that piques the Chancellor's curiosity but not his concern. In this regime, where conformity is god and individuality is treasonous, no act of defiance seems possible. Yet Wordsworth, unbowed, harbors a plan to prove otherwise, one that will expose the State's fragility through the smallest spark of freedom.

Escorted to his modest home, Wordsworth prepares for his final hour, surrounded by shelves filled with books—relics of a world the State has burned away. With calculated boldness, he extends an invitation to the Chancellor himself, daring him to join him in the library. The Chancellor, intrigued and eager to flaunt the State's fearlessness, accepts, dismissing warnings

---

* The tone of voice used by the subaltern as he reads the charges was a harsh monotone that, according to director Elliot Silverstein, was modeled after the speaking voice of Senator Joseph McCarthy.

The Obsolete Man

from his aides. "The State has no fears, none at all," he declares, stepping into Wordsworth's sanctuary: leather-bound volumes, a ticking clock, and Wordsworth's serene resolve.

Then Wordsworth springs his surprise on the Chancellor by announcing his choice of execution: a bomb, set to explode in this room at midnight. Oh, and by the way, the door to the study is locked and Wordsworth has the key, which means the Chancellor will die with him. Wordsworth's voice is steady as he speaks of death, "the great equalizer," stripping away titles and power until all stand equal: the rich and the poor, the ruler and the ruled. All must face it, with nothing to distinguish them. The Chancellor demands that Wordsworth let him out, but the State has no leverage over a man serving a death sentence, and Wordsworth refuses.

At first, the Chancellor puts on a bold front, confident and unconcerned, mocking Wordsworth's faith and his books, boasting that "the State is eternal." But as the minutes tick away, his bravado begins to fade; by contrast, Wordsworth, sits composed, reading from the forbidden Bible: "The Lord is my shepherd. . . " With the proceedings being broadcast live to the nation, Wordsworth knows that the State will not risk a loss of face by rescuing the Chancellor. "No one will come," he says. "The act of rescue would be very demeaning to them."

The Chancellor's composure cracks. Sweat beads on his brow; his voice rises, sharp with panic. "You can't do this!" he shouts, pounding the door; meanwhile, Wordsworth watches, not with malice but with pity. As midnight looms—mere seconds away—the Chancellor collapses into desperation. "In the name of God, let me out!" he cries. Wordsworth, his point proven, nods softly. "Yes, Chancellor, in the name of God, I will let you out." He tosses him the key, and the Chancellor scrambles, fumbling it into the lock. The door swings open; he stumbles into the night as the bomb detonates, engulfing the library—and Wordsworth—in a blaze of light.

The Chancellor has survived, but his victory is hollow. He returns to the courtroom, expecting to reclaim his podium, only to find the subaltern now occupying the seat of power. His show of weakness, of appealing in the name of God, has disgraced the State. "You therefore have no function. You are obsolete." In the end, the followers of the State turn on him and tear him to shreds, the revolution once again consuming its own.

II

Each of the three visits made to *The Twilight Zone* has addressed the issue of totalitarianism from a different point of view. "The Monsters Are Due on Maple Street" dealt with the mistrust and isolation that are a product of modern culture, while "Number 12 Looks Just Like You" reflects the oppression used to ensure conformity. "The Obsolete Man" touches on those subjects as well, but the primary focus is on the dehumanization—much of it self-sustaining—that is an inevitable part of the process in creating a repressive regime.

Burgess Meredith, a *Twilight Zone* veteran, shines as Romney Wordsworth, a character quite different from those that he plays in his other three appearances on the program. And yet, it seems to me, those four characters can all be seen as parts of a totalitarian society. His hapless bank teller in "Time Enough at Last," a good and decent man, is also a meek, bookish man who would like nothing better than to simply be left alone—the man who, when society starts to change, doesn't want to get involved. When the men in the brown shirts come around to collect his books, he'll be among those who are the most surprised.

"Mr. Dingle, the Strong," is cut from the same bolt of cloth: a weak man, easily taken advantage of, possibly even thinking that he doesn't deserve anything better from life. Lacking confidence, it's easy to see him as one of the subservient slaves, content to serve at the pleasure of the regime, as long as they don't harm him.

In "Printer's Devil," he presents us with the other side of the coin: the suave, smooth con artist who knows how to close the sale, willing to parlay to get what he wants, maintaining a façade of reasonableness while continuously inching toward his ultimate goal. By the time you realize what he's up to, it will be too late; you'll have already given your freedom away.

That brings us to Romney Wordsworth, the obsolete man who proves that he is not obsolete at all. As with his other three characterizations, the obsolete man—the man who resists, the man who, in the words of William F. Buckley Jr., stands athwart history shouting "Stop![2]"—is a part of every totalitarian society. We don't know much about his life prior to this episode; for all we know, he was another Henry Bemis, a man who wanted nothing more than to live in the world of his books. But something happens to him along the way; the timid little man becomes someone determined to stand on his principles, to "cling" to those old-fashioned ideals that make life precious to him. (One of the "deplorables," as a former presidential candidate once described them.)[3] He is well aware of the risks he takes with his hidden books, especially his Bible. It's a risk that he obviously feels is worth taking. And when he receives a sentence of death, he is equally determined to make that death mean something, to exact from the regime a price that may one day bring it down.

I could be completely wrong here, but I'd like to think it provides some food for thought.

III

We're never given a glimpse of life under the regime, whether its citizens are tortured, beaten, starved, or herded like cattle. We only see the rigidity of the law: harsh, oppressive, unforgiving, absolute. It's possible that intimidation and fear alone are sufficient to maintain such total control over the populace. After all, those kinds of tactics don't leave any marks. Outwardly, at least. But when you think about it, it's not really necessary for the State to resort to such brutality in order to maintain societal order; as a matter of fact, it's much easier than "The Obsolete Man" makes it appear.

Take religion, for instance. There's no need to actually ban it; all it takes is a few well-chosen words: talk about how *judgmental*, how *exclusionary*, how hateful it is, how it can create *divided loyalties*, breed an attitude of *defiance*, distract from the goals of the *State*—an institution, mind you, dedicated to preserving the rights of every citizen, not just a select few who refuse to go along with what is best for the whole. You don't have to abolish it, just use shame to make sure it no longer has a place in the public square.[4]

All it takes is the right word whispered in the right ear, the right accusation shouted by the mob in the streets. There's no need to resort to firemen to burn books. After all, everyone knows that there are some things too dangerous, too inflammatory, to appear in print, or online. People can't be allowed to fall victim to falsehoods, disinformation, fake news; it might contradict the advice of the State's experts, and after all, it's the state that knows what is best for the masses. No, it's best to protect the public from such ignorant ideas. And so, just a little pressure applied in the right places, and *voilà!* Publishers will refuse to print such degenerate information, bookstores will refuse to carry it, social media companies will ban any accounts trying to disseminate it. You might be able to find it somewhere, wrapped in a brown paper bag.

And the best part of it is, if you play your cards right, the people will do all the dirty work for you. I mean, think about it. Why bother with the messy threat of jail to keep people in line—excuse me, I mean, to preserve a peaceful society? No, you just make sure to understand the inherent vulnerabilities of people. Nobody wants to lose their job or have their business closed, just because of something they said or did when they were young; no one wants to risk having their credit lowered or find themselves unable to buy or rent a home, based on a candidate they supported for public office or a comment they made online.

Most importantly, nobody wants to face social ostracism, to have the people you considered friends turn their backs on you, to be airbrushed right out of the scene. It just takes a little cooperation from the public, and that's no problem when you've built a network of informants out of your true believers, the ones with the right pedigree and education, the ones who understand what the threat is, whether it's spreading false information—that is, something contrary to the official line—or an act of manifest disobedience, such as going out in public without a mask. It doesn't matter if it's the unnamed State of "The Obsolete Man" or an organization such as the Chinese Communist Party, or one that goes under a made-up name— oh, I don't know, let's just say something like ANTIFA.

Pretty soon, after a little of this, people will learn to censor themselves. You might call it being cowed into submission; others might see it as people learning to act in their own self-interest. Isn't that what we all do anyway? And who's to say that the people aren't fine with that?

Which is why someone like Romney Wordsworth is anything but obsolete—one might even call him indispensable.

IV

The old chestnut: *"What difference can one man make?"*

It's usually asked rhetorically, with varying degrees of cynicism, despair, sarcasm, or indifference. The answers often seem remote, detached, abstract.

What difference can one man make?

That's the central question answered in "The Obsolete Man." It could have been called "The Obsolete Men," after all, for Romney Wordsworth is hardly alone in his fate. Why else would the State take such delight in his televised execution, if not to provide a lesson, a deterrent, to those who might be tempted to follow in his disobedience?

How can a resistance be effective when it's comprised of just *one* man?

And yet it's singular, the obsolete *man*.

You've probably seen the photograph taken during the ill-fated Tiananmen Square protests in 1989, of the lone Chinese protester—"Tank Man," he's called—standing in front of a column of tanks, almost defying them to run him over. We don't know who he was, what happened to him, what was said when he climbed on top of the lead tank to talk with its commander. There were a million people in the Square during the protests, and yet what we remember is that one man, staring down the tanks. It remains an iconic image, one of the most influential photographs of the 20th century, so potent in its effect that it's still censored by the Chinese government.[5]

A photograph of one man.

Were it make-believe, this gesture would have led to the downfall of the communist government in Beijing, ushering in (we hope) a new era of freedom and justice for all. Instead, the story ends as it began, with the State firmly in control. We don't even have the visceral satisfaction of seeing the Chancellor torn to pieces by former followers, although you'd have to think that something almost certainly happened to some poor functionary within the government; such protests and demonstrations never occur in the perfect State.

Yes, it ends where it begins. For now.

When John F. Kennedy and Ronald Reagan gave their speeches at the Berlin Wall, it must have seemed to observers as wishful thinking that the Wall would ever fall, and yet it did, less than three decades after Kennedy's speech. [6] We don't know how "The Obsolete Man" ends because we don't see the end. It may have come a year or two later, or a decade or two later. The unfortunate citizens of that fictional country might still be living under totalitarian rule, for all we know. It doesn't always happen at once.

What difference can one man make?

One man may not be able to bring a regime down, to end it, all by himself. But one man can begin it; you can even argue that one man has to begin it, for change generally comes from the vision of an individual, his foresight, his desire to make his dream come true. Whether for good or ill, it takes the determination of one man to make it happen.

Romney Wordsworth is one man who, when confronted with the inevitable, decided to turn that fate into an opportunity. Knowing that his action may—just may—cause a crack in the otherwise impenetrable façade built by the regime. Knowing that he will not live to see the result, knowing that the end may take years, even generations, before it finally happens. Knowing, nonetheless, that once the snowball has been set in motion, it will, inevitably, continue along its path, picking up speed and size along the way, until, as Ellis tells Gordon in "The Sound of Different Drummers," the crack widens enough that someone will smash it.

V

Justice delayed is not justice denied, however.

The ultimate triumph of Romney Wordsworth—yes, *triumph*—is that he demonstrates, for one and all to see, that the authority of the State sits upon a foundation of sand. "No man is obsolete," Wordsworth says at his trial, and it is true; no human being can be obsolete as long as he maintains his humanity; it is what gives him life.

As Wordsworth and the Chancellor await the bomb blast, with the former increasingly serene and the latter increasingly frantic, Wordsworth reads from his forbidden Bible, and the state is exposed once and for all as a paper tiger. "The Lord is my shepherd, I shall not want," he quotes from the 23rd Psalm, but he could just as easily have been reading from the prayer for the dead, which asserts that "in death life is changed, not ended."[7]

He goes to his execution, not "cringing and pleading," as the Chancellor had predicted, "the end of a rather fruitless life." No, by facing death with such confidence and, dare I say it again, joy, he denies the State its ultimate victory. You do not control me, Wordsworth says through his words and his actions. I refuse to bend to your will. I refuse to live in fear. It is, in fact, the Chancellor who, in the face of death, cringes and pleads for his life—first, when he begs Wordsworth to let him go "in the name of God," and second, when he finds that he has himself been declared obsolete. His appeals, based on his history with the State, fall on deaf ears. "I've worked for the State. I've helped the State. I helped give the State strength." Ironic, isn't it, that it is the State that has declared that "history teaches you nothing."

Wordsworth's act of defiance proves that his death, and therefore his life, has not been meaningless. He has exposed a crack in the State, the first crack perhaps, but anyone observing how a crack in a cement sidewalk expands and spreads over time can predict how it will all end. Not, perhaps, in the lifetime of the new Chancellor; not even, perhaps, during the lifetimes of anyone in the story. Nevertheless, it will happen.

It is often said that only a fool fears nothing; it is fear that triggers the necessary instinct for survival. So it is with any government as well; a state that does not know fear issues an open invitation for its own downfall. As Serling wrote for his concluding narration, "Any state, any entity, any ideology which fails to recognize the worth, the dignity, the rights of Man...that state is obsolete."

And that final lesson of Romney Wordsworth's death, the one that most becomes his life, can be found in that book he holds in his hands, where the Apostle Paul, in his words to the Corinthians, asks, "O death, where is thy sting?"[8] For to fear death is to fear life, and to fear life, one might as well be dead. There's another line that Rod Serling wrote for his conclusion, one that wasn't used but sums up the lesson of "The Obsolete Man" quite well. "Any state, entity, or ideology becomes obsolete when it stockpiles the wrong weapons: when it captures territories, but not minds; when it enslaves millions, but convinces nobody. When it is naked, yet puts on armor and calls it faith, while in the Eyes of God it has no faith at all."[9] Just as tyranny is timeless, so is truth.

All dialogue quoted is from "The Obsolete Man" (*The Twilight Zone*).
1. Keller, "The Open Door," 17.
2. Buckley, "Mission Statement," para. 2.
3. Chozick, "Clinton Calls Trump Backers 'Deplorables.'"
4. Neuhaus, *Naked Public Square*.
5. Ray, "Tank Man," para. 2.

7. Kennedy, "Ich bin ein Berliner," and Reagan, "Brandenberg Gate," both American Rhetoric
7. *Roman Missal*, Preface for the Dead.
8. 1 Corinthians 15:55 (*KJV*).
9. Sirota, "Obsolete Man," para. 11.

Dialogues of the Carmelites (*Dialogues des Carmélites*)

Music and Libretto by Francis Poulenc
English translation by Joseph Machlis
Produced by Samuel Chotzinoff
Directed by Kirk Browning
Orchestra conducted by Peter Herman Adler
First broadcast on *NBC Opera Theatre*, December 8, 1957

Why are we so afraid when we think about death? Death is only dreadful for those who live in dread and fear of it. Death is not wild and terrible, if only we can be still and hold fast to God's Word. Death is not bitter, if we have not become bitter ourselves. Death is grace, the greatest gift of grace that God gives to people who believe in Him.

— Dietrich Bonhoeffer[1]

After silence, that which comes nearest to expressing the inexpressible is music.

— Aldous Huxley[2]

It is often the case that music can reveal truth in a way unlike that of any other form of communication. It has the ability to move people to action, to change the way they see and understand the world around them; in modern parlance, music can make a statement.

Which is why we so often find ourselves turning to the masters—the "Dead White Europeans," some call them—when we seek to understand something at its deepest, most intimate level. Bach, for instance, often called the "Fifth Evangelist";

Handel, most especially in "Messiah"; Mozart through his Requiem, which, even if he didn't write it all himself, could only have been the work of genius. Music can strike a sympathetic chord within our natural biorhythms, to convey emotion—as opposed to emotionalism—in such a way as to allow the listener to transcend the corporeal world and exist, even for a short time, on a higher plain.

I

Paris, 1789: Blanche de la Force (Elaine Malbin) is a young woman from an aristocratic family who, as her brother says, is fearful of everything, including fear itself. After being confronted by a violent mob on the streets of Paris, she determines to seek escape as a member of the Carmelites, despite the warnings of the dying Prioress (Patricia Neway) that "the Carmelite Order is not a refuge," and that it is the duty of the nuns to guard the Order, not the other way around. Blanche, fragile but resolute, joins anyway, grasping for some purpose in life.

In the convent, Blanche becomes a friend of another young novice, Sister Constance (Judith Raskin). One day, as the two are doing their chores, Constance shares a vision she has had that the two of them will die young, and on the same day. Blanche, greatly disturbed by what Constance tells her, rejects the idea. Her fear deepens when the Prioress, despite a lifetime of faith, dies in great pain and agony, expressing her feeling that God has abandoned her. Constance speculates that perhaps the Prioress, in her death, underwent suffering that was meant for another, and that consequently someone else might experience death in an unexpectedly easy way—a thought that haunts Blanche.

As the Revolution's anti-Catholic fervor swells, Blanche's brother, urgent and protective, visits, pleading with her to flee while she still has time. She refuses, telling him that this is now her home and that she is happy. But alone with Mother Marie (Rosemary Kuhlmann), her guardian, she confesses that while she is afraid of what might happen to her in the convent, she's even more afraid to leave.

One morning, after celebrating Mass, the chaplain delivers grim news to the sisters: the government has banned his preaching, forcing him into hiding. Before leaving, he tells them not to fear, that he'll try to return as often as he can. Constance, indignant, wonders how a nation could become so cowardly as to allow priests to be persecuted. Sister Mathilde replies that fear now governs the country; the people pass it along one to another, "just as they might give each other smallpox or cholera." When Constance asks if there are no men remaining to defend the priests, the new Mother Superior, Madame Lidoine (Leontyne Price), assures her that when there are no priests, there are plenty of martyrs. Yet when Marie proposes seeking martyrdom to save France, the Mother Superior reminds her that it is not for *them* to decide whether or not they will be martyrs; rather, one has to *accept* martyrdom as a gift from God.

The storm breaks when a mob surrounds the convent, demanding entry. An officer announces that the government has abolished religious orders and seized their property: the nuns must get rid of their "ridiculous costumes" and vacate the premises, or they will be executed. Mother Marie insists that "No matter what we wear, "we shall always be humble and devoted servants."

The officer scornfully dismisses her vow: "The people have no need of servants."

"No," Marie replies, "but it has a great need for martyrs."

"In times like these," he declares, "death is nothing."

"*Life* is nothing," she answers, "when it is so debased."

When Mother Superior Lidoine is called to Paris, Marie rallies the sisters to take a vow—not to *chase* martyrdom, but to *accept* it if God wills it. She will not, however, force it on any of them; if even one objects, they will not do it. The secret vote reveals one dissenter. Eyes turn to Blanche, but Constance, quick to shield her, claims that *she* was the one who voted no, but quickly changed her mind and now desires to stand with them. Blanche, weeping and in a panic, afraid of both life and death, flees to her family's estate.

Time passes. Mother Marie has left the convent to find Blanche, tracking her down in her father's library; Blanche tells her that her father has been taken away and guillotined, and that she has been reduced to working as a servant for those who used to serve her. Marie gives Blanche an address, where she is in hiding with the chaplain, and urges her to join them there, where she will be safe; Blanche, governed by fear, says that she cannot go.

Meanwhile, the remaining sisters are now in prison, sentenced to death, their convent plundered. Mother Lidoine, who was absent when the vow was taken but had returned from Paris in time to be arrested, tells them that she will not desert them, but will die with them. Constance, because of her dream, remains confident that Blanche will rejoin them. Marie, in hiding, says that she cannot let them die without her, but the chaplain forbids her from doing this: God has released her from her vow by absenting her when the sisters were imprisoned, and she cannot voluntarily join them in prison.

Comes the day of execution, and the Place de la Révolution looms under a leaden sky. In the public square, the sisters, one by one, mount the scaffold, their voices rising in the Salve Regina: "*Hail, Holy Queen, Mother of Mercy, our life, our sweetness, and our hope...*" Each fall of the blade—Sister Mathilde, Sister Ruth—reduces the number of voices, until only Constance remains. As she is about to ascend the steps, Blanche—at peace and free from all fear—makes her way through the crowd. Constance smiles at her and takes her turn at the guillotine. Blanche, calm and resolute, picks up the chant where Constance is cut off, and mounts the scaffold to keep her own appointment with destiny.

II

Although the personal stories of the sisters in "Dialogues of the Carmelites" are fictional, their martyrdom is not. The sixteen Martyrs of Compiègne in northern France—nuns, lay sisters, and novices—faced relentless pressure after the 1790 ban on religious life. Authorities interrogated and threatened them, demanding they break their vows of obedience, chastity, and poverty. Before the Revolution's storm, the Carmelites lived in disciplined serenity—rising for dawn prayers, laboring in silence, serving the poor. Their cloistered days, steeped in contemplation, instilled in them a faith and resilience that stood in stark contrast to the blood-drenched fury of the mob, demonstrating a strength drawn not from power but from surrender to God's will.

Arrested in 1794 for "religious fanaticism" and "hostility to the Revolution," they were charged with treason and undermining public freedom. On July 17, 1794, convicted and sentenced, they faced execution with defiance, their faith unshaken. Led by their Prioress, Mother Teresa of St. Augustine—her name in secular life had been Madame Madeleine-Claudine Lidoine—they resolved to die for France and its Church rather than renounce their faith. Their vow of martyrdom, rooted in the Carmelite charism of contemplative prayer and self-offering, was not simply defiance but a spiritual act, uniting their suffering with Christ's for the nation's redemption.

They were taken on an open cart through the streets of Paris, where onlookers hurled insults at them and pelted them with objects. Arriving at the site of their execution, the sisters sang hymns and forgave their executioners. As they were led to the guillotine, each one approached Madame Lidoine, kissed a small statue of the Virgin Mary, and asked the prioress for "permission to die." "Permission granted," she replied. Kneeling before the blade, they chanted Psalm 117, Laudate Dominum: O praise the Lord, all ye nations: praise him, all ye people. / For his merciful kindness is great toward us: and the truth of the Lord endureth for ever. / Praise ye the Lord.[3]

The chant was cut short in each case by the falling of the blade. Madame Lidoine, having granted each of her charges permission to die, was the last to be executed. The crowd, raucous only a few minutes earlier, fell silent.

It has been said that the shocking brutality of the execution of the Martyrs of Compiègne, along with the serenity and faith with which they accepted their fate, was a turning point in the Revolution. The leader of the revolutionaries, Robespierre, was himself executed ten days later, leading to the end of The Terror. The sisters were collectively canonized by the Catholic Church in 2024.[4]

They were not the only martyrs of the Revolution. A group of 191 Catholics executed at the Carmes Prison in the "September Massacres" of 1792 are collectively known as the Holy September Martyrs, and were beatified in October 1926. The French revolutionaries were nothing if not thorough.[5]

III

In 1953, hoping to write an opera on a religious theme, the French composer Francis Poulenc was introduced by his publisher to *Dialogues des Carmélites*, an unpublished screenplay by Georges Bernanos that told a fictional story based on the martyrs. Bernanos intended *Dialogues* as an allegorical comparison between the Revolution and the twin contemporary threats of Fascism and Communism.*[6]

Poulenc found it "a moving and noble work," and immediately began work on the opera, completing it in October 1955. His score, austere yet piercingly emotive, evokes the Carmelites' spiritual rigor, the melodies and harmonies bringing to life the inner lives of the nuns, while the dissonance prefigures their impending sacrifice—a testament to music's ability to touch the divine where words alone fell short. The final scene, in which the nuns are led off-stage to the guillotine while singing the Salve Regina, is described as "one of the most shattering experiences in all musical theatre."[7]

The opera premiered in January 1957 at La Scala in Italy, and almost immediately secured a place in the international repertory, which it still holds today. Following La Scala, *Dialogues* triumphed in Paris in June and debuted in America in San Francisco in September. On December 8, the Feast of the Immaculate Conception, it opened the NBC Opera Company's 1957–58 season. Choosing a new, uncommissioned work was a bold move by the company—it was the first time an opera not written specifically for television had debuted on TV before playing at the Metropolitan Opera—reflecting the opera's rapid acclaim and the power of its story.

---

* Such are the parallels between the French Revolution and Communism that these martyrs have been referred to as "The Protomartyrs of Communism."

The two-hour live color broadcast, in Joseph Machlis's English translation*, starred Leontyne Price, in her third appearance on *NBC Opera Theatre*; she had played Madame Lidoine in *Dialogues*' San Francisco debut, and would reprise the role often in her storied career. She was joined by Patricia Neway (Madame de Croissy), Rosemary Kuhlmann (Mother Marie), Judith Raskin (Constance), and Elaine Malbin (Blanche), conducted by Peter Herman Adler, NBC Opera's Music and Artistic Director.

Price's performances with the NBC Opera Company are not insignificant in American culture; in 1955, she had become the first black American to appear in a televised opera when she'd played the lead role in *Tosca*. Although several NBC affiliates in the South declined to carry the broadcast, Price's appearance broke barriers at a time when racial strife was coming to the fore in America, and it's difficult not to draw comparisons between her Madame Lidoine, standing firm against religious persecution, and the struggle for civil rights.

Robert Steinfirst, in the *Pittsburgh Post-Gazette*, immediately grasped the opera's significance. "Poulenc's message extends far beyond the confines of Paris in the revolution or, for that matter, the Nuns of the Carmelites," he wrote. "There have been other stories, books and even operas in which the faith has been upheld, but I doubt that it has been done as poignantly as in this version of Poulenc's."[8]

Television's intimacy also amplified the opera's impact, with director Kirk Browning's close-ups drawing viewers into the sisters' faces in a way that could not be done in the theater and thereby turning a potential liability into a strength. "The production intensified the personal values of the opera," noted

---

* NBC Opera Company's productions were always performed in English; it was also Poulanc's desire that "Dialogues" be performed in the vernacular of the local audience.

Howard Taubman in *The New York Times*. "The terror of the first Mother Superior as she confronted death in protesting doubts had memorable impact. The moment when the nuns chose martyrdom as their fate was done uncommonly well." He also praised the talent of the singers; "Elaine Malbin was moving as Blanche de la Force. Patricia Neway caught the terror of the first Mother Superior, and Leontyne Price the natural integrity of the humble woman who was her successor. Rosemary Kuhlmann's Mother Marie was forceful and understanding. Judith Raskin was touching as a young nun."[9]

IV

The French Revolution (1789-99) was hardly the time of enlightenment that its supporters have made it out to be, particularly the Satanic two-year period known as "The Reign of Terror." It came by its nickname honestly, writing its legacy with rivers of blood from the guillotines used in the wholesale slaughter of political opponents, and in particular the persecution of the Catholic Church.

Mind you, freedom of religion was guaranteed—theoretically—under the Declaration of the Rights of Man, which had been passed in 1789. According to Article X, "No one may be disturbed for his opinions, even religious ones, *provided that their manifestation does not trouble the public order established by the law.*"[10] (Emphasis added.) The devil was, if not in the details, at least in the italics: since the Church was, by definition, seen as "a counter-revolutionary force," anyone who professed religious belief could be seen to be troubling "the public order." It was, one might say, an early example of attempting to bar religion from the public square.

In 1790, the State outlawed religious life—that is, the monastic life practiced by priests, monks, and nuns. By Easter 1794, few of France's forty thousand churches remained open; many had been closed, sold, destroyed, or converted to other uses. Christianity had been denounced as "superstition" and replaced by the Cult of the Supreme Being. Approximately 30,000 French priests were forced to flee the country.

And what did this horror, described by historian William Bush as "sheer butchery," accomplish? The rise to power of Napoleon, and a war that swept the continent. It is, in its way, so typically French.

V

"Dialogues" is set in 1792, but as Robert Steinfirst understood in his *Pittsburgh Post-Gazette* review, the meaning of the story extended far beyond the French Revolution. Religious persecution didn't end then, just as it didn't end with the Puritans or the Know-Nothings or the Ku Klux Klan or—irony of ironies—the election of a "Catholic" president; not by a long shot. Not when one of the dominant political parties in the United States actively pursues a policy that says, in effect, that you're free to believe whatever you want, provided you don't try to put those beliefs into action.

Not when religious organizations are forced to hire people who don't share their beliefs, provide medical benefits that violate their core principles, deny the teachings they profess every Sunday under fear of government investigation. Not when the former speaker of the U.S. House of Representatives boasts that "I do my religion on Sundays," reducing faith to little more than a private hobby. (The buck may stop there, but not the Cross.)

Not when the state of Washington approves a law requiring priests to violate the Seal of Confession (a seal they are bound to protect to the death) if told by a penitent of sexual abuse.[11] Or in Houston, where the city council attempted to pass a law requiring a group of pastors to "turn over any sermons dealing with homosexuality, gender identity[,] or Annise Parker, the city's first openly lesbian mayor."[12] (The law was later withdrawn amid a public outcry, but not before it exposed the State's desire to police the pulpit.)

Not when members of the United States Senate blatantly ignore the Establishment Clause of the Constitution, when one senator criticizes a judicial nominee by saying, "When you read your speeches, the conclusion one draws is that the dogma lives loudly within you," while another asks, "If confirmed, will you recuse yourself from all cases in which the Knights of Columbus has taken a position?"[13]

The people have no need of servants, but they have a great need for martyrs.

It is impossible to ignore the undercurrent of hostility to religion that radiates from certain government bodies. Religion, which the State had already sought to remove from the public square and relegate to private life, becomes even more endangered; individuals seeking a role in public life are interrogated regarding their faith, their values, their beliefs, with the threat that to hold the wrong set of beliefs is to disqualify one from service. Law enforcement authorities discuss how religious belief might pose a threat to the state's power, and embed their agents in churches, hoping to infiltrate their congregations.[14] Silent prayer, when performed in the wrong place, becomes an act punishable by arrest, as does language that offends.[15]

Once you've decided religion no longer has a place in the public square, how long before you decide it has no place at all?

Will the day come when churches are taxed out of existence because of their beliefs, or charged with hate crimes because a pastor reads from the Bible[16], or closed altogether because of laws seeking to "protect" the public from things like the virus? When Christians must deny what their religion teaches in order to show "solidarity" with the State? Supreme Court Justice Samuel Alito, in his dissent in *Obergefell v. Hodges*, wrote, "I assume that those who cling to old beliefs will be able to whisper their thoughts in the recesses of their homes, but if they repeat those views in public, they will risk being labeled as bigots and treated as such by governments, employers, and schools."[17]

The anti-clericalism that drove the Reign of Terror may have started as a reaction to the relationship between the aristocratic class and the Church, but it sure as hell didn't end there, whipped up into a frenzy by Robespierre until it wound up even consuming him. "Are there any men remaining to defend the priests?" Constance asks at one point. Replies Madame Lidoine, "When priests are few, martyrs are many." Will Americans one day be required to choose between renouncing their beliefs and facing martyrdom? Only God decides who will be a martyr.

We die not for ourselves alone, Constance tells Blanche early on, *but for each other*.

Life is nothing, Marie tells the government lackey, *when it is so debased*.

The triumph of the Martyrs of Compiègne is the crowning glory of "Dialogues of the Carmelites," its effect on the viewer one not of sadness, but of joy: the joy of Blanche conquering her fears, of finding the meaning of her life with her death; the triumph of life over death is moving, stirring, and ultimately heroic.

Sometimes, the courage to do the right thing is more important than to simply go on living. Willa Cather, in a letter to her brother, wrote that "The test of one's decency is how much of a fight one can put up after one has stopped caring."[18] When one has stopped caring about protecting one's life, when one has stopped caring about what the masses think. The Martyrs of Compiègne stopped caring about those things; they persevered all the more because of it. The crown of martyrdom was their reward.

Life is nothing when it is so debased. Today, the questions hang in the air. How much more debasement will it take? How far will the descent into Hell continue?

All dialogue quoted is from "Dialogues of the Carmelites" (*NBC Opera Theatre*).

1. Metaxas, Bonhoeffer, 531.
2. Huxley, *Music at Night*, 17.
3. Psalm 117 (KJV).
4. Mares, "Martyrs of Compiègne saints," para. 1.
5. Beutner, "Protomartyrs of Communism."
6. Voegelin, " 'Dialogues of the Carmelites,'" para. 14.
7. Abbott, "Life of Poulenc."
8. Steinfirst, "Season Opens with 'Carmelites'."
9. Taubman, "'Carmelites' on TV," 39.
10. *Elysée.fr.*, "Declaration on Religious Liberty," Art. X.
11. Graham, "New Law Threatens Pastors," para. 1-2.
12. Starnes, "Houston Demands Sermons," para. 3.
13. Shackelford, "Senators Ask IRS," para. 2.
14. Palmer, "FBI Targeting Pro-Lifers," para. 2.
15. ADF, "UK Woman Arrested," para. 2.
16. Buckingham, "Ban the Mob"
17. *Obergefell v. Hodges*, 576 U.S. 644, 725 (2015) (Alito J. dissent).
18. Cather to Cather, in *Selected Letters*, 539.

Murder in the Cathedral

Written by T.S. Eliot
Produced by E. Martin Browne
Directed by G. More O'Ferrall
First broadcast on *Theatre Parade*, December 7, 1936

The disciples are to overcome fear of death with fear of God. Disciples are in danger, not from human judgment, but from God's judgment, not from the decay of their bodies, but from the eternal decay of their bodies and souls. Anyone who is still afraid of people is not afraid of God.

—Dietrich Bonhoeffer[1]

The year is 1935, Adolf Hitler is chancellor of Germany, and a somber mood engulfs the nations of Europe; the drums of war sound in the distance, moving ever closer, sounding ever louder. The people are gripped by a sense of unease, the feeling that something monumental is about to happen, to themselves and to the world they know, after which nothing will again be the same. At that time, every man will be asked to choose his own fate: to surrender to power, fraud, and corruption, or stand for one's beliefs and principles; to live as a slave or die as a free man.

Amidst this uncertainty, T.S. Eliot looked back more than 750 years, to another time when fear gripped the land, when a man was forced to choose whether to accept safety in exile or to remain faithful to his conscience, even if it meant persecution. Or death.

The man was Thomas Becket, Archbishop of Canterbury. The story was that of his "Murder in the Cathedral."

Darkness in Primetime

I

December 2, 1170: England trembles under the weight of discord, with Church and Crown locked in a bitter struggle. Thomas Becket, Archbishop of Canterbury, steps onto native soil after seven years exiled in France, sheltered by King Louis VII. Once King Henry II's confidant, Becket rose from Lord Chancellor to Archbishop at Henry's bidding, a bond forged in laughter and trust. But as Archbishop, Becket's loyalty shifted to God, fiercely guarding the Church's autonomy against Henry's hunger for control. His excommunication of Henry's allies—nobles bowing to the Crown—ignited a feud that drove him across the Channel. Now, returning, he knows the cost may be his life.

A Greek chorus of Canterbury women, their voices woven with dread, laments his arrival. They foresee blood, a clash of Church and State that could shatter their fragile peace. Becket's priests, though joyful at his return, hover with unease, their greetings tinged with fear for his safety. Becket, resolute, harbors no illusions. Martyrdom, to him, is not a specter but a calling—a testament to principles he'll die to uphold. He moves through the cathedral's shadowed halls, his steps echoing his purpose, unafraid of what awaits.

Four Tempters materialize, each a mirror to Becket's soul, probing his resolve. The First dangles safety: compromise, blend into obscurity, reclaim the ease of his youth. Becket brushes it aside—retreat betrays his vow. The Second offers power: return to Henry's side, wield influence to shape a better state. Becket scorns the lure, knowing servitude to man corrupts. The Third tempts rebellion: join the barons, topple Henry, reform the realm. Becket sees the trap—violence breeds chaos, not justice. The Fourth, most insidious, whispers of martyrdom's glory: die a saint, revered forever, your name a beacon. Becket pauses, confronted by the truth. "The last temptation is the greatest treason: to do the right deed for the wrong reason." Martyrdom, he realizes, must spring from humility, not pride—a surrender to God's will, not a grab for immortal fame. Casting off this final snare, he finds peace, ready for whatever divine path unfolds.

On Christmas morning, Becket ascends the pulpit, his sermon a mixture of joy and sorrow. He speaks of Christ's birth, a moment to rejoice, yet shadowed by the Cross's certainty. So too, he says, Christians mourn martyrs while celebrating their triumph in Christ's name. His words carry a quiet prophecy: "It is possible that in a short time you may have yet another martyr." The congregation stirs, sensing his acceptance—not seeking death, nor fleeing it, but standing open to God's design. Becket descends, his heart unburdened, his spirit steeled.

Act Two dawns on December 29, the air thick with foreboding. Four Knights, their faces eerily familiar—the same actors as the Tempters—stride into Canterbury, claiming Henry's mandate. They brand Becket a traitor, accusing him of disloyalty for his excommunications and defiance. "Come to the King," they demand, "answer for your crimes." Becket, unflinching, refutes them: "I'll face public charges, before the people, not in secret." His voice rings with conviction, denying their authority. The Knights, enraged, lunge, but priests rally, driving them back. The Knights retreat, snarling promises to return. The priests beg Becket to flee—hide in the countryside, seek sanctuary elsewhere. Becket, calm as stone, refuses. "I am in God's hands," he says, his gaze fixed on the cathedral's altar.

Night falls, and the Knights return, armored and resolute, swords gleaming with intent. The priests, desperate, bolt the cathedral doors, a barrier against death. Becket halts them, his voice commanding: "A cathedral's doors are never barred to those who seek entry." Reluctantly, they obey, swinging the great doors wide. The Knights storm in, their demand a final ultimatum: lift the excommunications, bow to Henry. Becket stands tall, his refusal absolute: "The Church answers to God alone." Steel flashes, and the Knights strike, their blades cutting down the Archbishop in his sacred hall. Blood pools on the stone, the chorus's wail rising like a tide. In the aftermath, the Knights step forward, their voices cold with justification. One claims Becket's pride drove him to ruin, another insists his crimes warranted death, a third pleads they merely followed orders for England's good. Their words, hollow, echo in the cathedral's silence. The Greek chorus re-emerges, their lament now laced with resolve. They accept the weight of Becket's sacrifice, and with it the assurance that spiritual good will come from it.

II

T.S. Eliot's decision to write his verse drama "Murder in the Cathedral" came about as the result of a commission from George Bell, Bishop of Chichester and former Dean of Canterbury Cathedral. Bell had previously worked with Eliot on the play "The Rock," a meditation on life and religious faith, and subsequently asked Eliot to write another play for the 1935 Canterbury Festival.[2] Taking as his inspiration the looming threat of Nazi Germany, Eliot turned to the story of St. Thomas of Canterbury and his resistance to the authority of King Henry II, culminating in the Archbishop's assassination in Canterbury Cathedral. The actual circumstances of the dispute between Thomas and Henry—the Crown's jurisdiction over criminal cases involving clerics being most prominent—are of less importance today than what they symbolize: the authority of the State over the Church; the conflict between Caesar and God.

The play was first performed in June 1935 in the Chapter House at Canterbury Cathedral—an on-location production in the truest sense, since it took place only 50 yards from the very spot on which Becket had been murdered. Following the premiere, the production moved to the Mercury Theatre in London, where the critic for *The Times* praised it as "the one great play by a contemporary dramatist now to be seen in England."[3] The play made its way to radio in January 1936, and then, during a revival at the Mercury, it was chosen by the British Broadcasting Company for a test broadcast prior to the rollout of its regular television service, securing a place in history as the world's first television drama.[4]

The broadcast, originating from the BBC's small studio at Alexandra Palace in London, consisted of several scenes transplanted from the stage production, with members of the cast reprising their roles. Starring as Becket was Robert Speaight, whose performance in the role won him critical acclaim and launched him on a long and prominent career as an actor and writer. He was joined by Guy Spaull as the First Tempter and First Knight, G.R. Schjelderup as the Second Tempter and Knight, Norman Chidgey as the Third Tempter and Knight, and the play's producer, E. Martin Browne, as the Fourth Tempter and Knight. It is impossible to know for certain which scenes were presented in the half-hour, but based on the cast list, it presumably centered on Becket's confrontations with the tempters and the knights, eliminating the Greek chorus of women and the priests attending to Becket. Having successfully passed the test, the play was broadcast live at 3:30 p.m. on December 7 on a program called *Theatre Parade*, and was repeated on December 21.

It seems self-evident to talk of innovations associated with the broadcast of "Murder in the Cathedral", given the newness of television—at this point, *everything* could be said to be an innovation. But new technology demands a new way of thinking, and, even at this early date, we were seeing the first signs of how television productions of the future would be done. In his book *Adventures in Vision*, John Swift referenced the significance of the broadcast and how producer George More O'Ferrall realized television's potential to become a new and distinct medium. "Murder in the Cathedral", Swift wrote, "marked the beginning of the use of symbolic effects. In the stage version, Becket sees the temptations in flesh and blood; in television, these were presented as ghosts whispering in his ear, by skillful positioning and 'double takes.'"[5] O'Ferrall himself explained how the scene allowed the production "to get away from both theatre and film."

> We saw Thomas Becket in close-up, soliloquizing about his temptations, and, as he weakened, the temptation appeared, whispering into his ear. As Thomas strengthened in purpose, the vision vanished. For, by placing the tempter before a separate camera, it was possible to superimpose the tempter on to the picture of Becket and fade it in and out at will.[6]

There were other innovations as well. For instance, O'Ferrall was the first to utilize scenery in a studio, "to fashion the interior of Canterbury Cathedral as it would appear at the time of Thomas à Becket." "Of course we have had shows in which the actors have been in costume," a BBC official was quoted as saying. "It has been our custom in the past just to use black and white drop curtains."[7]

O'Ferrall achieved this effect through the use of a device called a Penumbrascope, which cast shadows onto backcloth, creating the illusion of architectural features such as archways—ideal for the 12th century period. It was simple, quick, and created a much greater effect than the traditional use of black and white drop curtains. Already, in the very first television drama, the medium was laying the groundwork for its own unique production values.

III

All well and good, true, but there are more reasons to include "Murder in the Cathedral" than its contributions to television history.

Recall, for a moment, George Bell, who commissioned Eliot to write the play. Bell was a major figure in the World Council of Churches, and as an active proponent of the Ecumenical Movement in Europe, he had been an eyewitness to Hitler's rise to power. Through this work, he had become a close friend and confidant of Dietrich Bonhoeffer, the German theologian and pastor who was a staunch opponent of Hitler and his persecution of the Jews. Bonhoeffer's resistance to Hitler gradually escalated from words to action; he would become involved in the plots to assassinate Hitler, and was eventually arrested and, just a month from the end of the war, was executed on Hitler's personal orders. His courageous willingness to accept an unsought and unwanted martyrdom has since become a symbol of conscientious resistance to unjust or corrupt authority, the willingness to pay the ultimate price as a disciple of Christ.

Although Bonhoeffer's death was a decade in the future when Eliot wrote "Murder in the Cathedral", Bonhoeffer and Bell had been friends and colleagues for two years; Bell would have been much too perceptive not to see the parallels between the lives of the two men, leading some to speculate that Bell and Eliot may have seen the play as a response to the Nazis.[8] Was Bell thinking of Bonhoeffer in making such a suggestion?

Did Bell and Eliot ever discuss the confluence of principles of Bonhoeffer and Becket? It would not be surprising if they had; it may have been more surprising if they had not.

IV

Power is a strange and addictive quality: the more one has, the more one wants. And those who possess it, whether individuals or governments or other institutions of authority, are reluctant to ever give it up, even a fraction, even if the granting of that power was meant to provide a temporary solution to a temporary problem. What's more, they're likely to view anyone or anything that attempts to deny them that power—to resist, in other words—as a threat.

Bonhoeffer and Bell shared a growing concern about Hitler's consolidation of power, and the threat his socialist policies posed to religious and personal freedom, at a time when many others either failed to recognize it or refused to accept it for what it was. They understood that the situation was bound to precipitate a crisis sooner or later.

It's been said that people show their true colors during a crisis. It's where the rubber meets the road, where we see what people are truly made of when there's no place to hide. Some rise to levels of greatness that few thought possible, displaying both leadership and vision; others, overwhelmed by the magnitude of the challenge facing them, shrink away, leaving the task to others. And then there are those who seek to exploit the crisis for personal or political gain.

Former presidential advisor Rahm Emanuel, riffing off of Winston Churchill's famous quote that a good crisis should never go to waste, elaborated that a crisis gives one "an opportunity to do things that you think you could not do before."[9]

One of those opportunities, perchance, came about during the charade of COVID Theater.

The great American mantra of separation of church and state is enshrined as one of the fundamental principles of the nation, yet it appears nowhere in the Constitution. Thomas Jefferson made the phrase famous in a letter he wrote to the Danbury Baptist Association in 1802 when he used it to describe the practical implication of the Establishment Clause in the Bill of Rights, which states that "Congress shall make no law respecting an establishment of religion."[10]

But what does this mean? To Roger Williams, founder of Rhode Island, the wall of separation was intended to safeguard the church from the corruptions of the state, not the other way around.[11] Certainly Benjamin Franklin, perhaps the most famous deist in American history, would agree; he believed that religion was "an example of universal benevolence, humility, and piety," a necessary inspiration for the average American to do good.[12] The Founders, then, saw the State as being informed by, rather than protected from, religion.

The state has viewed the church as a threat to its authority for as far back as either of them goes: it was how the Egyptians saw Moses, how Rome regarded Jerusalem, how Herod perceived the Messiah, how the Sanhedrin judged Christ, how Henry II viewed Becket. Few institutions guard their power as jealously as does the State, and anything that even remotely vies for the hearts of the people—a description that certainly fits religion—becomes a potential adversary. The State has always found something threatening in Christ's admonition to "render unto Caesar," given that the State generally views *everything* as being within its possession.

The ultimate issue in "Murder in the Cathedral", though, is not one of religious persecution so much as it is the primacy of individual conscience, and one's commitment to stand on it regardless of threats and coercion. Their opponents are the State and its four knights: Big Business, Big Pharma, Big Tech, and Big Politics. They act to bribe, to censor, to drug, to bully, to conserve and consolidate, to force people into a betrayal of that conscience—or else. They couch their efforts in vague language, accusing someone of having violated someone else's "rights," while neglecting the fact that the rights of those being punished—their right to act based on their personal religious beliefs—are being violated as well.

And so doctors are paid by pharmaceutical companies to shoot people full of drugs and turn them into addicts;[13] meanwhile, hospitals offer operations to mutilate the young and confused;[14] in both cases, the name of the game is to exploit patients to add to the bottom line. Small business owners are threatened with loss of their livelihood should they decline to bake wedding cakes for homosexual couples.[15] Religious agencies are forced to end their involvement in facilitating adoptions if they refuse to place children with homosexual couples.[16] Parents are told they don't have the "right" to know that their children are being taught (or is it brainwashed?)—to accept dogmas that violate their beliefs.[17] Social media, following the instructions of the State, regulates and erases people who are told that their religious beliefs constitute hate speech, people who are to be ostracized, put at risk of losing their jobs, threatened with cancellation or even imprisonment, unless they conform to the correct set of beliefs, one approved by secular authorities.[18]

And in that most egregious of scandals, COVID Theater, people were faced with losing their jobs, losing their freedom to move about, even threats of internment camps, just for refusing the jab.[19] (Enthusiastic supporters of the restrictions favored even more.[20]) It didn't matter that the vaccine might have been developed through the use of the fetal cell lines procured through abortion.[21] It was of no consequence that the vaccine was unproven, that people could be putting themselves and their loved ones at risk by taking it. One could apply for a religious exemption if their pastor had the courage and conviction to provide them with one, but even then, there was no guarantee that the exemption would be honored.[22] Concern for your neighbor trumped any such conscientious objections, we were told, even by some religious leaders, who were only too eager to cede that moral high ground to the State.[23]

The suppression of church services was perhaps the height of this drama, this theater of the absurd. In some places, they were banned altogether; other, more enlightened communities, limited them to a laughably small number of attendees. Some governments, both in America and abroad, took the opportunity to eliminate any recourse to sacramental life, such as confession and communion, driving both ministers and parishioners underground. Only a few courageous clergymen dared to take the government to court over the restrictions.[24] As the absurdity of this position became increasingly apparent, the justifications used by political leaders to keep such restrictions in place became increasingly contorted.

Shockingly, the response from the religious establishment to the COVID scare was, for the most part, meek acquiescence. Doubtless, some accepted the rationale offered by the authorities, and, though acting out of fear, were at least sincere in their beliefs. Others turned to creative ways of ministering to their flocks, to the point of being shut down or even arrested. The vast majority, however, complied: not only with the closing down of their churches, but with vaccine and mask mandates as well, often with an enthusiasm bordering on unseemliness; any objections they offered to these restrictions were mild and tentative, more for public consumption than anything substantial.[25]

This, then, is the greatest of the scandals of COVID Theater. After all, the behavior of the State is hardly surprising, given that its authority rests largely on power and the consolidation of power. But one expects more from the religious—morals, principles, a backbone. Principled resistance to unjust or corrupt authority, in other words. Instead, too many of them abandoned their flocks to the wolves at a time when they were most needed, leaving them adrift to face a world increasingly falling into suspicion and alienation, one Maple Street after another. And when confronted with this fact, they fell back on the excuse that they were merely "following orders," as if no other explanation was necessary. Which was true; it told you everything you needed to know about their character, or lack thereof. We've seen how it's been used through the ages, by weak and fearful men more interested in conserving what they have, in preserving their existing power base within the status quo, than taking any kind of risk.

This fight for the right to follow one's conscience, regardless of the pressure brought to bear by society and the State to give in, to conform—this is what Thomas Becket fought for, what he gave his life for.

V

It occurs to me that the 1936 broadcast of "Murder in the Cathedral," primitive as it might have been, serves as a perfect metaphor for our times. For just as George More O'Ferrall's superimposed images prefigured today's special effects, St. Thomas Becket's confrontation with King Henry II prefigured today's confrontation between church and state, not just in America but in the world as well.

There is an interlude between Acts 1 and 2, a scene which was likely omitted from the broadcast, which Eliot took from Becket's actual Christmas Day sermon of 1170, four days before his death. In that sermon, Becket reflects on "the strange contradiction that Christmas is a day both of mourning and rejoicing, which Christians also do for martyrs," and tells his flock that "it is possible that in a short time you may have yet another martyr."[26] Coming as it does after Becket's rejection of the Fourth Tempter, it demonstrates his acceptance of his death as the price of discipleship, and his faith that good will eventually come from it. About twenty years later, Eliot's poem "The Cultivation of Christmas Trees" hearkens to that Christmas Day sermon. Eliot tells the story of a child who will, with age and wisdom, come to understand that "the joy of Christmas is disturbed not only by the premonition of the Passion, but also by the uncertainty of the Second Coming."

> The accumulated memories of annual emotion
> May be concentrated into a great joy
> Which shall be also a great fear, as on the occasion
> When fear came upon every soul:
> Because the beginning shall remind us of the end
> And the first coming of the second coming.[27]

And if Eliot is right that the Second Coming casts a shadow over the joy of Christmas, so also does it overshadow everything we do today. After all, it was another Thomas—Thomas Jefferson, you know, the guy who talked about the separation of church and state—who also said, "Indeed I tremble for my country when I reflect that God is just: that his justice cannot sleep for ever."[28]

Darkness in Primetime

All dialogue quoted is from the play *Murder in the Cathedral* by T.S. Eliot (New York: Harcourt, Brace & Company, Inc., 1935.)
1. Bonhoeffer, *Discipleship*, 216.
2. Badenhausen, *Eliot in Context*, 128-9.
3. "Mercury Theatre," *The Times*.
4. Wyver, "BBC's first drama," para. 2.
5. Swift, *Adventures*, 50.
6. O'Ferrall, "Televising Drama."
7. Wyver, "BBC's first drama," para. 6.
8. Dixon, "Eliot's Murder," para. 2.
9. Emanuel, quoted in Seib, "Crisis," para. 2.
10. Caldwell, "Wall of Separation."
11. Williams, *Bloudy Tenent*.
12. "Williams's Sermon," *Scots Magazine*, 490.
13. Ornstein, "Documents on Williams."
14. Do No Harm, "Child Trans Industry."
15. *Masterpiece Cakeshop v. Colorado Civil Rights Comm'n*, 584 U.S. 617 (2018).
16. Higgins, "Court Sides with Baker," para. 1
17. Butcher, "Schools Defy Gender Rules," para. 3
18. Facebook, "Community Standards."
19. Greene, "Workers Fired."
20. Ashworth, "Conscience Rights."
21. Wallis, "Fetal Cell Lines," para. 2.
22. Hadro, "Conscience Exemptions Upheld."
23. Di Corpo, "Dioceses Suspend Mandates," para. 1
24. Hanneman, "Priest Prevails."
25. Schiffer, "Give Us Sacraments."
26. Eliot, *Murder in the Cathedral*, 44.
27. Eliot, *Imaginative Conservative*.
28. Jefferson, *Notes on Virginia*, 163.

A Feasibility Study

Written and Produced by Joseph Stefano
Directed by Byron Haskin
First broadcast on *The Outer Limits*, April 13, 1964

For scarcely for a righteous man will one die: yet peradventure for a good man some would even dare to die.

—Romans 5:7[1]

If eternity exists, it is available not on the basis of how hard you hold to life but how generous you are with it.

—Harry Reasoner[2]

Luminos: a planet in a distant star system. Our scientists have concluded that the planet is too close to its sun to support any form of life, but life exists there nonetheless—a strange and suffering form of life that now searches the galaxy for a planet with a healthy population. One that can be enslaved. Cut to an average neighborhood, one such as you or I might live in. A man prepares to go to the office, while his wife lovingly chides him about spending too much time at work. Next door, another man breaks off a continuing argument with his wife and looks for refuge in church, but finds his car will not start. Outside, a mist settles over the area—is it radioactive? Such are the mundane features of an everyday Sunday morning on Midgard Drive in Beverly Hills, USA, Earth, a neighborhood that is about to become the subject of a most unusual experiment—a feasibility study.

Darkness in Primetime

I

The day dawns crisp on Midgard Drive,* a quiet suburban enclave where ambition hums beneath manicured lawns. Ralph Cashman (David Opatoshu), a businessman tethered to success, kisses his wife Rhea (Joyce Van Patten) goodbye, heading to the office despite Sunday's calm. Outside, he spots neighbor Dr. Simon Holm (Sam Wanamaker) wrestling with a dead car. Ralph offers a lift to church, a gesture of neighborly duty. Simon's wife, Andrea (Phyllis Love), lingers in their doorway, her farewell heavy—she'll be gone before Simon returns. In the car, Simon confesses that he and Andrea are separating. They've only been married a year and a week, but that's long enough, Simon says, to discover it was a mistake.

After dropping Simon off, Ralph finds himself swallowed up by a thick, cloud-like fog. He stops, steps out, and looks around at a barren, rocky plain. Three shadowy stone-like figures close in on him. A commanding hand, from an unseen body, freezes him in terror.

Back in the neighborhood, Simon returns to find Andrea still home, unable to call a taxi because their phone is out of order. Their rift deepens as she demands autonomy: "I need part of my life to live my own way." Simon insists he's not controlling, only prioritizing their shared life, but she retorts, "No matter how benevolent or secure you'd make it, it's slavery!"

Their argument is interrupted by Rhea's—someone staggers toward her door. It's Ralph, his skin blighted with grotesque sores, mirroring the alien figures. "Don't touch me," he rasps, voice unearthly. "*We're not on Earth,*" then vanishes. A noise

---

* The word "Midgard" comes from Norse legend, where Midgard describes "the world inhabited by men"; and J.R.R. Tolkien derived from it the term Middle-earth. Midgard was said to be surrounded by Jotunheim: the world of the hostile giants.

from the tool shed draws Simon's attention. A boy's voice, panicked, warns him off: "I came through the shield. I'll be punished if I spoil the experiment." Barely 16, he calls himself "almost an old man." Emerging, his skin shows early eruptions. He forces Andrea to drive him back through the fog, threatening contagion. Simon chases them, plunging into the mist.

Beyond the fog lies Luminos, a desolate world of jagged stone. Simon stumbles into the same alien terrain Ralph saw, confronted by ponderous beings, their bodies encased in rocky shells, blending with the landscape. Andrea, suspended in a glowing tube, is unharmed but captive. Simon is led before a council, presided over by The Elder (voice of Ben Wright, physically Robert H. Justman), whose presence looms like the planet itself. The truth unfolds: Midgard Drive, six square blocks, has been teleported to Luminos. The Luminoids, cursed by a genetic disease that encrusts them in stone, grow immobile with age, reliant on slaves. Earthlings are their experiment—a test to enslave humanity. The disease, contagious through touch or air, is their leash; infection means transformation into Luminoid form, useless for labor. "You'll be happy," the Elder intones, "secure, if you avoid us." Andrea, sterilized by gas after sharing air with the boy, will return home. Simon is to tell his neighbors to "fear no fears and dream no dreams of escape—for there is no escape."

Back on Midgard, Andrea waits, shaken but resolute. The sterilizing gas spared her immediate infection, but the boy's breath lingers as a risk. The event has caused them to realize that they never stopped loving each other, and each asks forgiveness for having tried to change the other. The truth of her earlier words—*No matter how benevolent or secure you'd make it, it's slavery!*—is now a literal truth. They resolve to fight, not just for themselves but for all. Simon will set up a meeting at the church to alert the neighbors and discuss their options. Andrea promises to join him, but alone, she glimpses her shoulder in the mirror—a faint eruption blooming, the first sign of the disease.

At the church, as Simon explains what the Luminoids plan for them, Ralph appears outside, fully transformed, his body a grotesque shell, weeping in desolation. Father Fontana (Frank Puglia) moves to embrace him, but Simon holds him back—contagion is certain death. Andrea arrives, standing behind Ralph, her own infection advancing. The congregation recoils in fear.

Simon, turning to the group, tells them there is no way of escape, no way back to Earth. Their future is as slave labor. They don't have to suffer the same fate as Ralph, not as long as they remain in their homes and don't travel more than six blocks in any direction; even if some, like Andrea, catch the disease through the air, enough of them will survive to make the experiment feasible. And then the Luminoids will teleport the entire population of Earth to the planet to be enslaved. "We will live in labor camps," he says, "we will toil and sweat and die in controlled areas."

But they have a choice, he reminds them. *Human choice.* They can let the Luminoids know that they will not simply stand by while the entire human race is enslaved. They can choose to voluntarily expose themselves to the disease, to become what the Luminoids are. "My wife has already been infected," he tells them. "I'm going to take her hand. Will someone take mine?" After a moment's hesitation, Andrea does; Father Fontana grasps Rhea's other hand, and in turn the others, one by one, form a human chain, hand in hand. A chain forged by love, and a resolution to thwart the Luminoid plan.

A final image shows the crater that marks where the Midgard neighborhood once stood. An official sign has been posted telling people not to enter the area due to threat of possible radioactive dirt or rocks, and asks anyone with knowledge concerning the disappearance to contact the police. We are told that the Luminoid feasibility study has concluded. "Abduction of human race: infeasible."

II

"A Feasibility Study" was the ninth episode in the production cycle of *The Outer Limits*, wrapping up in August 1964, but it would not air until eight months later, as the series' 29th episode. The delay was unwelcome, but not exactly unexpected. "There was enough thinking going on in *The Outer Limits* to worry people,"[3] recalled the show's creator, Leslie Stevens, and approval from the network's Standards and Practices department was unusually slow in coming. ABC was particularly nervous about the ending, which network censor Dorothy Brown read as condoning mass suicide. "She saw the act of martyrdom as a negative gesture rather than a noble one," producer/writer Joseph Stefano said. "But I probably proved my point when ABC saw the finished film, with everyone joining hands. It was very moving and inspirational, and that's when they approved it."[4]

A few words about the performances of the principals in the cast. Sam Wanamaker (yet another Blacklist victim!) and Phyllis Love, as Simon and Andrea Holm, display a quiet vulnerability that, once they reunite, turns to strength and courage. David Opatoshu and Joyce Van Patten, as Ralph and Rhea Cashman, inject their brief scenes together with the comfortable affection born of a successful marriage; Opatoshu's reappearance as the infected Ralph is heartbreaking, and Van Patten's response is both touching and inspiring. Ben Wright, providing the voice of The Elder, is appropriately superior and disdainful; Frank Puglia, in the small but not unimportant role of Father Fontana, projects a quiet power and spirituality, particularly in the closing scene.

The unsettling atmosphere of the planet Luminos, its oppressive fog and darkness contrasting with the everyday normality of the human neighborhood to create a growing sense of impending doom, is portrayed in stunning, glorious black and white by cinematographer John Nickolaus; the poignancy of the episode's final scene, as the humans commit to their heroic sacrifice, is enhanced by the lovely, heartrending music of Dominic Frontiere—and, surprisingly, it wasn't even composed specifically for the episode, instead consisting of musical cues composed for other *Outer Limits* episodes.[5]

While *Outer Limits* critics have been divided on the merits of the story, "A Feasibility Study" struck a note in viewers that made it one of the most-remembered episodes of the series, a moving meditation with a singularly memorable ending. If there isn't a moment in it that causes you to think about your life and the lives of your family and loved ones—well, there's something about you that just isn't human.

III

We've seen three themes that constantly reappear throughout the stories in this book: freedom, slavery, and fear. In "A Feasibility Study," all three themes come together: the loss of freedom suffered by the Luminoids due to their disease; the loss of freedom felt by the Earthlings as the Luminoids enslave them; and the loss of freedom that comes when one becomes a slave to fear and inaction. Joseph Stefano's powerful and complex script continues to play with these themes throughout: Andrea feels herself a slave to Simon's desires, while Simon fears her loss; the Luminoids become slaves to their bodies, and can obtain a modicum of freedom only by enslaving others; the Earthlings struggle internally between the fear of slavery and the fear of death; and, ultimately, the freedom over fear—and death—purchased by love.

Much of the power in Stefano's script comes from the fact that the horror of slavery is never seen. There are no scenes of torture, of beatings, of vengeful masters whipping helpless slaves trying to escape. These masters are literate, even eloquent, not the monsters of "1984" or "Darkness at Noon." And they're most accommodating—or at least practical, for as Simon tells his fellow humans, slaves are no good to them dead.

No, Stefano trusts the viewer to understand this; he never even bothers to explain what type of work the slaves are to carry out, and in truth it makes no difference, for the kind of slavery he's talking about doesn't require work; it merely requires people to let themselves be led around like sheep—unthinking, uncaring, unfeeling. As the Elder tells Simon, "You will be happy. Your lives here will be comfortable and secure, and you will be free to worship and love and think as haphazardly as usual." Kind of like "You will own nothing, and you will be happy," don't you think? I can't remember who said that, but I'm sure you know who I mean.[6]

There's only one catch in all this: you lose your freedom in the process. Not the freedom of anarchy, licentiousness, or indulgence; those are just illusions of freedom, but in reality, they're simply different forms of slavery. No, this is the kind of freedom that helps define what it means to be human: free choice.

In a critical scene, Simon and Andrea come to understand and appreciate how loving someone means choosing to make sacrifices. Earlier, she had complained to Simon, "I can't live with you if life has to be lived according to your prescriptions. No matter how benevolent or secure you'd make it, it's slavery!" Now, faced with the prospect of actual slavery, and no apparent way to escape from it, they contemplate the choice they're left with:

SIMON: That's the whole bright mystique of life, choice. Maybe that's what the soul is. Choice.
ANDREA: Can we live with the loss of it?
SIMON: Perhaps. But I think it would be better to die trying to win it back.

Of course, if one *chooses* to be a sheep, there is nothing stopping them, and no way to free them.

IV

There can be no return, Simon tells his fellow slaves. No escape, no way back to Earth and their former lives. It does not, however, mean that there is no alternative. "We can choose to make their enslavement of our Earth infeasible. We can choose not to escape infection. We can deliberately become what they are."

This climactic scene takes place, appropriately, in a church. It is there that we are saturated with the symbols of religion: burning candles, statues, Rosaries. And at the heart of it, looming ever-present in the darkness as Simon makes his impassioned plea, is the symbol of the ultimate sacrifice, the Crucifix.

And the choice made by the humans demonstrates something the Luminoids, for all their advanced knowledge, could not anticipate: the power of caring, of loving, of sacrifice; of overcoming fear and uncertainty; most of all, the power of choice. For Stefano, human beings by definition cannot be sheep, are incapable of being sheep, as long as they have free will and an intellect, as long as they are capable of choice.

Whether we like it or not, free will is a gift to us and for us, one that asks us to exercise it thoughtfully. It tests our mettle, shows what we're made of, appeals to both the best and the worst in us. Most of all, it requires us to choose. "That's the whole bright mystique of life, isn't it?" Simon muses. "Choice. Maybe that's what the soul is: choice." Those people I mentioned above all had something in common: they were given a choice, and their choices were driven by their faith.

Consider the stories preceding "A Feasibility Study" in this section on martyrdom: "Dialogues of the Carmelites," "Murder in the Cathedral," and "The Obsolete Man" all end with the protagonists accepting their deaths with courage, defiance, and faith—a reminder that death is not the end of life.

For the Carmelites, the choice was to offer their own lives in an act of martyrdom, secure in their faith that, by being persecuted for their beliefs, the fire of hatred that inflamed the revolution would become uncontrollable, consuming and burning itself out, leading to divine graces for the people and for France. And for Blanche, the young sister who had first fled to save her life and then returned to give it up, her choice meant she would no longer be ruled by fear.

For Thomas Becket, the Archbishop of Canterbury locked in a struggle with King Henry II, he could have chosen to submit to the authority of the king to avoid death. Instead, he returned home from a safe haven in France and stationed himself in an unlocked Canterbury Cathedral, despite the pleadings of his monks to either flee or barricade himself inside, to await the knights he knew would assassinate him.

For Romney Wordsworth, the obsolete man, his choice was to accept death as an act of resistance, echoing the words of St. Paul, "Death, where is thy sting?" And, as he sat in his room reading from his banned Bible and honoring a faith he refused to renounce, he might have hoped that the people would realize that the emperor had no clothes, that the Chancellor was driven by fear just like they were; and that, therefore, they could defeat him, bring down the State, and show that no man is obsolete.

All of them faced execution as punishment for their choice. By contrast, the deal offered to the humans on Luminos seems to be a pretty good one. The Luminoids "don't intend to harm us," as Simon points out. "They want us strong and well. They need our strength." True, you could die just from breathing the same air, but we can chalk that up to the same risks we face every day; after all, getting out of bed in the morning is a risk. Whatever it is that they have to do as slaves to the Luminoids, one could envision living a good life, or at least a tolerable one. Get up in the morning, go off to work, come back in the evening, have dinner, catch up with the wife and kiddies, and go to bed. You can even go to church on Sunday! And anyway, aren't we all just wage slaves already, working for The Man every night and day?

But the Carmelites, Becket, Wordsworth, and the Luminoid captives: they're human beings, and, as Simon tells them, they have the freedom to make a choice.

In a way, Dorothy Brown, the ABC censor, was correct: without that faith, and without that freedom to choose, there is no sacrifice: it simply amounts to mass suicide.

V

As we have seen throughout this book, the totalitarian state is constructed on fear; it is what the despot counts on—what he depends on—to remain in power. Ever the double-edged sword, fear is also what propels him to act: fear of the loss of power.

For fear to be overcome, it first has to be acknowledged, recognized for what it is. The phrase "Be not afraid," or variations thereof, appears more often in the Bible than any other admonition.[7] Sammy Davis Jr. once said that "You always have two choices: your commitment versus your fear."* In the British science fiction series *Doctor Who*, the Doctor tells one of his companions that one must accept the possibility of death as the price for overcoming fear; "I had to face my fear. That was more important than just going on living."[8]

In "A Feasibility Study," the Luminoids bank on the human fear of death, and the consequent willingness to do anything to avoid that death. The Elder astutely sizes up Earthlings as "vain fleshmen who love their bodies above all else that nature has given to them," and concludes that, "you will obey. At the threat of our touch, you will obey." And in truth, it's hard to blame them for coming to that conclusion. After all, look at what we did in the name of a virus that had a survival rate of over 90 percent: we subjected ourselves to an untested "vaccine" without regard to the possible side effects, closed down society and business, demonized anyone who "questioned the science."[9]

But that's not all. Over the last few decades, humans have become so sensitive to any kind of risk that it's almost pathological. From food allergies to antibacterial soap, fear and disease lurk around every corner. Not to diminish those who actually suffer from such maladies, but one has to wonder if the preventive actions we take aren't, in fact, responsible for the ailments in the first place; a basic exposure to germs, for

---

* The quote might be apocryphal—there's no solid proof he said it—but the idea rings true either way.

example, is necessary to the development of a functioning immune system.[10]

No, for all the bluster about how savage humans are at heart (a theme of many a science-fiction story), we're really quite timid, so risk-averse that one wonders what value there is to a life that doesn't allow for taking chances. In a self-reflective mood, the legendary television newsman Harry Reasoner once remarked that

> The idea of trying to outguess life, to avoid everything that might conceivably ever injure your life is a peculiarly dangerous one, I think. Pretty soon you are existing in a morass of fear and you have given up not only cigarettes, prime beef, good butter, fine whiskey, spinach, tennis, sleeping on your side, riding without seat belts, air travel, train travel, chiropractors—maybe, next month, love.
>
> Life asks a great deal of man in exchange for what it provides, but if life asks him to cringe in front of all reasonable indulgence, he may at the end say life is not worth it. Because for the cringing he may get one extra day or none; he never gets eternity. If eternity exists, it is available not on the basis of how hard you hold to life but how generous you are with it.

"It may not be wise or manly to act only to stay alive," he concludes: "the odds are that you will die anyway."[11]

Reasoner, being a man of uncommon common sense, can hardly be said to speak for the majority anymore. So the Luminoids can hardly be blamed for believing that their human captives would accept slavery rather than suffer the consequences. They would have looked at this as manna from heaven, absolute proof that they could exploit that fear into creating a slave race.

But there is one thing that can overcome fear, and that is love. It is the equalizer, the great healing power, because without love there can be no sacrifice, not really. And a very interesting thing about "A Feasibility Study" is that it is about love as much as it is fear. The first half of the story highlights the absence of love, or at least the relegation of love to a lesser status. Despite their words, it's obvious that Simon and Andrea love each other, but they won't let that love breathe through layers of ambition and disappointment and cynicism. It's only when they're confronted by something bigger than either of them that they realize they can face it only by coming together.

And if the first part of the story is about the absence of love, then the conclusion shows us what happens when love is allowed to overcome fear. It's what happens when Simon and Andrea support each other and, in doing so, gain the strength to defeat it. It's what happens when Father Fontana approaches the church doors and, with a simple gesture, is able to move aside the two men barring entrance, reminding them that the church closes its doors to no one. It's what happens when, in one of the story's most affecting scenes, the weeping Ralph is comforted by his wife Rhea, who is not afraid to go to him.

You might have noticed that when Father Fontana opens the door and finds Ralph standing there, his first instinct is to reach out to him until he is restrained by Simon. We don't know if anyone involved in makeup for the show had this in mind, but the effect of Ralph's appearance evokes an image of someone infected by leprosy—a disease which, similarly, caused people to recoil in horror for fear of contamination. And I was reminded of Fr. Damien, the Catholic priest who treated the lepers of Molokai and eventually was infected himself; it is said that in his first sermon after the diagnosis, instead of his usual greeting of "My fellow believers," he began, "My fellow lepers."[12] A small moment, perhaps.

Perhaps the most inhuman thing the human race did during COVID Theater was to intentionally isolate itself from each other, to cut off the most vulnerable of us from human companionship and contact. How many times did we hear of those not allowed to see their loved ones in a hospital or nursing home, not able to furnish them with companionship, not able to be with them in their last hours of life. They not only reacted out of fear—fear that had been imposed on them—they stoked that fear, added to it until it became hysteria.

That contact, the human touch and the love that comes with it—so simple, and yet we deliberately, willingly removed it from use. There was a lot of talk thrown around at the time about caring for others, about this isolation being an act of love. In some specific cases, there may well have been a medical justification for it. But make no mistake—this was no act of love. There was no love involved in it.

VI

Death does not mean that life has ended, but merely changed.[13]

Certainly, "A Feasibility Study" can be seen as a commentary on the civil rights fight that continued throughout the 1960s. However, the issues that Joseph Stefano explores—freedom, choice, love, fear—go far beyond what would have been necessary to make that simple plea. For that reason, I'm convinced Stefano did not want the episode to be seen purely through the lens of then-contemporary events. For him, the idea of martyrdom, the voluntary sacrifice of life in order to preserve the human race, seems to have been his main interest, and there's no way to fully understand and appreciate that aspect without looking at everything else. And those are timeless themes, applicable to any era.

Watching "A Feasibility Study," it's hard not to be reminded of the passengers of United Airlines Flight 93, the flight that crashed in Stonycreek Township, Pennsylvania, on September 11, 2001. You remember: the passengers, having learned from their phones of the attacks on the World Trade Center and the Pentagon, fought back against their hijackers, forcing the plane to crash well short of its intended target. Like the humans held captive by the Luminoids, they knew that they could not escape, that there would be no return to their former lives, their friends and loved ones.

But those passengers understood—their actions indicate they must have understood—that even though the fact of their deaths could not change, the meaning of their deaths could, and would. They would die at the hands of their captors, or they would sacrifice their lives to prevent their captors from accomplishing their goal, taking yet more innocent lives. Either way, they would be dead—but nothing else would be the same. One can choose to die as a slave, or as a free man.

We can choose.

There is one major difference in these sacrifices. The whole world would know soon enough about what happened on Flight 93, and that their rebellion, directly or indirectly, would lead to the failure of the terrorists' mission. The sacrificial act made on Luminos, on the other hand, will go unknown by the billions on Earth, including many who may not have merited it. Their martyrdom will supply no encouragement, will raise no flag under which others can choose to fight back; and there will be no shrine constructed in their honor. In fact, were you to ask Simon, he might tell you that this is the way it had to be, for it would mean that their rebellion had succeeded, that the continued teleportation of Earthlings had been found to be infeasible, that no one on Earth would ever know about it.

And while those on Earth might remain ignorant of what happened, we can observe that there is a lesson to be taken from it all, which is that freedom is something intrinsic in the human spirit. It may lie submerged, deep in the recesses of the psyche, perhaps for generations at a time; nevertheless, it exists, waiting for the moment when it will be called on, when a spark will bring it to life.

"For freedom Christ has set us free," St. Paul writes to the Galatians. "Stand fast, and be not entangled again with the yoke of bondage."[14] The apostle was writing about the slavery of sin, but there is more than one kind of slavery, just as there is more than one kind of freedom. The Luminoids did not understand that, but we do, because humans have always had to fight for their freedom.

We can choose.

Some people will see the ending as sad or depressing, but I don't think Stefano intended it that way, nor is it how I understand it; in fact, I'm rather encouraged by it, because it suggests the indomitable spirit of the human being, the desire for freedom, and the ability to love. Even in these times, it's comforting to think that this spirit is ingrained in us, that if we're put to the test, we'll respond the way we hope we would.

The Luminoids would have accused their would-be slaves of having chosen death, but in reality, they chose freedom. They chose *life*. Possibly—just possibly—we will, too.

All dialogue quoted is from "A Feasibility Study" (*The Outer Limits*).
1. Romans 5:7 (*KJV*).
2. Reasoner, *Before the Colors Fade*, 165.
3. Schow, *Outer Limits Companion*.
4. Ibid.

5. Beam, "A Feasibility Study," para. 19.
6. *Cf. Schwab and Malleret*, "Welcome to 2030."
7. Isaiah 41:10, among others (*KJV*).
8. *Doctor Who*, "Planet of the Spiders," May 4–June 8, 1974
9. Devine, "Vaccine Reckoning."
10. Castaneda and Schroeder, "Soil and Sin"
11. Reasoner, *Before the Colors Fade*, 165.
12. Murray, "The Touch."
13. *Roman Missal*, Preface for the Dead.
14. Galatians 5:1 (*KJV*).

JOURNEY'S END

The Horn Blows at Midnight

By Leo Davis, Leonard Gershe, Howard Snyder and Hugh Wedlock Jr.
Based on the 1949 radio play and 1945 movie of the same name
Directed by Ralph Levy
First broadcast on *Omnibus*, November 29, 1953

This is the way the world ends
Not with a bang but a whimper.

—T.S. Eliot[1]

There's a thin line between comedy and tragedy; it's why the theater's symbols are the laughing mask of Thalia and the crying mask of Melpomene: always together, two sides of the same coin. We're not used to looking to comedies for our heavy moral lessons, although the absurdity of what we've allowed ourselves to be subjected to would be laughable if it weren't so tragic. So perhaps it's fitting that this final one—the only one to deal with the actual end of the world—is a comedy. One with strings attached, however, because it ends with mankind being given another chance—a last chance.

I

In the gleaming halls of Heaven's Department of Small Planet Management, the Chief (Lester Matthews) sighs over a directive from the Front Office. Planet 33974, a speck of trouble dubbed Earth, has vexed celestial patience too long—wars every two decades, two million crimes yearly, greed and intolerance festering like weeds. The order is blunt: destroy it. His assistant, Elizabeth (Dorothy Malone), hands over Earth's file, her eyes flickering with unease. The plan is simple: an angel will descend to the Waldorf-Biltmore's top floor in New York City, blow five notes on a sacred trumpet precisely at midnight, and Earth will vanish. Elizabeth nominates her boyfriend, Athanael, for the task. The Chief groans—Athanael, Angel Junior Grade, 3rd Phalanx, 15th Cohort, is a perennial bungler. "A nincompoop," he mutters, recalling Athanael's string of flops. Elizabeth insists he's perfect, a trumpeter in the Heavenly orchestra, "The Sweetest Music the Other Side of Heaven." The Chief relents, skeptical but swayed.

Athanael (Jack Benny) is mid-rehearsal, fumbling Beethoven's Fifth Symphony, when the summons arrives. Beethoven, exasperated, is ejecting him for mangling the opening notes—again. The call to destroy Earth, his home 300 years ago, gives Athanael pause. His mortal life flashes—music, dreams, mistakes—but duty beckons. The Chief hands him the trumpet, its golden curves heavy with fate. "Midnight exactly," he warns. "Not 11:59, not 12:01." Success means a leap to Angel Senior Grade, a prize Athanael craves. He nods, masking doubt, and descends to Earth, trumpet case in hand.

New York City buzzes, its 1950s pulse a mix of neon and hustle. Athanael, dressed in an oddly timeless suit, blends into the crowd near the Waldorf. Voices catch his ear—a young couple, Danny (Lee Millar) and Helen (Jeff Donnell; real first name Jean Marie), bickering on the sidewalk. Danny, a trumpeter scraping by in a radio orchestra, clings to his art. Helen, practical and yearning for marriage, presses him for a "real job." The scene touches Athaneal, reminding him of a similar argument he'd had with Elizabeth. He interjects, urging them to cherish their love, but Danny stalks off, mistakenly grabbing Athanael's trumpet case. Realizing the error, Athanael hails a cab, heart racing. The driver, weathered and wry, catalogs Earth's woes: I've already gone through one war, he tells Athaneal, and my kid went through another. "Einstein says the next war will be fought with atomic bombs, and then the next war after that will be fought with rocks."

The cab weaves through Manhattan, delivering Athanael to the Waldorf's rooftop garden, where Danny's orchestra plays under twinkling stars. With midnight approaching, Athanael spots Danny and retrieves his trumpet. Helen joins them, her eyes soft with worry. Athaneal reveals to them his true identity and that he is about to blow his trumpet and destroy the Earth. "You only have four minutes to live. Are you going to spend those four minutes just fighting with each other?" Danny is skeptical, but Helen tells him that with the world as it is, anything could happen at any minute. "Suppose we *did* have only four more minutes to live," she asks him. "We've wasted all our precious time." If only they knew when the world would end, they could make every second a happy one. "Holding each other close would be the most important in all the world." Realizing the truth of what Athaneal has said, they return inside arm-in-arm, leaving the angel alone in the garden, holding his trumpet as the minute hand moves toward midnight. And here he pauses.

At every act of kindness he has encountered, Athaneal's doubts about his mission have increased, leaving him to wonder if The Chief realizes the true nature of the situation. Now, speaking directly to him, Athaneal pleads for the lives of those on Earth. Take Danny and Helen—"They're not bad people, and they're so much in love—how can they be bad? They shouldn't be destroyed." He thinks back to the others he's encountered during his mission: two young shoeshine boys he met upon his arrival, who were so nice to him; the friendly news dealer who helped him find Danny; the little old lady he sat next to in the hotel lobby, planning a trip around the world after winning a contest. There are millions like them all over the world, just looking for a little happiness; don't they all deserve another chance?

Moved by Athaneal's plea, The Chief relents, giving the planet and its people that one—final?—chance.

II

Jack Benny's self-deprecating humor turned the theatrical version of *The Horn Blows at Midnight* (1945), a box-office disappointment, into a legendary gag, alongside his stinginess and eternal "39" age. The film underperformed, overshadowed by President Roosevelt's death eight days prior and the Broadway triumph of Rodgers and Hammerstein's "Carousel," which better handled spiritual themes.[2] Critics, like Winston Archer of the *New York Post*, called it an "overworked" comic fantasy that never came together.[3]

Yet Benny embraced the flop, joking about it across his career, boosting the film's fame and recouping its costs. In a 1957 TV skit, he asks a studio guard (Mel Blanc) if he saw it. "Saw it? I directed it!" Blanc quips, cementing Benny's knack for mining failure for laughs.[4] "When the horn blew at midnight" Benny later said, "it blew taps for my cinema career"[5]—his final starring role, yet one of his best-known, even among those who've never seen it.

A radio adaptation of *The Horn Blows at Midnight* was produced for *Ford Theater* on March 4, 1949, with Benny starring once again as Athanael.[6] It wasn't *quite* the same version of the story as that seen in the movie theaters, though; for one thing, the movie had a running time of 78 minutes, while *Ford Theater* had a one-hour timeslot (minus commercials); obviously, changes would have to be made.

The biggest change involved a framing device used in the movie's beginning and ending, which presented Benny as a musician named Athaneal, a trumpet player in a studio orchestra performing for a radio program. Athaneal falls asleep during a commercial for the show's sponsor, Paradise Coffee (the coffee "that makes you sleep"), and *dreams* that he is an angel, thus triggering the story to follow. The movie concludes with a chase scene ending with Athaneal falling off the roof; the sense of falling causes him to fall off his orchestra chair and awaken from the dream.

This framing device was eliminated in the radio adaptation: Benny no longer dreams that he is an angel; he *is* the angel Athaneal, selected by The Chief (God? St. Peter? Edward Platt?) to bring down the curtain on Earth by blowing his trumpet at midnight. The radio version then continued with a storyline similar to that in the movie, minus some secondary characters and plotlines, as well as many of the slapstick elements that would be meaningless on radio.

However, without that dream sequence, the radio version would need a new ending, and that ending, containing Athaneal's dramatic and moving appeal to The Chief to give Earth one more chance, produced a subtle but marked difference, not only in the tone of the story but in the conclusions to be drawn from it.

The changes made in the radio version improve the story in other ways as well. The framing structure meant that audiences knew from the beginning that this was all just a dream; the movie essentially served as its own spoiler, ruining whatever suspense there might have been. The elimination of excess characters and storylines also makes the overall presentation tighter and more dramatically effective. And when the story makes its way to television four years later, it is the radio version, not the theatrical one, that serves as the basis for the teleplay, broadcast live on CBS's Sunday afternoon cultural variety show *Omnibus*, three days after Thanksgiving, 1953.

The story remains a comedy, with many funny moments, most centering on Benny's reputation for stinginess. For instance, while waiting in the hotel lobby for Danny to appear, there's a page for "Jack Benny." The old woman sitting next to Athaneal mentions that she never misses Benny's show, adding that he must be "the sweetest, kindest, most generous man in the whole world." Athanael is also a big tipper, giving the two shoeshine boys (one of them played by Harry Shearer) a dollar each; "It's such a wonderful feeling to give money away," Benny says, with his trademark pause as he looks at the studio audience. There's also a scene poking fun at his age; when a little girl at the Waldorf asks Athanael how old he is, he replies that he's 357, but adds "I tell everybody up there that I'm 339."

These moments ensure that "The Horn Blows at Midnight" maintains a lightheartedness that keeps it from ever becoming preachy, and makes maximum use of Benny's comedic talent. But the slapstick and the broad comedy of the movie have now been replaced with a humor that is at once both gentle and very human, underlining man's foibles while at the same time looking at him with a patient affection.

It also makes possible the story's most dramatic moment, the one that provides its moral center: Athaneal's plea for mercy on behalf of the people of Earth.

III

The eighteenth chapter of Genesis consists in large part of a conversation between God and Abraham, during which God not even ten righteous men, warn Lot and his family to leave the town at once, after which the cities are laid waste; "the smoke of the country went up as the smoke of a furnace."[8]

IV

The programs discussed in this book often were met with skepticism when they originally aired; scattered among the reviews from critics and viewers are terms such as "far-fetched," "paranoid," "heavy-handed," "unrealistic," and "improbable." And in a dramatic sense, this may have been true.

But what about in a prophetic sense?

Some stories, such as "Dialogues of the Carmelites," "Murder in the Cathedral," or "Darkness at Noon," used historical events to remind viewers that the unimaginable was once all too real. Others—"The Year of the Sex Olympics," "They," "Sounds of a Different Drummer"—were logical extensions of a future that had already been glimpsed, prophecies of what could happen if events continued without being altered.

"The Horn Blows at Midnight" is a different animal altogether. Ever since receiving his assignment, Athanael has been warned about the "nasty little globe" he's about to help obliterate. Upon his arrival, he sees the headlines of investigations, wars, murders—even smog! The taxi driver rushing him to the hotel expresses his concerns about the world; for him, another war is a given. But the people he meets are good and decent, dealing with their own thoughts and fears, their hopes and dreams for the future—problems that, as Humphrey Bogart's Rick says in *Casablanca*, "don't amount to a hill of beans in this crazy world."[9]

And yet, those beans prove to be quite important to Athanael, who is so moved by them that he is compelled to question his mission, and ultimately challenge the orders given to him by The Chief. His plea is based not on tolerance or acceptance, and expresses not sympathy or pity, but something more overwhelming and essential: a deeply felt sense of compassion. Someone once described compassion as love put into action, and it's hard to find a better description for the feeling Athaneal comes to have for these humans and their planet.

It is that compassion that emboldens him to speak so frankly with The Chief, to intercede with him on behalf of all those who will die without even having had a chance to build a world of their own. This ending—quite unlike that of the original movie—is what gives "The Horn Blows at Midnight" its gravitas, its moral weight. Having once seen it, it becomes more and more difficult to imagine the story without it, and perhaps that's one reason why the movie didn't fare so well.

It is also that compassion that seems to be in such short supply nowadays. We've become a world in which it's one strike and you're out, leaving no room for forgiveness, for understanding, for rehabilitation and reclamation—for humanity. The world seems to be caught in the grasp of a sickness today, one greater than that which existed in the time of "The Horn Blows at Midnight." Depending on the day, we have the potential to look at the news and read about some new moral depravity, something that might have been thought unthinkable a few years ago, but now has become accepted as the new normal. We see screaming mobs consumed by hatred—hatred for others, which ultimately traces its roots back to hatred for themselves. One need only look at reactions to the Israel-Hamas war to see this, but in reality, it has been growing steadily in the past few years, and if the growth now seems to be exponential, I'm sure there's a mathematical explanation for that.

V

It is compassion, not pity or tolerance, that drives Athanael's plea—love in action, interceding for Earth's millions. Like Abraham haggling for Sodom's ten righteous, Athanael faces a Chief poised to end things, but open to persuasion. In 1953, wars and greed were everywhere, but so was goodness: a shoe-shine boy's grin, a news dealer's help, an old lady's travel dreams. These points of light swayed The Chief to grant one more chance. But the world of today feels darker, colder, its moral rot deeper. Schools prize relativism over reality, while churches live in the world rather than seeking the divine. While Danny and Helen choose to spend those precious moments of life treasuring their love for each other and God's love for them both, we seem to be content exchanging the thrill of everyday life for the safety of the mundane, science for spirituality, the impersonal for the human touch.

Our headlong rush toward iconoclasm and nihilism tears at the roots of existence. We dismantle beliefs and codes that have sustained humanity for millennia, crafting alternative realities where truth becomes a mere observation, where biology itself is denied. Athanael's taxi driver feared atomic wars; ours dread cancellation, coerced shots, or silence. Whereas Jack Benny's humor masked courage, the masks we wear hide our own cowardice.

We seem hell-bent on self-destruction, a path Sodom trod to ruin; Lot barely escaped, and we may not. And so, we should be hoping that The Chief shows as much compassion for us today as he did in 1953. Either that, or we have someone as eloquent as Jack Benny pleading our case for us.

Meanwhile, night falls, and the clock continues to go tick, tick, tick . . .

All dialogue quoted is from "The Horn Blows at Midnight" (*Omnibus*).
1. Eliot, "Hollow Men," 87.
2. Crowther, "Horn Blows," 15.
3. Archer, "Horn Blows at Midnight," 18.
4. Perrin et al., quoted in *The Jack Benny Program*, "Jack's Life Story," December 1, 1957.
5. Benny, quoted in Josefsberg, *Jack Benny Show*, 416.
6. "The Horn Blows at Midnight," *Ford Theatre Archive*.
7. Genesis 18:20–32 (*KJV*).
8. Genesis 19:28 (*KJV*).
9. *Casablanca*

Bibliography

Abbott, Graham. "The Life and Work of Francis Poulenc." *Graham's Music* (blog), May 9, 2020. Accessed June 10, 2025. https://www.grahamsmusic.net/post/the-life-and-work-of-francis-poulenc.

Aeschylus. *Aeschylus, 1: The Oresteia*. Translated by David R. Slavitt. Philadelphia: University of Pennsylvania Press, 1998.

Allen, Stewart. "'Investigation' Nightmarish in Detail." *Arizona Republic*, April 15, 1967.

Alliance Defending Freedom. "UK Woman Arrested for Silent Prayer Outside Abortion Clinic." *ADFInternational.org*, December 6, 2022. Accessed April 19, 2025. https://adfinternational.org/news/uk-woman-arrested-for-silent-prayer-outside-abortion-clinic.

America in Class. "After Shays' Rebellion." National Humanities Center. Accessed June 4, 2025. https://americainclass.org/after-shays-rebellion/.

Anderson, Jack E. "'The Investigation' A Provocative Drama," *Miami Herald*, April 18, 1967.

Anti-Defamation League. "From the River to the Sea: Decoding a Genocidal Slogan." ADL.org. Accessed June 12, 2025. https://www.adl.org/resources/blog/river-sea-decoding-genocidal-slogan.

Archer, Winston. "The Horn Blows at Midnight' and All Day at the Strand." *New York Post*, April 21, 1945.

Ashworth, Nate. "Poll: 45% of Dems Support Internment Camps for Unvaccinated, 59% Support Home Lockdowns." Election Central, January 19, 2022. Accessed June 6, 2025.

https://www.uspresidentialelectionnews.com/2022/01/poll-45-of-dems-support-internment-camps-for-unvaccinated-59-support-home-lockdowns/.

Atlanta Journal. "'Studio One' Sets Gripping Drama." January 4, 1958.

Auken, Ida. "Welcome to 2030: I Own Nothing, Have No Privacy, and Life Has Never Been Better." World Economic Forum, November 10, 2016. https://www.weforum.org/agenda/2016/11/welcome-to-2030-i-own-nothing-have-no-privacy-and-life-has-never-been-better/.

Badenhausen, Richard. "Drama", in Jason Harding, ed., *T.S. Eliot in Context* (Cambridge, 2011), 128-9.

Baur, Joe. "What makes Germans so orderly?" *BBC*, June 1, 2020. Accessed June 11, 2025. https://www.bbc.com/travel/article/20200531-what-makes-germans-so-orderly.

Beam, Craig. "Episode Spotlight: 'O.B.I.T.'" *My Life in the Glow of The Outer Limits* (blog). November 4, 2013. Accessed June 11, 2025. https://theouterlimits1963.blogspot.com/2013/11/episode-spotlight-obit.html.

———. "Episode Spotlight: 'A Feasibility Study' (4/13/1964)" *My Life in the Glow of The Outer Limits* (blog). April 13, 2014. Accessed June 11, 2025. https://mylifeintheglowoftheouterlimits.blogspot.com/2014/04/episode-spotlight-feasibility-study.html.

Beley, Gene. *Ray Bradbury Uncensored! The Unauthorized Biography.* New York: iUniverse, 2006.

Berlau, John. "Debanking: Cancel Culture's Extreme New Form." *Competitive Enterprise Institute*, June 15, 2023. Accessed April 19, 2025. https://cei.org/studies/debanking-cancel-cultures-extreme-new-form/.

Berry, Wendell. *The Unsettling of America: Culture & Agriculture.* San Francisco: Sierra Club Books, 1977.

Beutner, Dawn. "The Protomartyrs of Communism: The Martyrs of September." *Catholic World Report,* September 2, 2022. Accessed June 10, 2025. https://www.catholicworldreport.com/2022/09/02/the-protomartyrs-of-communism-the-martyrs-of-september/.

BFI. "Nigel Kneale: The Year of the Sex Olympics." Accessed June 10, 2025. https://bfidatadigipres.github.io/nightmares%20&%20daydreams%3Cbr%3Ea%20centenary%20celebration%20of%20screenwriter%20nigel%20kneale/2022/04/12/year-of-the-sex-olympics/.

Billingsley, Kenneth. "Hollywood's Missing Movies." *Reason,* June 2000.

Birnbaum, Emily. "Trump Officials Defend Use of Facial Recognition Amid Backlash." *The Hill,* July 2, 2019. Accessed April 19, 2025. https://thehill.com/policy/technology/452529-trump-officials-defend-use-of-facial-recognition-amid-backlash/.

Blum, Christopher O. "C.S. Lewis and the Religion of Science." *National Review,* September 30, 2019. Accessed June 11, 2025. https://www.nationalreview.com/magazine/2019/09/30/c-s-lewis-and-the-religion-of-science/.

Boakes, Philip. Introduction to *One,* by David Karp. Richmond, VA: Valancourt Books, 2017.

Bolt, Robert. *A Man for All Seasons.* London: Heinemann, 1960.

Bonhoeffer, Dietrich. *Discipleship.* Edited by Martin Kuske, Ilse Tödt, Heinz Eduard Tödt, and Ernst Feil. Translated by Barbara Green and Reinhard Krauss. Dietrich Bonhoeffer Works, vol. 4. Minneapolis, MN: Fortress Press, 2003.

Bradfield, Scott. "Why '1984' is still relevant today—but not for the reason you may expect." *Los Angeles Times,* June 13, 2019. Accessed June 10, 2025.

https://www.latimes.com/books/la-ca-jc-review-ministry-truth-george-orwell-1984-20190613-story.html.

Brodsky, Katherine. "Canadians Without Life Threatening Diseases Are Being Encouraged to Consider Suicide." *Newsweek*, February 12, 2024. Accessed June 11, 2025. https://www.newsweek.com/canadians-without-life-threatening-diseases-are-being-encouraged-consider-suicide-opinion-1868692.

"Brotherhood of the Bell." *TV Guide* (New England edition). January 6, 1958. Philadelphia: Triangle Publications, Inc. Accessed June 12, 2025. https://archive.org/details/tvguide-scan-january-4-1958-mp-ia/page/4/mode/1up?view=theater

Buckingham, Janet Epp. "Ban the Mob, Not the Bible." *Christianity Today*, June 6, 2024. Accessed June 10, 2025. https://www.christianitytoday.com/2024/06/hate-speech-bible-pakistan-finland-canada-united-nations/.

Buckley, William F., Jr. "Our Mission Statement." *National Review*, November 19, 1955. Accessed June 6, 2025. https://www.nationalreview.com/1955/11/our-mission-statement-william-f-buckley-jr/.

Bush, George W. *A Charge to Keep*. New York: William Morrow, 1999.

Butcher, Jonathan. "Some Schools Don't Want You To Know What They Are Teaching Your Kids. That's a Problem." *The Heritage Foundation*. September 10, 2020. Accessed June 5, 2025. https://www.heritage.org/education/commentary/some-schools-dont-want-you-know-what-they-are-teaching-your-kids-thats-problem.

Caldwell, James. "Jefferson's Wall of Separation Letter." *U.S. Constitution.net*. April 23, 2024. Accessed June 10, 2025. https://www.usconstitution.net/jeffwallhtml/

Cammaerts, Émile. *The Laughing Prophet: The Seven Virtues and G.K. Chesterton*. London: Methuen & Co. Ltd., 1937.

Campbell, Douglas R. "Self-Motion and Cognition: Plato's Theory of the Soul." *The Southern Journal of Philosophy* 59, no. 4 (December 2021).

Capital Research Center, "When Schools Go Secret: How Oakland Unified and Teachers Unions Are Undermining Parental Rights." June 6, 2025. Accessed June 7, 2025. https://capitalresearch.org/article/when-schools-go-secret-how-oakland-unified-and-teachers-unions-are-undermining-parental-rights/.

Castaneda, Ruben, and Michael O. Schroeder. "Could Getting Dirty and Being Exposed to Germs Boost Your Health?" *U.S. News & World Report*, September 19, 2019. Accessed June 5, 2025. https://health.usnews.com/wellness/articles/hygiene-hypothesis-could-more-dirt-and-germs-boost-your-health.

Cather, Willa. To Roscoe Cather, July 10, 1938. In *The Selected Letters of Willa Cather*, edited by Andrew Jewell and Janis Stout, 539. New York: Knopf, 2013.

Catholic Answers. "Individual." Accessed April 17, 2025. https://www.catholic.com/encyclopedia/individual.

Cedrone, Lou. "It Was Better on TV." *Baltimore Evening Sun*, April 19, 1967.

Chatterbox. "The Skulls (and Bones) Prequel." *Slate*, March 21, 2000. Accessed June 11, 2025. https://slate.com/news-and-politics/2000/03/the-skulls-and-bones-prequel.html.

Chozick, Amy. "Hillary Clinton Calls Many Trump Backers 'Deplorables' and G.O.P. Pounces." *The New York Times*, September 10, 2016. Accessed June 6, 2025. https://www.nytimes.com/2016/09/11/us/politics/hillary-clinton-basket-of-deplorables.html.

Christenson, Josh. "Nearly 6,000 US public schools hide child's gender status from parents." *New York Post*, March 8, 2023. Accessed June 7, 2025. https://nypost.com/2023/03/08/us-public-schools-conceal-childs-gender-status-from-parents/.

Clavell, James. *The Children's Story*. New York: Delacorte Press, 1981.

Code of Canon Law Annotated. Edited by Ernest Caparros. Montreal: Wilson & Lafleur, 2004.

Coffey, Sarah. "What is Debanking? Political and Religious Discrimination by Financial Institutions." *The Foundation for Government Accountability*, August 21, 2023. Accessed June 9, 2025. https://thefga.org/blog/what-is-debanking-political-and-religious-discrimination/.

Craig, Kit. "'Darkness' Shows What Can Be Done In Studio." *St. Petersburg Times*, May 5, 1955.

Crosby, Joan. "TV Scout: 'Investigation' Compelling Drama." *Pittsburgh Press*, April 14, 1967.

Crosby, John. "Radio and Television: We Wash Their Brains." *The Portsmouth Times*, September 28, 1953.

Crowther, Bosley. "The Screen; 'Horn Blows at Midnight,' With Jack Benny as Trumpeter, of Strand—'Circumstantial Evidence' New Rialto Feature." *New York Times*, April 21, 1945.

"The Declaration of the Rights of Man and of the Citizen." *Elysée*, December 14, 2022. Accessed June 10, 2025. https://www.elysee.fr/en/french-presidency/the-declaration-of-the-rights-of-man-and-of-the-citizen.

de Jong, Loe. *Het Koninkrijk der Nederlanden in de Tweede Wereldoorlog*. Vol. 3. The Hague: Martinus Nijhoff, 1970.

Delatiner, Barbara. "TV's New Sensitivity to Holocaust Themes." *Newsday*, April 10, 1967.

Devine, Miranda. "A COVID-19 vaccine reckoning is coming for the DOJ over federal mandates." *New York Post*, November 12, 2023. Accessed June 10, 2025. https://nypost.com/2023/11/12/opinion/a-covid-19-vaccine-reckoning-is-coming-for-the-doj-over-federal-gov-mandates/.

Di Corpo, Ryan. "U.S. dioceses suspend Masses and close churches as coronavirus pandemic escalates." *America Magazine*, March 13, 2020. Accessed June 6, 2025. https://www.americamagazine.org/faith/2020/03/13/us-dioceses-suspend-masses-and-close-churches-coronavirus-pandemic-escalates.

Dixon, Wheeler Winston. "Cinema and Poetry: T. S. Eliot's *Murder in the Cathedral*." *Senses of Cinema* (blog), September, 2016. Accessed June 6, 2025. https://www.sensesofcinema.com/2016/feature-articles/murder-in-the-cathedral/.

Do No Harm. "Do No Harm Launches First National Database Exposing the Child Trans Industry." October 8, 2024. Accessed June 6, 2025. https://donoharmmedicine.org/2024/10/08/stop-the-harm-national-database-child-trans-industry/.

Dockrill, Peter. "China's Chilling 'Social Credit System' Is Straight Out of Dystopian Sci-Fi, And It's Already Switched on." *Science Alert*, September 20, 2018. Accessed April 19, 2025. https://www.sciencealert.com/china-s-dystopian-social-credit-system-science-fiction-black-mirror-mass-surveillance-digital-dictatorship.

Doux, Billie. "The Outer Limits: O.B.I.T." *Doux Reviews* (blog). Accessed May 1, 2025. https://www.douxreviews.com/2012/03/outer-limits-obit.html.

Downey, Caroline. "Biden Claims School Children Don't Belong to Parents 'When They're in the Classroom'." *National Review*, April 27, 2022. Accessed June 7, 2025.

https://www.nationalreview.com/news/biden-claims-school-children-dont-belong-to-parents-when-theyre-in-the-classroom/.

Drennan, Kathryn M. "A Test of Character." *Starlog*, December, 1989.

Du Bois, W. E. Burghardt. "The Economic Aspects of Race Prejudice." *The Editorial Review* 2 (May, 1910). Accessed June 8, 2025. https://babel.hathitrust.org/cgi/pt?id=njp.32101076424934&seq=503.

Du Brow, Rick. "Show Presents An Awesome Description of Inhumanity." *Williamson Daily News*, April 15, 1967.

Dube, Bernard. "Tviewing." *Montreal Gazette*, May 4, 1955.

Ehrlich, Paul R., and Anne H. Ehrlich. *The Population Bomb*. New York: Ballantine Books, 1968.

Eliot, T.S. "The Cultivation of Christmas Trees". *The Imaginative Conservative*. December 24, 2024. Accessed June 5, 2025. https://theimaginativeconservative.org/2024/12/cultivation-of-christmas-trees-ts-eliot.html.

———. *Collected Poems, 1909–1962*. New York: Harcourt, Brace & World, 1963.

"Eloquent Cast Dramatizes Chilling Story of Future." *St. Petersburg Independent*, April 16, 1970.

Emerson, Faye. "'Noon' Is Big Step For TV." *Pittsburgh Press*, May 1, 1955.

Emerson, Ralph Waldo. "Self-Reliance." *Essays: First Series*, 1841, The Essential Writings of Ralph Waldo Emerson, edited by Brooks Atkinson, Modern Library, 2000.

Epstein, Julius J., with Philip G. Epstein and Howard Koch, *Casablanca*. Directed by Michael Curtiz. Warner Bros., 1942.

Facebook. "Community Standards." https://www.facebook.com/communitystandards.

Fanning, Win. "Radio and TV: 'Showcase' Achieves Technical Miracle." *Pittsburgh Post-Gazette*, May 3, 1955.

Fenton, Andrew. "Longevity expert: AI will help us become 'biologically immortal' from 2030." *Cointellegraph*, June 6, 2024. Accessed June 4, 2025. https://cointelegraph.com/magazine/longevity-escape-velocity-jose-luis-cordeiro-biological-immortality-2030/.

Fidelity Investments. "How is Your Credit Score Calculated?" Accessed April 17, 2025. https://www.fidelity.com/learning-center/smart-money/how-is-credit-score-calculated.

The Ford Theatre Archive. *Audio Classics Archive*. Accessed June 5, 2025. http://www.audio-classics.com/ltheford theater.html.

Francis, Bob. Quoted in David Ryan, *George Orwell on Screen: Adaptations, Documentaries and Docudramas on Film and Television*. Jefferson, NC: McFarland, 2018.

Franklin, Benjamin. "Pennsylvania Assembly: Reply to the Governor, 11 November 1755." Printed in *Votes and Proceedings of the House of Representatives*, 1755–1756, Philadelphia, 1756, pp. 19–21. Accessed June 8, 2025. https://founders.archives.gov/documents/Franklin/01-06-02-0107#BNFN-01-06-02-0107-fn-0005.

Frymer, Murray. "Dialogue With Writer Marya Mannes." *Newsday*, May 25, 1971.

Fulton, Roger. *The Encyclopedia of TV Science Fiction*. 3rd ed. London: Boxtree, 1997.

Gallagher, Paul. "The Lure of Forced Utopia: Twilight Zone's 'Number 12 Looks Just Like You'." *Shadow & Substance* (blog). Accessed April 17, 2025. https://thenightgallery.wordpress.com/2018/02/09/the-lure-of-forced-utopia-twilight-zones-number-12-looks-just-like-you/.

Gardner, John. *On Moral Fiction*. New York: Basic Books, 1978.

Gatiss, Mark. "Nigel Kneale: The Man Who Saw Tomorrow." *The Guardian*, November 1, 2006. Accessed April 19, 2025.

https://www.theguardian.com/media/2006/nov/02/broadcasting.arts1.

Gerrold, David. *The World of Star Trek*. New York: Ballantine Books, 1973.

Goodrick, Edward W., and John R. Kohlenberger III, eds. *NIV Exhaustive Concordance*. Grand Rapids, MI: Zondervan, 1990.

Gorner, John. "Assisted Dying and Inheritance: What Does the Law Say?" *SlaterHeelis Solicitors*, October 17, 2024. Accessed June 11, 2025. https://www.slaterheelis.co.uk/articles/wills-probate/assisted-dying-inheritance-uk-high-court-ruling/.

Gould, Jack. "Television in Review: Orwell's '1984'; 'Studio One' Presents Masterly Adaptation in Opening Program Eddie Albert Cited for Portrayal—Nickell Scores as Director" *New York Times*, September 23, 1953.

———. "TV: 'Darkness at Noon' Impresses." *New York Times*, May 3, 1955.

———. "TV: A Powerful Drama: 'Playhouse 90' Offers 'Sound of Different Drummers,' Anti-Conformity Protest The Real McCoys" *New York Times*, October 4, 1957.

———. "TV: A Drama of Power; 'One,' by David Karp, Receives Effective Revival on 'Matinee Theatre'." *New York Times*, February 8, 1957.

Grace, Arthur. "Studio One Clinker; Ellis Has Rebuttal." *The Miami News*, January 8, 1958.

Graham, Ruth. "New Law Requires Priests to Break Seal of Confession to Report Child Abuse." *New York Times*, May 8, 2025.

Greene, Jenna. "Why workers fired for refusing Covid vaccines are starting to win in court." *Reuters*, November 1, 2024. Accessed June 6, 2025.

https://www.reuters.com/legal/government/column-why-workers-fired-refusing-covid-vaccines-are-starting-win-court-2024-11-01/.

Greenwald, Glenn. "The Patriot Act's Pernicious Legacy." *The Intercept* (blog), May 22, 2015. https://theintercept.com/2015/05/22/patriot-acts-pernicious-legacy/.

Gries, Phil. *Archival Television Audio, Inc.* Accessed April 19, 2025. https://www.atvaudio.com, March 15, 2023.

Hadro, Matt. "Bioethicist: There Must be Conscience Exemptions to Vaccine Mandates." *National Catholic Register*, August 5, 2021. Accessed April 19, 2025. https://www.ncregister.com/cna/bioethicist-there-must-be-conscience-exemptions-to-vaccine-mandates.

Haines, Tim. "NPR CEO Katherine Maher: A Reverence For The Truth Might Be Getting In The Way Of Getting Things Done." *Real Clear Politics*, April 17, 2024. Accessed June 2, 2025. https://www.realclearpolitics.com/video/2024/04/17/npr_ceo_katherine_maher_a_reverence_for_the_truth_might_be_getting_in_the_way_of_getting_things_done.html.

Hamburger, Philip. "Television: Stunning '1984.'" *New Yorker*, September 26, 1953.

Hanneman, Joseph M. "SSPX priest in California prevails in challenge to COVID closure order." June 3, 2021. Accessed June 5, 2025. https://www.catholicworldreport.com/2021/06/03/sspx-priest-in-california-prevails-in-challenge-to-covid-closure-order/.

Harris, Harry. "Screening TV." *Philadelphia Inquirer*, October 10, 1957.

Hayden, Sterling, quoted in 1984 interview with Gerald Peary. Accessed October 3, 2023. http://www.geraldpeary.com/interviews/ghi/hayden.html.

Hayden, Sterling. Interview by David Kobal. *Film Comment* 10, no. 2 (March–April 1974).

Heck, Alfons. *A Child of Hitler: Germany in the Days When God Wore a Swastika.* Phoenix, AZ: Renaissance House, 1985.

Herrick, James A. "C.S. Lewis, Science, and Science Fiction." *Evolution News*, August 23, 2020. Accessed June 11, 2025. https://evolutionnews.org/2020/08/c-s-lewis-science-and-science-fiction/.

———. "The Abolition of Man and the Advent of the Posthuman." Evolution News, 2012. Accessed June 11, 2025. https://evolutionnews.org/2020/08/the-abolition-of-man-and-the-advent-of-the-posthuman/.

Higgins, Bill. "Hollywood Flashback: One in Three TV Sets Tuned In to 'Shogun' in 1980." *The Hollywood Reporter*, June 24, 2020. Accessed June 4, 2025. https://www.hollywoodreporter.com/tv/tv-news/hollywood-flashback-one-three-tv-sets-tuned-shogun-1980-1298878/.

Higgins, Tucker. "Supreme Court sides with Catholic adoption agency that refuses to work with LGBT couples." *CNBC*, June 17, 2021. Accessed June 6, 2025. https://www.cnbc.com/2021/06/17/supreme-court-sides-with-catholic-adoption-agency-that-refuses-to-work-with-lgbt-couples.html

Hoffer, Eric. *The True Believer: Thoughts on the Nature of Mass Movements.* New York: Harper & Row, 1951.

Huxley, Aldous. *Brave New World.* London: Chatto & Windus, 1946.

Huxley, Aldous. *Music at Night.* London: Chatto & Windus, 1931.

Internet Broadway Database. "The Investigation." Accessed June 6, 2025. https://www.ibdb.com/broadway-production/the-investigation-3292.

Jefferson, Thomas. *Notes on the State of Virginia*. Edited by William Peden. Chapel Hill: University of North Carolina Press, 1955.

Josefsberg, Milt. *The Jack Benny Show*. New Rochelle, NY: Arlington House, 1977.

Juvenal. *Satires*. Translated by G.G. Ramsay. Cambridge, MA: Harvard University Press, 1918.

Kaplan, Milton K., editor. "Television Drama: A Discussion." *The English Journal* 47, no. 9 (Dec., 1958).

Karp, David. *The Brotherhood of Velvet*. New York: Lion Books, 1952.

———. *One*. New York: Vanguard Press, 1953.

———. Script notes for "One," 1955. *David Karp Collection*, Box 58 #4, Boston University Howard Gotlieb Archival Research Center.

Keller, Helen. *The Open Door*. Garden City, NY: Doubleday, 1957.

Kennedy, John F. "Ich bin ein Berliner (I am a 'Berliner')" *American Rhetoric*, June 26, 1963. Accessed June 6, 2025. https://www.americanrhetoric.com/speeches/jfkberliner.html.

———. Address to the American Newspaper Publishers Association, April 27, 1961, in *Public Papers of the Presidents of the United States*: John F. Kennedy, 1961 (Washington, DC: Government Printing Office, 1962), 335.

Kirkley, Donald. "'Boldest' New Venture on the Air." *The Baltimore Sun*. April 9, 1967.

———. "Look and Listen" *The Baltimore Sun*, April 20, 1970.

Kirsch, Adam. "The Desperate Plight Behind 'Darkness at Noon'." *New Yorker*, September 9, 2019. Accessed April 19, 2025. https://www.newyorker.com/magazine/2019/09/30/the-desperate-plight-behind-darkness-at-noon.

Kleiner, Dick. "Old Price Squeeze Bugaboo Prompts Hollywood Shrug of Television." *Sarasota Journal*, April 13, 1967.

Koutsobinas, Nick. "Biden Labeled COVID-19 Opposition 'Domestic Violent Extremists'" *Newsmax*. May 24, 2025. Accessed June 5, 2025. https://www.newsmax.com/newsfront/biden-covid-domestic/2025/05/24/id/1212222/.

Kundera, Milan. *The Unbearable Lightness of Being*. Translated by Michael Henry Heim. New York, Harper & Row, 1984.

Lee, Mary Ann. "TV News and Views." *Memphis Press-Scimitar*, April 29, 1970.

Lee, Robert E. Attributed statement following the Battle of Fredericksburg, December 1862.

Lewis, Sinclair. *It Can't Happen Here*. New York: Doubleday, Doran & Co., 1935.

Lifton, Robert Jay. *The Nazi Doctors: Medical Killing and the Psychology of Genocide*. New York: Basic Books, 1986.

Lincoln, Abraham. "House Divided Speech," June 16, 1858. In *The Collected Works of Abraham Lincoln*, edited by Roy P. Basler, 2:461. New Brunswick, NJ: Rutgers University Press, 1953.

Lincoln, Benjamin. To George Washington, February 22, 1787. In *The Papers of George Washington*, W. W. Abbot, ed., 5:45. Charlottesville: University Press of Virginia, 1993.

Llewellyn, Jennifer, and Steve Thompson, "*The Einsatzgruppen*." Alpha History, August 12, 2020. Accessed June 9, 2025. http://alphahistory.com/holocaust/schutzstaffel-ss/.

Loughery, David. *Star Trek V: The Final Frontier*. Directed by William Shatner. Paramount Pictures, 1989.

Lowry, Cynthia. "Flip Wilson Gets His Own TV Star," *The Robesonian*, September 18, 1970, page 11.

Lyons, Leonard. "Lyons Den." *Post-Standard* (Syracuse, NY).

Mallet du Pan, Jacques. *Considérations sur la Révolution de France*. London: J. Edwards, 1793.

Mankiewicz, Don M. "A Heretic In Utopia; ONE. By David Karp." *The New York Times*, October 11, 1953.

Mannes, Marya. *They*. Garden City, NY: Doubleday, 1968.

Mares, Courtney. "Pope Francis declares French Martyrs of Compiègne saints via equipollent canonization." *Catholic News Agency*, December 18, 2024. Accessed June 10, 2025. https://www.catholicnewsagency.com/news/261097/pope-francis-declares-french-martyrs-of-compiegne-saints-via-equipollent-canonization.

Marshall, Jack. "A Symptom of Creeping Totalitarianism: The Left's Embrace of Newspeak." *Ethics Alarms*, August 12, 2024. Accessed April 19, 2025. https://ethicsalarms.com/2024/08/12/a-symptom-of-creeping-totalitarianism-the-lefts-embrace-of-newspeak/.

Marx, Karl. *A Contribution to the Critique of Hegel's Philosophy of Right*, translated by A. Jolin and J. O'Malley. Edited by J. O'Malley. Cambridge: Cambridge University Press, 1970.

Maslin, Janet. "TV: Defeat's Cost, 'Children's Story.' *New York Times*, February 18, 1982.

Masterpiece Cakeshop v. Colorado Civil Rights Commission, 584 U.S. 617 (2018).

McQuiston, John T. "Lee J. Cobb, the Actor, is Dead at 64. *The New York Times*, February 12, 1976.

Meet the Press, NBC, February 8, 2004.

Mercer, Charles. "Studio 1 Fades in Reputation As Fine Drama.'" *Associated Press*, January 9, 1958.

"The Mercury Theatre: Mr. T.S. Eliot's New Play," *The Times* (London), November 5, 1935.

Merriam-Webster's Collegiate Dictionary. 11th ed. Springfield, MA: Merriam-Webster, 2003.

Metaxas, Eric. *Bonhoeffer: Pastor, Martyr, Prophet, Spy*. New York, Thomas Nelson, 2010.

Mill, John Stuart. *Autobiography, Essay On Liberty*. New York: F. F. Collier and Son Company, 1909.

Morris, Nigel. "Keeping It All in the (Nuclear) Family: Big Brother, Auntie BBC, Uncle Sam and George Orwell's Nineteen Eighty-Four." *Frames Cinema Journal*. November 19, 2012. Accessed June 8, 2025. https://web.archive.org/web/20190511162341/http://framescinemajournal.com/article/keeping-it-all-in-the-nuclear-family-big-brother-auntie-bbc-uncle-sam-and-george-orwells-nineteen-eighty-four/.

Murphy, Francis. "Behind the Mike." *The Oregonian* (Portland), April 17, 1970.

Murray, John F. "The Touch: On Saint Damien of Molokai and the Love of Christ." *Catholic World Report*, May 10, 2024. Accessed June 5, 2025. https://www.catholicworldreport.com/2024/05/10/the-touch-on-saint-damien-of-molokai-and-the-love-of-christ/.

Murrow, Edward R. "RTNDA Speech, October 15, 1958." *In In Search of Light: The Broadcasts of Edward R. Murrow, 1938–1961*, edited by Edward Bliss Jr., 364–71. New York: Knopf, 1967.

National Academies of Sciences, Engineering, and Medicine. "Toxicologic Assessment of the Army's Zinc Cadmium Sulfide Dispersion Tests." Washington, DC: The National Academies Press, 1997.

Naval Medical Center, "Impact of Internet Pornography," *Journal of Sexual Research* 49, no. 2 (2012). Accessed June 10, 2025. https://pmc.ncbi.nlm.nih.gov/articles/PMC5039517/.

Navasky, Victor S. *Naming Names*. New York: Viking Press, 1980.

NBC. "Vice President Nixon Commends NBC for Presenting 'Darkness at Noon' as Effective Answer to Question; 'What Makes a Communist Tick?'" May 2, 1955.

https://ia800605.us.archive.org/30/items/nbctra-derelease1955nati_3/nbctraderelease1955nati_3.pdf.

"NET Playhouse; They." American Archive of Public Broadcasting, Library of Congress and GBH, accessed June 11, 2025, https://americanarchive.org/catalog/cpb-aacip-512-hq3rv0dx0z.

Neuhaus, Richard John. *The Naked Public Square: Religion and Democracy in America*. New York, Wm. B. Eerdmans Publishing Co., 1988.

New Advent. "Individualism." Accessed April 17, 2025. https://www.newadvent.org/cathen/07762a.htm.

———. "Summa Theologiae > First Part > Question 75." Accessed June 11, 2025. https://www.newadvent.org/summa/1075.htm.

New American, "The 60th Anniversary of Orwell's 1984." November 27, 2009. Accessed June 8, 2025. https://thenewamerican.com/us/culture/history/the-60th-anniversary-of-orwell-s-1984/.

New York Daily News, "Cancels Raines; Cobb In." Tuesday, April 12, 1955.

Newton, Dwight. "'Murder Was My Duty. . .'" *San Francisco Examiner*, April 15, 1967.

Nietzsche, Friedrich. *Twilight of the Idols, or, How to Philosophize with a Hammer*. Translated by Walter Kaufmann. New York: Penguin Books, 1990.

Norris, J.F. "FFB: The Brotherhood of Velvet - David Karp." *Pretty Sinister Books* (blog). June 22, 2012. Accessed June 4, 2025. https://prettysinister.blogspot.com/2012/06/ffb-brotherhood-of-velvet-david-karp.html.

O'Ferrall, George More. "The Televising of Drama." *Radio Times*, March, 1937.

Obergefell v. Hodges, 576 U.S. 644, 725 (2015).

Oliver, Wayne. "'Darkness at Noon' Marks High Point in TV Drama." *Spencer Daily Reporter,* May 5, 1955.

Olmstead v. United States, 277 U.S. 438 (1928).

Ornstein, Charles. "New Documents Show How Drug Companies Targeted Doctors to Increase Opioid Prescriptions." *ProPublica*, May 17, 2022. Accessed June 6, 2025. https://www.propublica.org/article/pharmaceuticals-pay-doctors-drugs.

Osborn v. United States, 385 U.S. 323 (1966).

Orwell, George. *Nineteen Eighty-Four*. London: Secker & Warburg, 1949.

———. "For what am I fighting?": George Orwell on Arthur Koestler's 'Darkness at Noon'." *The New Statesman*, January 4, 1941. Accessed June 11, 2025. https://www.newstatesman.com/culture/2013/01/what-am-i-fighting-george-orwell-arthur-koestlers-darkness-noon.

Oviatt, Ray. "On The Beam: TV Drama On Flaws Of Communism." *Toledo Blade*, May 5, 1955.

Palmer, Ewan. "FBI Under Pressure for Targeting Catholics in Leaked Document." *Newsweek*, February 10, 2023. Accessed April 19, 2025. https://www.newsweek.com/fbi-memo-catholics-radical-traditional-leaked-1780379.

Pearson, Howard. "Florence Type Cast." *Deseret News*, September 18, 1970.

———. "TV Highlights 'Documentaries for Utah'." *Deseret News*, April 10, 1970.

Pentin, Edward. "Communist Crackdown in China is 'Beyond George Orwell's Imaginings'—and It's Only Getting Worse." *Catholicism Pure & Simple* (blog), January 20, 2021. Accessed April 21, 2025. https://catholicismpure.wordpress.com/2021/01/20/communist-crackdown-in-china-is-beyond-george-orwells-imaginings-and-its-only-getting-worse/.

Perrin, Sam, with George Balzer, Al Gordon, Hal Goldman. "Jack's Life Story." *The Jack Benny Program*. Aired December 1, 1957, on CBS-TV.

Pew Research Center. "Beyond Distrust: How Americans View Their Government." November 23, 2015. Accessed June 7, 2025. https://www.pewresearch.org/politics/2015/11/23/1-trust-in-government-1958-2015/.

Philosophy Break. "Nietzsche on Why Suffering Is Necessary for Greatness." Accessed June 10, 2025. https://philosophybreak.com/articles/nietzsche-on-why-suffering-is-necessary-for-greatness/.

Pine, Lisa. *Education in Nazi Germany*. Oxford: Berg, 2010.

Pius XII. *Humani Generis*. Encyclical letter, August 12, 1950. Accessed April 19, 2025. http://www.vatican.va/content/pius-xii/en/encyclicals/documents/hf_p-xii_enc_12081950_humani-generis.html.

Pixley, Andrew. "Flashback: The Year of the Sex Olympics." *TV Zone* no.162 (May 2003) pp.46-51.

Plato. *Republic*. Translated by Benjamin Jowett. Oxford: Clarendon Press, 1871.

Postman, Neil. *Amusing Ourselves to Death: Public Discourse in the Age of Show Business*. New York: Viking Penguin, 1985.

Quiñones, Peter R. "They Want You Dead But They'll Settle For Your Obedience." *The Pete Quiñones Show*, July 26, 2021. Accessed April 19, 2025. https://petequinones.substack.com/p/they-want-you-dead-for-your-lack.

Rand, Ayn. *The Fountainhead*. Indianapolis: Bobbs-Merrill, 1943.

Rascoe, Burton. "Spine-Chiller on Kraft Theatre Tonight." *Staten Island Advance*, October 26, 1955.

Ray, Michael. "Tank Man," *Britannica.com*, March 14, 2025. Accessed April 19, 2025. https://www.britannica.com/biography/Tank-Man.

Reagan, Ronald. "Remarks at the Brandenburg Gate." *American Rhetoric*, June 12, 1987. Accessed June 6, 2025. https://www.americanrhetoric.com/speeches/ronaldreaganbrandenburggate.htm.

Reasoner, Harry. *Before the Colors Fade*. New York: Alfred A. Knopf, 1981.

Reice, Sylvie. "Swinging Set." *Syracuse Herald Journal*, April 11, 1967.

Roman Missal. Vatican City: Libreria Editrice Vaticana, 2011.

Rooney, Andy. *Andy Rooney: 60 Years of Wisdom and Wit*. New York: PublicAffairs, 2010.

Roosevelt, Franklin D. *The Public Papers and Addresses of Franklin D. Roosevelt*. Vol. 10 New York: Random House, 1941.

Rösler, Paula. "What makes Germany and the Germans special?" DW, February 10, 2018. Accessed June 9, 2025. https://www.dw.com/en/what-makes-germany-and-the-germans-special/a-45656679.

Roxborough, Scott. "80 Years After Auschwitz Liberation, 'The Investigation' Bears Witness to Nazi Atrocities." *The Hollywood Reporter*, January 27, 2025. Accessed June 6, 2025. https://www.hollywoodreporter.com/movies/movie-features/the-investigation-film-nazi-atrocities-auschwitz-liberation-80-1236118942/.

Russo, Charles J. "Massachusetts Bill will eliminate 'mother' and 'father' from parenting laws." *Catholic World Report*, August 6, 2024. Accessed June 7, 2025. https://www.catholicworldreport.com/2024/08/06/massachusetts-bill-will-eliminate-mother-and-father-from-parenting-laws/.

Ryan, David. *George Orwell on Screen: Adaptations, Documentaries and Docudramas on Film and Television*. Jefferson, NC: McFarland, 2018.

Schiffer, Kathy. "Faithful to Bishops: 'Give Us Sacraments During Coronavirus — They Are Essential'" *National Catholic Register*, April 3, 2020. Accessed June 6, 2025. https://www.ncregister.com/blog/faithful-to-bishops-give-us-sacraments-during-coronavirus-they-are-essential.

Schow, Ashe. "Flashback: Walz Implemented COVID Hotline to Snitch on Neighbors." *Daily Wire*. Accessed June 3, 2025. https://www.dailywire.com/news/flashback-walz-implemented-covid-hotline-to-snitch-on-neighbors.

Schow, David J. *The Outer Limits Companion*. Berkeley, CA: Gingko Press, 1998.

Scoleri, John. "The Outer Limits at 55: O.B.I.T." *Films from Beyond the Time Barrier* (blog). November 4, 2018. https://www.filmsfrombeyond.com/2018/11/the-outer-limits-at-55-obit.html.

Seed, David. *Brainwashing: The Fictions of Mind Control*. Kent, OH: Kent State University Press, 2004.

Seib, Gerald F. "In Crisis, Opportunity for Obama." *The Wall Street Journal*, November 21, 2008.

Shackelford, Kelly. "When senators ask a nominee about their religious beliefs, they should give this simple answer." *Washington Examiner*, February 20, 2019. Accessed April 19, 2025. https://www.washingtonexaminer.com/opinion/384070/when-senators-ask-a-nominee-about-their-religious-beliefs-they-should-give-this-simple-answer/.

Shain, Percy. "The concluding suicides were almost welcome." *Boston Globe*, April 20, 1970.

Shapiro, Ben. "The Ben Shapiro Show." *The Daily Wire*, 2021. Accessed April 19, 2025. https://www.dailywire.com/show/the-ben-shapiro-show.

Sheen, Fulton J. "Signs of Our Times." Broadcast on *Light Your Lamps*, January 26, 1947. Accessed June 10, 2025. https://www.virgosacrata.com/antichrist-signs-of-our-times.html.

Shull, Richard K. "An Investigation Into 'The Eichmann Impulse." *Indianapolis News*, April 15, 1967.

Simpson, Robert. "A Tribute to Nigel Keale." *Hammer Web* (blog), February 10, 2007. Accessed June 9, 2025. http://www.hammerfilms.com/features/tributes/nigel_kneale.html

Sirota, Mike. "'The Obsolete Man'—A Warning." *Swords and Specters: The Novels of Mike Sirota* (blog), August 19, 2019. Accessed June 6, 2025. https://mikesirota.com/the-obsolete-man-a-warning/.

Sloman, Robert. *Doctor Who*. "Planet of the Spiders," season 11, episode 5, aired May 4–June 8, 1974. BBC.

Smith, Cecil. "Views on Television." *The Victoria Advocate*, September 6, 1970.

Starnes, Todd. "City of Houston Demands Pastors Turn Over Sermons." *Fox News*, October 14, 2014. Accessed April 19, 2025. https://www.foxnews.com/opinion/city-of-houston-demands-pastors-turn-over-sermons.

Steinfirst, Donald, "NBC Opera Season Opens With Poulenc's 'Carmelites.'" *Pittsburgh Post-Gazette*, December 10, 1957.

Stern, Stewart. "Heart of Darkness." *Playhouse 90*, season 3, episode 7, directed by Ron Winston, aired November 6, 1958. CBS.

Swift, John. *Adventures in Vision: The First 25 Years of Television*. London: John Lehmann, 1950.

Taubman, Howard. "Opera: 'Carmelites' on TV." *The New York Times*, December 9, 1957.

Television Academy. "1984 – 36th Emmy Awards." Accessed June 4, 2025. https://www.television-academy.com/awards/nominees-winners/1984/outstanding-lead-actor-in-a-miniseries-or-a-movie.

Tesla, Nikola. "Radio Power Will Revolutionize the World." *Modern Mechanics and Inventions*, July 1934.

Thesaurus.com. "Indoctrination." *Thesaurus.com*. Accessed April 21, 2025. https://www.thesaurus.com/browse/indoctrination.

"'They' Adapted as Haunting TV Drama." *New York Times*, April 18, 1970.

The Thinking Conservative. "Ronald Reagan statement on Liberalism during 1975 interview by Mike Wallace on 60 Minutes." April 27, 2024. Accessed June 11, 2025. https://www.thethinkingconservative.com/ronald-reagan-statement-on-liberalism-during-1975-interview-by-mike-wallace-on-60-minutes/

Thoreau, Henry David. "Life Without Principle." *The Atlantic Monthly* 12, no. 71 (October 1863).

Toner, James, PhD. "Currentism: The Perennial Life." *OnePeterFive*, February 9, 2021. Accessed June 9, 2025. https://onepeterfive.com/currentism-the-perennial-lie/.

"Tonight's Television Highlights," *Warsaw Times-Union*, September 17, 1970.

"Top 10 Twilight Zone Episodes." *Time Magazine*. October 5, 2009. Accessed April 14, 2025. http://time.com/top-10-twilight-zone-episodes.

Triplett, Gene. "A 'chilling' parable examines the vulnerability of children." *The Oklahoman*, February 18, 1982. Accessed June 4, 2025.

https://www.oklahoman.com/story/news/1982/02/14/a-chilling-parable-examines-the-vulnerability-of-children/62894131007/

Trombetta, Sadie. "Why The Last Line Of '1984' Is One Of The Most Devastating Lines In Literature." *Bustle*, March 21, 1018. Accessed June 4, 2025. https://www.bustle.com/p/the-last-line-of-1984-is-one-of-the-most-quietly-heartbreaking-lines-in-literature-8560347.

Tuskegee University. "About the USPHS Syphilis Study." Accessed June 4, 2025. https://www.tuskegee.edu/about-us/centers-of-excellence/bioethics-center/about-the-usphs-syphilis-study.

"TVKey Previews." *Bergen Evening Record*, February 7, 1957.

"TV Key Previews." *Pittsburgh Post-Gazette.* April 14, 1967.

"TV Key Previews." *Pittsburgh Post-Gazette*, April 17, 1970.

"TVKey Previews," *St. Joseph News-Press*, October 3, 1955.

"TV Time Previews," *Youngstown Vindicator*, September 17, 1970, p. 25

U.S. Congress. Senate. "The Invasion of Kevin Ireland." *Congressional Record*. 92nd Cong., 1st sess., vol. 117, pt. 26, October 5, 1971, 35003–35009.

Unger, Arthur. "A 'horror show' on classroom indoctrination" *Christian Science Monitor*, February 18, 1982. Accessed June 4, 2025. https://www.csmonitor.com/1982/0218/021801.html.

United Press. "Tough Problems Solved for Tonight's TV Show, '1984'". *Jeannette News-Dispatch,* September 21, 1953.

Van Horne, Harriet. "'Investigation' Painful." *Knoxville News Sentinel*, April 17, 1967.

Voegelin, Eric. "The Power of Francis Poulenc's 'Dialogues of the Carmelites.'" *Voegelin View* (blog), July 20, 2023. Accessed June 10, 2025. https://voegelinview.com/the-power-of-francis-poulencs-dialogues-of-the-carmelites/.

Wager, Walter. "'The Investigation': A Playwright's Program Notes." *TV Guide*, April 8, 1967.

Wallis, Jay. "Verify: Yes, fetal cell lines were used in the development of Johnson & Johnson's COVID-19 vaccine." WFAA-TV, Dallas-Fort Worth, Texas. March 5, 2021. Accessed June 6, 2025. https://www.wfaa.com/article/news/verify/verify-johnson-johnson-covid-19-vaccine-aborted-fetal-cell-lines-catholic-church/287-2f3a58f9-6cec-4426-b0a9-17c49502d76c.

Weiss, Peter. *The Investigation*. Translated by Ulu Grosbard. New York: Atheneum, 1966.

Wiktionary. "Sheeple." Accessed June 12, 2025. https://en.wiktionary.org/wiki/sheeple.

Wilde, Oscar. *The Soul of Man Under Socialism*. London: Arthur L. Humphries, 1912.

Williams, David. *A Liturgy on the Universal Principles of Religion and Morality*. London: Printed for the Author, 1776, viii. Quote from Psalms 49:1, 69:34, 30:4, 62:8 in Williams, *A Liturgy*, 1. On the "religion of Christ," see Williams, *Essays*, 3. On inclusion of scripture and English classics, see "Books: Williams's Sermon and Liturgy," *The Scots Magazine* 38 (September 1776): 490.

Williams, Larry. "Actor Finds 'They' Is Often Wrong." *Memphis Commercial Appeal*, April 16, 1970.

Williams, Roger. *The Bloudy Tenent of Persecution*. London, 1644.

Winchell, Walter. "Actress Working as Waitress." *The Spartanburg Herald*, September 29, 1953.

Wood, Mary. "A Contrast in Deejays." *Cincinnati Post*, October 5, 1957.

World Economic Forum. "Young Global Leaders." Accessed April 17, 2025. https://www.younggloballeaders.org.

Wyver, John. "BBC television's first drama: *Murder in the Cathedral* (1936)." *Screen Plays* (blog). December 5, 2015. Accessed June 11, 2025. https://screenplaystv.wordpress.com/2015/12/05/bbc-televisions-first-drama-murder-in-the-cathedral-1936/

Zicree, Marc Scott. *The Twilight Zone Companion.* New York: Bantam Books, 1982.

Index

Akins, Claude, 128, 130
Albert, Eddie, 12, 16, 19
alienation, 8, 12, 23, 284
Andersen, Hans Christian, 228
Aquinas, St. Thomas, 109
"The Architects of Fear," 39–50, 56, 241
assisted suicide, 164, 165, 190
Aurthur, Robert Allen, 93, 96, 97, 98, 99, 101, 106, 107, 203, 207
Austin, Pam, 69
Babcock, Barbara, 218
Baxter, Alan, 53, 56
Beaumont, Charles, 67, 69
beauty, 12, 13, 18, 68, 71, 73, 74, 75, 77, 82, 204
Becket, St. Thomas, 4, 273, 274, 275, 277, 278, 280, 281, 284, 285, 295, 296
Bell, George, 276, 279
Benny, Jack, 308, 310, 311, 312, 318
betrayal, 76, 142, 187, 206, 225, 282
Biden, Joseph, 62
Blacklisting, 58, 59, 101, 103, 151, 177, 211, 291
Bold Ones, 169, 172, 181
Bonhoeffer, Dietrich, 259, 273, 279, 280, 286
brainwashing, 15, 81, 88
Brandeis, Louis, 51, 57
Breck, Peter, 52, 56
Brooks, Geraldine, 40, 42
Cox, Brian, 232
Brotherhood of the Bell, 140–152
Browning, Kirk, 259, 266
Bush, George W., 61, 149
Campanella, Joseph, 170, 172
cancel culture, 5, 120
censorship, 2, 19, 35, 94, 151
"The Children's Story," iii, 81–91
Clavell, James, 81, 82, 84, 85, 89, 91
Clavell, Michaela, *see Ross, Michaela*
Cobb, Lee J., 204, 207, 209, 211
Coe, Fred, 109, 203, 209
communism, 4, 21, 209, 212, 265
conformity, 34, 35, 59, 77, 78, 97, 115, 151, 248, 250
conscience, 114, 273, 281, 282, 284
conspiracy, 29, 35, 52, 61, 143, 148, 152
Cordeiro, Jose Luis, 73
Corey, Jeff, 54, 56, 59
COVID, 5, 90, 98, 106, 122, 130, 131, 134, 179, 199, 228, 281, 282, 283, 284, 299
COVID Theater, 5, 90, 98, 122, 131, 199, 281, 282, 284, 299

Crane, Norma, 13, 16
Critical Race Theory, 90
Culp, Robert, 16n, 40, 42
Daniels, Marc, 155, 159, 160
"Darkness at Noon," iii, 4, 114, 203-214, 293
debanking, 177
deep state, 55
defiance, 13, 59, 62, 63, 72, 142, 157, 159, 205, 232, 247, 248, 252, 256, 263, 264, 275, 295
dehumanization, 119, 186, 237, 250
"Dialogues of the Carmelites," iii, 259-270, 295, 315
Dolinsky, Meyer, 39, 42, 51, 56
Doohan, James, 219
dystopia, 5, 99, 114, 115, 121, 135
education, 1, 5, 33, 34, 53, 71, 82, 87, 89, 91, 100, 120, 253
Elcar, Dana, 171, 173
Eliot, T.S., 4, 273, 276, 279, 285, 286, 307, 318
Evans, Maurice, 142, 146
fear, 12, 14–15, 18, 22, 24, 36–37, 41, 49, 51–52, 57–59, 63, 78, 102, 110, 119, 129, 131, 133, 135, 137, 147, 151, 179, 203, 206, 214, 241–242, 247, 249, 252, 256–257, 260–262, 268, 273, 283–284, 292–300 (main discussion)

Federal Bureau of Investigation, 102, 106, 107, 271
Farentino, James, 170, 172
"A Feasibility Study," 287-302
Ford, Glenn, 141, 145
Ford Theater, 310
Forsyth, Rosemary, 142, 146
Frankenheimer, John, 93, 96
Franz, Eduard, 141, 146
freedom, 5, 12, 20, 29, 34, 51, 60, 61, 62, 64, 68, 74, 77, 87, 93, 97, 98, 103, 119, 142, 200, 223, 243, 248, 251, 254, 263, 280, 282, 289, 292, 293, 296, 300, 301, 302
French Revolution, 189, 214, 264, 265n, 267, 268
Frontiere, Dominic, 43, 292
"The General," 5, 27-37
Gordon, Colin, 28
Gould, Jack, 18, 97, 115, 209
Greene, Lorne, 13, 16
Greifer, Lewis 27
Grosbard, Ulu, 185, 190, 343
Groupthink, 22, 34, 36
Haskin, Byron, 39, 42, 287
Hayden, Sterling, 94, 96, 101
Heilpern, Steve, 169, 173
Hill, George Roy, 109, 115
Holocaust, 4, 185, 189, 191, 195, 197, 200, 228
"The Horn Blows at Midnight," 307-317
Houghton, Buck, 127, 247

Index

Hugo, Laurence, 111, 114
Huggins, Roy, 173
humanity, 40, 45, 47, 48, 55, 56, 57, 72, 96, 120, 145, 155, 158, 173, 191, 194, 200, 242, 247, 256, 289, 316, 317
Huxley, Aldous, 8, 11, 235, 240, 243, 259, 271
individualism, 103, 110
individuality, 68, 72, 74, 78, 241, 248
indoctrination, 5, 22, 33, 81, 88, 89, 90
"The Invasion of Kevin Ireland," 5, 169-181
The Investigation, iii, 4, 7, 185-201, 222
Ireland, John, 94, 96
Ives, Burl, 170, 172, 173
Jackson, Felix, 11, 15, 16, 17, 18, 21
Jefferson, Thomas, 281, 285
Jones, Barry, 111, 114
Karp, David, 4, 109, 113, 115, 116, 140, 144, 145, 151, 152
Kennedy, John F., 55, 61, 140, 152, 255, 258
Kennedy, Robert F., 60
Kerry, John, 149
Kingsley, Sidney, 203, 207
Kneale, Nigel, 231, 234, 235, 236, 239
Koestler, Arthur, 4, 150, 203, 207, 210, 211, 212

Kraft Television Theatre, 109, 113, 114, 115, 116, 122
Kuhlmann, Rosemary, 261, 266
Lambert, Paul, 95, 96
language/Newspeak, 2, 20, 21, 22, 163, 212, 236, 269, 282
Lee, Robert E. 217, 221
Lewis, C.S., 47, 48, 49
Lincoln, Abraham, 137, 332
Lincoln, Benjamin, 130
Long, Richard, 68
love, 13, 14, 35, 36, 40, 42, 45, 46, 49, 69, 96, 113, 122, 131, 155, 158, 160, 163, 204, 205, 240, 241, 289, 290, 293, 297-302, 308, 309, 316, 317
Love, Phyllis, 288, 291
Lynn, Diana, 94, 96
Malbin, Elaine, 260, 266, 267
Malone, Dorothy, 308
"A Man for All Seasons," 76
manipulation, 2, 21, 45, 54, 176
Mann, Delbert, 203, 208, 209
Mannes, Marya 155, 159, 160, 161, 163, 165, 167, 235
Marley, John, 190, 194
martyrdom, 42, 95, 270, 275, 285
Mathews, Carmen, 156, 159, 160
Matthews, Lester, 307

McCarthy, Joseph, 15, 21, 58, 101, 102, 130, 151, 248, *see also Blacklisting*
McGavin, Darren, 170, 172, 173
McGoohan, Patrick, 27, 28, 31
media, 22, 25, 33, 55, 62, 64, 90, 102, 132, 143, 149, 151, 180, 201, 231, 235, 239, 252, 282
Meredith, Burgess, 248, 250, 251
Merrill, Gary, 156, 159, 160
Mill, John Stuart, 68, 77, 78
Mobil Showcase, 81, 85, 91
"The Monsters Are Due on Maple Street," 5, 127-138, 241, 250
More, St. Thomas, 76
"Murder in the Cathedral," iii, 273, 276, 277, 279, 281, 284, 286, 295, 315
Natwick, Mildred, 82
NBC Opera Theatre, 259, 265, 266
NET Playhouse, 155, 159, 167, 200
Neve, Suzanne, 232
Nickell, Paul, 11, 16, 21
Nietzsche, Friedrich, 75, 93, 103, 107
Nimoy, Leonard, 218
nonconformist, 68, 111
"Number 12 Looks Just Like You," 5, 67-78, 241, 250
"O.B.I.T.," 51-64

obedience, 119, 131, 141, 222, 223, 224, 263
"The Obsolete Man," 247-257, 295
O'Ferrall, G. More, 273, 278, 284
Omnibus, 307, 312
"One", 5, 109-122, 241
Opatoshu, David, 94, 96, 218, 288, 291
Orwell, George, 4, 11, 12, 15-25
Oswald, Gert, 51, 56
The Outer Limits, 5, 39, 42, 43, 48, 50, 51, 55, 57, 64, 287, 291, 302
overpopulation, 46, 165, 231, 237
overreach, 2, 23
paranoia, 128
Parker, Suzy, 68
persecution, 25, 196, 198, 266, 267, 268, 273, 281
Playhouse 90, 93, 96, 107, 114, 115
pornography, 231, 237, 238, 240
Postman, Neil, 231, 239
Poulenc, Francis, 259, 265, 266
Price, Leontyne, 261, 266, 267
The Prisoner, 25, 27, 31, 34, 35, 37, 119
privacy, 5, 12, 23, 51, 55, 57, 64, 119, 132, 147, 169, 175, 178, 179, 181

Producers' Showcase, 203, 206, 208, 210, 215
propaganda, 155, 248
Proxmire, WIlliam, 173, 174
Reagan, Ronald, 120, 255
Reasoner, Harry, 287, 298
reeducation, 24, 34, 70, 83, 120, 214
Roosevelt, Franklin D., 1, 36, 310
Ross, Michaela, 82, 85
Rossiter, Leonard, 232
Roman, Ruth, 204, 208
sacrifice, 8, 45, 76, 159, 179, 212, 219, 265, 276, 292, 293, 294, 296, 298, 300, 301
scientism, 47, 48, 49
secrecy, 40, 52, 140, 141
separation of church and state, 281, 285
Serling, Rod, 69, 86, 113n, 127, 130, 134, 136, 247, 257
Shatner, William, 217
Sheen, Fulton J., 236
sheeple, 227, 228, 229, 230
Silverstein, Elliot, 247, 248n
Singer, Alexander, 169, 173
Skinner, Cornelia Otis, 156, 159, 160
Skull and Bones, 149
Social Credit, 49, 176, 181
social media, 22, 55, 62, 64, 90, 102, 103, 132, 180, 252, 282
Socrates, 35

"A Sound of Different Drummers," 93-107
Sowards, Jack B., 169, 173
Star Trek, 35, 44, 75, 217, 221, 229
Stefano, Joseph, 39, 51, 287, 291, 292, 293, 294, 300, 302
Stevens, Leslie, 291
Stone, Leonard, 40
Studio One, 11, 15, 17, 18, 20, 21, 114, 144, 145
surveillance, 2, 5, 19, 23, 29, 53, 54, 55, 57, 64, 134, 151, 176, 180
"A Taste of Armageddon," 5, 217-229
Templeton, William P., 11, 17, 18
"They," 73, 155-167
Theatre Parade, 273, 277
Thoreau, Henry David, 11, 94
Tomerlin, John, 67, 69, 70
totalitarianism, 2, 4, 20, 21, 25, 201, 207, 250
Townes, Harry, 54, 56, 110, 114
The Twilight Zone, 5, 67, 69, 78, 86, 127, 130, 134, 135, 138, 247, 250, 257
Ustinov, Peter, 87, 91
vaccine, 46, 49, 77, 179, 199, 229, 282, 283, 297
Van Patten, Joyce, 288, 291
Venza, Jac, 155, 159
Vogel, Tony, 232
Wanamaker, Sam, 288, 291

Wayne, David, 204, 208
Weaver, Fritz, 248
Weiss, Peter, 4, 185, 188, 189, 190, 191, 192, 193, 194, 199, 200, 202, 222
Weston, Jack, 128

Wilcox, Collin, 68
Wiseman, Joseph, 156, 159, 160, 204, 208
"The Year of the Sex Olympics," 5, 231-243, 315

www.ingramcontent.com/pod-product-compliance
Lightning Source LLC
Chambersburg PA
CBHW031138020426
42333CB00013B/430